W9-BJV-378

READING EMBODIED CITIZENSHIP

Disability, Narrative, and the Body Politic

EMILY RUSSELL

Rutgers University Press

NEW BRUNSWICK, NEW JERSEY, AND LONDON

Visit our Web site: http://rutgerspress.rutgers.edu

Manufactured in the United States of America

LIBRARY OF CONGRESS CATALOGING-IN-PUBLICATION DATA

Russell, Emily, 1979–
    Reading embodied citizenship : disability, narrative, and the body politic / Emily Russell.
        p.   cm. — (American literatures initiative)
    Includes bibliographical references and index.
    ISBN 978-0-8135-4939-2 (hardcover : alk. paper)
    1. American fiction—20th century—History and criticism.   2. Human body in literature.   3. People with disabilities in literature.   4. National characteristics, American, in literature.   5. Human body—Political aspects—United States.   I. Title.
PS374.B64R87   2011
813'.540935287—dc22

                                                                        2010017321

A British Cataloging-in-Publication record for this book is available from the British Library.

THE
AMERICAN
LITERATURES
INITIATIVE

A book in the American Literatures Initiative (ALI), a collaborative publishing project of NYU Press, Fordham University Press, Rutgers University Press, Temple University Press, and the University of Virginia Press. The Initiative is supported by The Andrew W. Mellon Foundation. For more information, please visit www.americanliteratures.org.

CONTENTS

Acknowledgments

It seems only appropriate, in a work about anomalous bodies and their many forms, that I am indebted to a no-less-extraordinary body of colleagues, friends, and family for their support. Even before this project began to take shape, reading the work of Rosemarie Garland-Thomson opened my mind to the possibilities of disability as a field of inquiry. At an early stage, both Helen Deutsch and Rachel Lee modeled the value of intellectual generosity and the insights that can emerge from an open and rigorous engagement with seemingly far-flung sources. They brought a similarly careful eye to reading drafts of this work, through which the final product has improved immeasurably. I am fortunate to have both as mentors.

Each draft of this manuscript has benefited immensely from the insightful critique of Kate Hayles, Vivian Sobchack, Diane Price Herndl, Joyce Lee, Melanie Ho, Denise Cruz, Loren Blinde, and Meg Lamont. Samantha Pinto has served as a tireless sounding board and writing partner; her friendship, enthusiasm, and incisive mind have been a sustaining force at every stage of my academic life.

In addition to these individuals, I am grateful to have found support from institutions and intellectual communities. I have been particularly fortunate in the generous assistance of the Charlotte K. Newcombe Foundation and the Department of English at UCLA. The Embodiment Reading Group at UCLA provided invigorating intellectual cooperation and established a model I hope to replicate. I am thrilled to have landed among colleagues at Rollins College who are both challenging and supportive. I have been tremendously lucky in finding here an engaged cohort of young faculty—most notably, Vidhu Aggarwal, Martha Cheng, Paul Reich, and Anne Zimmermann. I owe a deep debt to the Department of English, and to Ed Cohen for his kind and generous mentorship. The students at Rollins have consistently reanimated my work with their humor and enthusiasm, and in asking for and offering fresh perspectives on American literature. I extend my enduring thanks to Leslie Mitchner at Rutgers University Press for her support and guidance and to Katie Keeran for her editorial assistance. I am also deeply indebted to Olan Quattro, who listened to my fumbling ideas and created the exquisite and monstrous art for the cover image.

My collaboration with these colleagues and friends would not be possible without the profound support of my family. I thank Philip Fibiger, who has been an enduring constant as our lives have taken us across thousands of miles to often surprising places. In the weeks before I completed this project, Will Fibiger joined our family, immediately enriching my life and deepening my understanding of what it means to be part of the social body. To my parents, Bill and Kathy Russell, I owe an enormous debt of love and gratitude. From the earliest age, they showed me the richness of intellectual life; I could not have imagined my way here without their example or their boundless confidence.

An earlier version of chapter 5, "Some Assembly Required: The Embodied Politics of *Infinite Jest*," was previously published in *Arizona Quarterly* 66, no. 2 (2010): 147–169. I appreciate the editors' permission to reprint this material.

Reading Embodied Citizenship

Introduction

In the political history of disability in the United States, 1990 serves as a watershed moment. The passage of the Americans with Disabilities Act (ADA), a broad legislative statement laid on the foundation of the Rehabilitation Act of 1973, affirmed the rights of disabled Americans in the last of that century's civil rights laws.[1] While each of the act's five titles covers specific spheres such as employment, public services, and communications technology, the conceptual reach of the ADA goes beyond these aspects of policy to impact the most fundamental concepts in American citizenship, including independence, individualism, and public responsibility to citizens. Crucial to the passage of the ADA was the insistence that disabled Americans were not seeking so-called special treatment, but demanding foundational civil rights. The need for this legislation two centuries after the Bill of Rights was enacted, however, captures an equally fundamental truth about American citizenship: the concepts that are central to U.S. national identity are not timeless, but uneven, compromised, and contested. *Reading Embodied Citizenship* explores how confronting figures of physical difference throws central concepts of American identity into crisis and examines the narrative revisions that take place in the face of these public encounters.

Not only did the ADA hold together decades of disability legislation under one central act, it also reaffirmed a basic statement about how to define disability. According to Jacqueline Vaughn Switzer's history of American disability policy, defining who would be covered by the protections of the act confounded many lawmakers. Some were anxious over users of illegal drugs; others raised the specter of homosexuality and bisexuality; Switzer relates that Senator Jesse Helms "questioned whether pedophiles, schizophrenics, kleptomaniacs, and transvestites would be considered disabled" (107). What lawmakers understood, however, is that the diversity of disability makes constructing an exhaustive list of impairments impossible. While legislators included a brief list of exclusions addressing the above complaints, arguing, for example, that "homosexuality and bisexuality are not impairments and as such are not disabilities" (sec. 12211), they largely preserved the broader definition laid out in the American Rehabilitation Act of 1973. According to the state, disability has three elements, with membership in any category constituting legal disability: "The term 'disability' means, with respect to an individual: A) a physical or mental impairment that substantially limits one or more life activities of such individual; B) a record of such an impairment; or C) being regarded as having such an impairment." Beyond its value in the courtroom, this definition of disability reflects a major shift in America's understanding of embodiment. As I will discuss in more detail below, enduring models of liberal citizenship imagine political independence through John Locke's concept of an inalienable "property in one's person." The ADA definition, by contrast, follows key work in disability studies in acknowledging that embodiment is not straightforward medical fact; the body is not simply a self-evident, physical truth.

While the language of "a physical or mental impairment" in the first part of the definition largely conforms to common expectations of disability as a medical truth to be diagnosed and treated, the ADA does not stop there. The definition pushes our public understanding of disability beyond physical or mental impairment to include a history or "record" of impairment (such as a history of cancer) and "regard" by others (such as a scar). Here, history and social perception exist on par with more conventional associations of disability as a strictly embodied condition. In a series of amendments intended to strengthen the force of the ADA after years of judicial dilution, legislators returned in 2008 to the question of definitions. The ADA Amendments Act of 2008 further challenges notions of disability as a static category by acknowledging the often-episodic nature of impairment in including conditions in remission (although not conditions that are considered "temporary"). The amendments similarly affirm the discriminatory power of social perception by stating that "being regarded as having such impairment" includes both cases of "actual or perceived" impairment (sec. 12102). Taken together, this definition captures more than a series of guidelines for implementing policy; it serves as a conceptual model for more thoroughly understanding how disability functions in the national imagination.

The three elements of this definition acknowledge a fundamental, but typically overlooked, homology of physical, social, and textual bodies as the terrain for constructing social narratives of disabled citizenship. The shared use of the word "body" in the common terms "physical body," "body politic," and "body of the text" is not merely a neat coincidence of language, but a sign of the often-forgotten dependence of each category upon the others. In the ADA definition, "impairment" (the body), "record" (the text), and "regard" (the social) act in concert to trace out the contours of disability in the discourse of American individualism.

Reading Embodied Citizenship captures the necessary interdependence of the textual, social, and physical body in imagining modern American democracy. While the courtroom might seem a more obvious battleground for studying the intersection of disability and citizenship, I argue that narrative has always been a central feature in constructing the public concept of disability that undergirds legislative efforts. Before the successful passage of the ADA, individuals were asked to send "discrimination diaries," documenting their quotidian experiences of inaccessibility. Hearings in Washington and across the country offered public venues for personal stories, constituting individual acts of citizenship that translated to policy change. In this book, I offer readings of narratives that dramatize similar acts of daily citizenship. In each of these texts, the encounter between an anomalous physical body and the body politic requires narrative strategies that can make sense of the unfamiliar. Whether it's conjoined twins entering a small-town Missouri boardinghouse or a disabled Vietnam veteran staging a public protest in his wheelchair, these moments highlight the intersection between physical and social bodies and, in turn, call upon narrative to make these encounters legible.

Just as physical difference calls for the public to construct new stories to manage disabled bodies, so do these encounters prompt an imaginative reconsideration of the body politic itself. Even as the crowd demands legibility from the embodied spectacle, its own identity shifts in response. In the case of the protesting Vietnam veteran, for example, disability not only is the mark of individual loss, but symbolizes national loss as well. By analyzing these textual moments of reciprocal reexamination, I explore how local, even intimate, expressions of citizenship capture the overlapping contours of textual, political, and physical bodies. Such a model places the disabled body at the center of analysis to explore the political stakes of embodiment in American literature. Throughout this book, I take up narratives that capture moments of crisis in the life of the nation—from the turmoil surrounding citizenship following the Civil War and failures of Reconstruction in the 1890s to anxieties over the influx of transnational influences in the 1990s—in order to demonstrate how our concept of the body politic is intertwined with figures of physical difference.

Locating Citizenship in the Body

While my literary analysis begins in the 1890s, the political foundations of embodied citizenship can be found at the origins of liberal political philosophy. I move from conventional understandings of the body as the unremarkable requirement of all citizenship to exposing embodiment as an unevenly distributed characteristic only made visible by its difference. As suggested above, in traditional models of liberal individualism, drawing from John Locke's call for the sanctity of "property in one's person," one's ownership of one's body—and one's capacity, or ability, to labor—stands as a founding concept in the construction of U.S. citizenship. But even if citizenship assumes corporeal self-possession for all its subjects, bodies read as normal slip back into a position of invisible neutrality. Consequently, it is particularly those with visible bodily difference whose political participation is read as inescapably embodied. The features that exclude those with anomalous bodies from full access to the national ideal are the same features that make their acts of citizenship legible. "Embodied citizenship," then, stands for the unacknowledged embodiment of all citizens, but more directly calls upon the ideological weight attached to bodily difference as the overdetermining force of political participation for those marked as different.

The long history of political marginalization of people with marked bodies should not, however, suggest their invisibility in the national imagination. Physical unruliness may exclude individuals from the subject position in foundational formulations of the human, but corporeal difference nevertheless acts as a frequent figure *against* which to define the human. C. B. Macpherson underscores Locke's work on the self-possessive subject in the central principle that "what makes a man human is freedom from dependence on the wills of others" (263). By making one's humanity contingent upon self-determination of one's person, this logic excludes all those who have been constructed as physically dependent. Of course it is not a new observation to challenge the uneven principles of freedom as applied to slaves, women, the poor, children, immigrants, and disabled people. While the laws governing the legal citizenship status of these groups all have their own complex histories,[2] the ideological legacies of their exclusions persist in how we understand access to national belonging and participation. In this regard, disabled citizens have long been the abject imaginary in the rhetoric of liberal individualism. In *Extraordinary Bodies: Figuring Physical Disability in American Literature and Culture*, Rosemarie Garland-Thomson turns to Ralph Waldo Emerson to make a similar case. In 1847, Emerson described the triumph of "self-reliance": "And now we are men . . . not minors and invalids in a protected corner, not cowards fleeing before revolution, but guides." For Emerson, conservatives are "effeminated by nature, born halt and blind" and can "only, like invalids, act on the defensive."[3] The triumphant figures of autonomous individualism that are emblematic of American citizenship construct and cast out their opposites from membership. As a persistent "not-me" figure in the rhetoric of American independence and the literal target of political prohibitions, people with marked bodily differences may easily complain of national exclusion. These complaints, however, are themselves an act of citizenship, in that they make a claim upon the state for civil rights. This book looks at the moments of narrative collision that emerge when excluded subjects expose the contradictions and gaps upon which citizenship is founded.

Where the preceding discussion demonstrates how bodies have been located simultaneously at the center and margins of citizenship and political representation, the following sections consider the tension between material embodiment and symbolic representation. These veins of inquiry begin to tease out the complex intersections between the physical and the political, the material and the metaphoric, the national and the symbolic. These intersecting spheres, in turn, lay the conceptual groundwork for the book as a whole.

The Trouble with Metaphor

The imaginative rejections that locate corporeal difference outside national ideals are perhaps the most expected deployment of disability in the national imaginary, but should not obscure equally pervasive metaphors in which the disabled physical body stands directly for the social body. Despite representative democracy's consistent exclusion of disabled *individuals*, *figures* of anomalous bodies are often pressed into service as a metaphorical representation of the body politic. In his 1868 sketch called "The Siamese Twins," Mark Twain imagines Chang and Eng's immediate physical proximity as a virtue of loyalty, not physical necessity, in order to offer a contrast to a nation at war with itself. Twain's essay offers a rare case in which the anomalous body stands as an idealized vision of the national body. More often, disability represents an indictment of a nation gone wrong. Heart-tugging images of children with cancer in popular films like *Erin Brockovich* or *20/20*-style news coverage offer an indictment of public policies and corporate practices that threaten national innocence. While powerful as a tool of protest, this kind of symbolism collapses any account of rich subjectivity among disabled individuals. Ultimately, the simplification required in these metaphors makes visible the imaginative violence required to even approximate a good fit.

Perhaps the most foundational visual symbol of the social body can be found in Thomas Hobbes's 1851 frontispiece to *Leviathan*. This image captures the sovereign with crown, sword, and staff ruling over both the land he gazes upon and the mass of citizens that make up his body. This striking figure reflects the contradictory realities of becoming a political subject, with its inclusion of the tools of coercion and the tension between the successful containment of the social body and its visual suggestion of a teeming, noisy crowd. Just as symbols of disability elide the complex nature of disabled citizenship, Hobbes's illustration limits itself to the difficulty in moving from the many to the one. These images are less eloquent about the ideological effects upon disabled people of being forced into service as the symbol for a nation.

The logic that seeks to align individual bodies with the nation—and its unavoidable unevenness—is an extension of the doctrine of the king's two bodies. Elizabethan jurist Edmund Plowden describes this split, "The king has in him two bodies, *viz*, a Body natural and a Body politic. His Body natural . . . is a Body mortal, subject to all infirmities that come by Nature or Accident. But his Body politic is a Body that cannot be seen or handled . . . and this Body is utterly void of Infancy, and old Age, and other natural Defects and Imbecilities" (qtd. in Kantorowicz 7). While the idea of an eternal body politic addresses the political problem of the king's death and succession, its relevance to embodied citizenship lies in its reciprocal relationship between physical bodies and political ideals. The king's body natural is that which animates and makes legible the intangible body politic. As an embodied stand-in for an abstract unity, conceptions of both the physical and the political body shift according to their mutual alignment. In Joseph Roach's work on cultural memory, the mingling of the national body in the king's body extends to a series of performative substitutes starting with actors playing kings on the stage and extending to a model of behavior in public spheres. By making legible an imitative category called kingliness (which is already coextensive with national identity), staged performance bleeds into the "performance of everyday life" to multiply the exemplary citizen beyond the body of the king and toward a property called "Englishness." The doctrine of the king's two bodies and its extension into national identification is not, however, limited to Britain's monarchy. Although the American Revolution was staged in part as a repudiation of the power of kings, Michael Rogin identifies the enduring legacy of this doctrine in the rhetoric of American presidents. Abraham Lincoln, Woodrow Wilson, and Richard Nixon, he argues, all speak of themselves as an embodiment of the nation. Just as Roach moves outward from kings to citizens, *Reading Embodied Citizenship* moves away from Rogin's U.S. presidents to explore the effects of this imaginative national alignment for figures of physical difference. I argue that taking on the mantle of the national body proceeds unevenly between normative subjects and citizens with marked bodies. When disabled people become candidates for this substitution, they carry with them the ideological burden of circulating as those with too much "body natural," as overly subject to "natural Defects and Imbecilities." Again, "embodied citizenship" carries two meanings: first, the traditional model in which the body politic is aligned with the physical body and, second, the typically overlooked ways in which embodiment carries an added ideological weight for visibly different citizens marked by disability, race, gender, and sexuality.

The persistent critical vitality of the tie between the anomalous body and the social body emerges from the unevenness inevitably found in representation—the king can never contain his two bodies. Figures of disability speak to a profound moment of interaction between the figurative and the material, an interaction that remains always incomplete. On one hand, as suggested by the image of a uniformed veteran in a wheelchair or conjoined twins Chang and Eng as a model of national fidelity, disability slips constantly toward the metaphoric. Images of anomalous bodies, often under the rubric of the grotesque, surface throughout cultural expression as a sign for largely abstract concerns. On the other hand, disability often performs a reductive role in accounts of identity formation, limiting both individuals and characters to the literal and material bounds of their physical condition. In the latter cases, disability seems relentlessly material and subjectivity emerges only through indenture to the abnormal body. As a product of these interconnected traditions, physical difference calls upon both metaphor and materiality, but it also argues that the relation between these spheres will necessarily involve imbalance and discomfort. The mingling of the physical, social, and textual body, then, captures a shifting and uneven terrain in which each element can become obscured and ignored. Figures of disability are read as striking pictures of inescapable physical realities—for example, the daily difficulty of dressing for a paraplegic—or mere signs of abstract anxieties. These poles, however, exist on a spectrum in which the material and the abstract are mutually reliant.

Language and the body exist in a supplemental relation in which neither category can be conceived without recourse to the other. Contemporary theorists, most notably David Wills, capture this phenomenon under the disability-resonant term "prosthesis." In Wills's sprawling and speculative 1995 volume, *Prosthesis*, he grounds his exploration of the term's abstract resonances in the recollection of his father's use of a prosthetic leg and cane. It is perhaps not surprising that Wills sees instances of prosthesis proliferating throughout history and culture since, at its core, the term captures for Wills the necessary mediation between language and the material. In their 2000 work, *Narrative Prosthesis: Disability and the Dependencies of Discourse*, David Mitchell and Sharon Snyder take up Wills's foundational theorization of prosthesis, but yoke their examination more thoroughly to the context of disability. For Mitchell and Snyder, prosthesis points to the social construction of a normal body as the prosthetic seeks to restore the "deficient" body to this ideal of somatic wholeness. This restoration, however, remains incomplete, and "the ruse of prosthesis always fails in its primary objective: to return the body to the invisible status of a normative essence" (8). Much of the rich value and force of Mitchell and Snyder's prosthetic model lies in its emphasis on the moments of discomfort and poor fit that denaturalize ideals of the complete body.

When read in conjunction with *Narrative Prosthesis*, Vivian Sobchack's work inserts a helpful caution about the risks of using prosthesis solely as a metaphor. Each of these three critics retains the material roots of prosthesis while exploring its suggestive theoretical implications. In her essay "A Leg to Stand On: Prosthetics, Metaphor, and Materiality," Sobchack takes on critics outside disability studies who use prosthesis strictly as a metaphor that mediates a series of binaries including "self/

other, body/technology, actor/ground, first world/third world, normal/ disabled, global/local, male/female, West/East, public/private" (Diane Nelson, qtd. in Sobchack, *Carnal Thoughts* 208). I quote this list in full to prompt the response I share with Sobchack: "This is a tall order for a metaphor to fill" (208). In its use as the great mediator, Sobchack argues that the material origins of prosthesis as the replacement of a missing body part have themselves been lost. Sobchack looks to reseat studies of prosthetics through a phenomenological approach that emphasizes the lived body. Her essay goes on to describe the experience of embodiment in terms of "figuration," in which metaphorics offer more than a linguistic tool, but serve as a model by which to understand somatic form. In another and related critique of the celebratory turn to pain, technology, and prosthetics exemplified by Jean Baudrillard's vision of the transcendent escape from the body as "meat," Sobchack rejects this deflating read of the body as object ("Beating the Meat" 211). She offers the ethically and intellectually charged reminder that one's corporeal experience is important to subjectivity. While my own readings are less explicitly grounded in the term, I find prosthesis helpful to hold in mind because it recalls Mitchell's, Snyder's, and Sobchack's acknowledgment of the naturalized and repressive notion of bodily wholeness. Here, prosthesis serves as the specific starting ground of an analysis that seeks to hold in mind the mutually defining spheres of metaphor (the text) and materiality (the physical) in constructions of the body. Prosthesis exists both literally and conceptually to demonstrate the uneven relation between bodies and the ideal of completeness they never reach. Sobchack, Wills, Mitchell, and Snyder take divergent paths in their studies of prosthesis, but each holds in mind the notion that linguistic form and embodiment act in mutually reinforcing ways. In *Reading Embodied Citizenship*, I argue, similarly, that the alliance between the body politic and the physical body is more than a mere coincidence of terms, but can open up readings of both the material and the metaphoric.

Materiality as Cultural Capital and Burden

As Captain Ahab or Richard III or Tiny Tim might testify, however, the national imagination is much more comfortable exploiting disability as a symbol than it is accustomed to considering the disciplinary effect of cultural norms upon disabled individuals. According to this logic, the material elements of embodiment seem divorced from history or culture and disability assumes the status of unshakeable truth. In fact, much of the early ground gained among disability theorists has been to wrench disability from its position as a seemingly obvious property of the body. One of the first steps in this process occurred in 1976 with the articulation of the social model of disability, conceived as a rejection of medical narratives that see disability as residing in natural physical flaws.[4] The social model argues for a conceptual break between disability and impairment, in which disability is a discriminatory social effect "imposed on top of one's impairment."[5] This split in terminology between "impairment" and "disability" argues that cultural forms are the social grid laid over the natural body. The model relies on an identifiable category called impairment that is located in the body and understood as distinct from the social. One legacy of this distinction is that physical impairment becomes, for some, the limit case of social constructionism. Despite the ground gained in dislodging race and sex from biological essentialism, studies of the body that couch disability within a similarly anti-essentialist framework must work against the widespread cultural assumption that there is something more "real" about physical impairment. Rosemarie Garland-Thomson, who stages her 1997 book *Extraordinary Bodies* explicitly as a "reframing of disability as another culture-bound, physically justified difference to consider along with race, gender, class, ethnicity and sexuality" (5), demonstrates the complexities of materiality by a tension in her language between disability as discursive representation and the "raw materials of bodily variation" and "physiological facts" (6, 7). This widespread conceptual persistence of the "raw" body and its "facts" demands that any account of the body that relies upon a discursive model must offer an answer to the skeptical question, "How can not being able to walk [see, speak, hear] be socially constructed?" For those committed to a discursive model, the answer would be to argue that there can be no understanding of a raw body detached from the disciplinary practices that make it legible. For me, as important as the content of the question itself is the incredulity with which it is asked. This skepticism, both within and outside disability circles, points to the phenomenon I am interested in here, namely, what are the political and ideological effects of this belief in the body's overdetermining "reality"? The perceived limits of the social construction model prompt responses on two fronts: First, what might be a productive model for understanding the relation between bodies and subjectivity? And second, what intellectual currency is gained by those who argue from a position granting priority to the perceived irreducible reality of the disabled body?

The ideological split between the physical and the social evokes familiar ground for theorists of embodiment who are used to challenging divisions between body and subject. To return to the logic of citizenship, the doctrine of "property in one's person" suggests that while the body is necessary, it assumes the secondary position of possession. Writing against this assumption, both Vivian Sobchack and Barbara Duden draw from phenomenology to press for a reformulation from the body that we *have* to the body that we *are*. In addressing a similar problem, Elizabeth Grosz's *Volatile Bodies* offers a way to conceive of embodiment as it differs from the persistent philosophical models of dualism and monism. In dualist perspectives, the mind and body are seen as distinct categories, typically with the mind as the active subject in control of the body as object. A monist approach would see mind and body as aspects of a single, irreducible substance. Grosz rejects both traditions in favor of a model that deconstructs the clarity of a split between body and subject. She writes,

> Bodies and minds are not two distinct substances or two kinds of attributes of a single substance, but somewhere in between these two alternatives. The Möbius strip has the advantage of showing the inflection of mind into body and body into mind, the ways in which, through a kind of twisting or inversion, one side becomes another. This model also provides a way of problematizing and rethinking the relations between the inside and the outside of the subject, its psychical interior and its corporeal exterior, by showing not their fundamental identity or reducibility but the torsion of the one into the other, the passage, vector, or uncontrollable drift of the inside into the outside and the outside into the inside. (xii)

In this formulation, Grosz denies the possibility of a disembodied mind. She insists on a model in which bodies are produced by and productive of subjectivity.[6] The twisting, never-ending Möbius strip frustrates attempts to finally approach a pure or prediscursive body, but it also requires us to hold onto the material conditions of the body. Instead of arguing for a natural body onto which social meanings are imposed, Grosz offers a way of troubling the split between the body and the mind without collapsing either category.

If Elizabeth Grosz offers an antidote to persistent turns to the physical as reality, then by contrast, other theorists of disability argue for the body's materiality and, in doing so, gain academic ground. In *Narrative Prosthesis*, David Mitchell and Sharon Snyder share Rosemarie Garland-Thomson's interest in charting the relation between disability and race,

gender, and sexuality. In their introductory essay, "Disability and Identity," Mitchell and Snyder acknowledge their debt to multicultural studies
but argue that "disability occupies a unique identity that must navigate
the terrain between physical/cognitive differences and social stigma.
No purely constructivist reading can adequately traverse this political
and experiential divide" (3). While I would argue against the notion that
ideologies of race or gender can be understood as any less reliant on assumptions of physical difference than disability,[7] I am even more struck
by the rhetorical recourse made to materiality in order to establish legitimacy in an emerging field of study. Seeking to avoid the posterior
spot in a simultaneously contested and wearying line of identity categories—gender, race, class, sexuality, religion, nationality, age—disability
theorists often seize upon the social importance granted to the body as
that which "really matters."

The cultural capital generated from claims to materiality in Mitchell and Snyder's work, however, also demonstrates the compromising
effects of institutionalized knowledge production. As standard bearers
in a nascent field, scholars in the first wave of disability studies must
locate themselves in a tradition of claims upon the state or the academy
while also distinguishing themselves from what has gone before. As the
title suggests, Simi Linton's *Claiming Disability* performs this function
as a manifesto for the legitimacy of disability studies in the humanities.
Similarly, Michael Bérubé's "Citizenship and Disability" grounds itself
in declarations of the value of centering disability in political policy and
discourse. His language tends toward strong, flag-planting claims such
as "Without a sufficient theoretical and practical account of disability, we
can have no account of democracy worthy of the name" or "A capacious
and supple sense of what it is to be human is better than a narrow and
partial sense of what it is to be human, and the more participants we as a
society can incorporate into the deliberation of what it means to be human, the greater the chances that that deliberation will in fact be transformative in such a way as to enhance our collective capacities to recognize
each other as humans entitled to human dignity" (56). While it serves to
inspire more broad-based support for a disability rights movement—itself an important goal—the investment in "human dignity" and a liberal
project seeking to resuscitate the promises of the democratic state seem
at odds with the theoretical underpinnings of disability, which challenge
not just the capaciousness of the category "human," but its construction
and deployment as a social and political tool. Perhaps the not-surprising
response to this tension is that the need for institutional legibility as an

academic program or civil rights agenda requires a rhetorical and conceptual move that sets aside the radical theoretical challenges of disability in favor of something like shared democratic values.

While the extension of democratic values creates a clear path toward liberal reformation, it should not be undertaken without acknowledging the costs. In Simi Linton's discussion of the institutionalization of multiculturalism, she recounts Henry Louis Gates Jr.'s argument that the "extended face-off with conservatism has had a deforming effect, encouraging multiculturalism to know what it is against but not what it is for" (qtd. in Linton 88). I use or quote the disability-inflected language of both "institutionalization" and "deforming effect" deliberately in the previous sentence. Gates's use of "deforming effect," when read through a disability studies lens, reemphasizes the relational or social nature of physical difference. The claims of disability studies, like the compromises and concessions of ethnic and women's studies programs, necessarily shift and "deform" in order to make themselves conform to state and academic narratives that have excluded disability and its interests from their value systems. This increasing academic and political institutionalization cannot be read as an uncomplicated victory. Like the medical model of institutionalization for disabled people, a coherent disability studies program can lead to visibility and coalitions, but it also requires compromises in self-determination and scholarship. In this sense, disability studies, in its "deforming" relation with academia and government, is tracing the same ground that race and gender has trod in the past forty years.[8] I do not want to dismiss the value of gains in institutional visibility that continue to be made by disability scholars and activists. I do, however, hope that disability studies can support the work of internal debate, a heterogeneous model of coalition that I develop in chapters 4 and 5 as finding its model in disability itself. This relationship between identity-based rights movements and the rhetorical postures demanded by social institutions in order to achieve legibility is another ground upon which to explore how each overlapping sphere puts pressure on the others.

Writing like Michael Bérubé's and Simi Linton's is particularly compelling because of the way both yoke their scholarly intervention to the heightened stakes of political discourse: who, after all, wants to be on the side of a narrow, unworthy democracy aligned against the value of human dignity? In taking democracy at its word, however, and insisting on an extension of promised rights and freedoms, this vein of argument participates in the universalist reasoning of the liberal state that has produced the exclusion of disabled people. While I take up the strategic value of such claims upon the state in chapter 3, as an introductory move I will dwell upon my sense of wariness at this union between disability studies and the foundational assumptions of the nation. As the preceding discussion of prosthesis suggests, this juncture inevitably entails both possibility and poor fit. Since its inception, disability studies has grappled with how to account for the body's physical properties, reacting against two long-standing and equally repressive traditions. The anomalous body is viewed either as without interior life and therefore entirely reducible to its form, or as purely symbolic, a stand-in for "larger concerns."[9] The emergence of the social model of disability, and with it the language of impairment, has sparked continued debates over the line between the "social" and the "material." These arguments form much of the important ground constituting disability studies, and their continued vitality speaks to a phenomenon that lies at the heart of my current inquiry: the uneven ideological distribution of embodiment. Rather than redraw the line between the metaphoric and the material, this book examines the mutually constitutive relationship between the physical, political, and textual body to reveal the imaginative constructions that emerge through the productive tension among these terms.

If we return to the foundational claims of liberal democracy, we find a similar mismatch between the universalized language of the body and the move to obscure the complex heterogeneity of an embodied population. The logic of "property in one's person" suggests that self-governing one's material body is intended as a universal principle, but the contradictory claims of liberty suggest an ideal where the body slips away from notice. Rosemarie Garland-Thomson's neologism, the "normate body," describes a similar phenomenon. In *Extraordinary Bodies*, Garland-Thomson argues, "The disabled figure operates as the vividly embodied, stigmatized other whose social role is to symbolically free the privileged, idealized figure of the American self from the vagaries and vulnerabilities of embodiment" (7). Certainly, national calls to liberty include a belief in freedom from excessive demands of the body. The fullest access to citizenship depends on mastery of the physical.

While the notion of liberty as both mastery of and freedom from the body relies on a universal norm, the practice of citizenship demonstrates that all bodies do not "matter" equally. Judith Butler's work in *Bodies That Matter* foregrounds the politically inflected consequences of embodiment in her title's play on "matter" as both materiality and social importance. Butler pitches her 1993 work as a response, in part, to common critical responses to *Gender Trouble*. In addition to taking on the misapprehension that gender performativity suggests a choosing subject, Butler attempts to address the (patronizing) question, "What about the materiality of the body, *Judy*?" (ix). This question comes from the sense that constructed categories may open up some kinds of analysis, but are limited to only ever being seen as artificial and dispensable (xi). Butler transforms the question of materiality from this notion of an indispensable or prediscursive category into a process she calls "materialization." The stakes of this turn from "matter" to "materialize" are the chance to call attention to the problem of trying to reference any kind of pure body. Butler is interested in the process by which the boundaries of bodies become legible and naturalized and, consequently, how this process depends on an abject and constitutive outside consisting of abnormal bodies.[10] She writes, "How, then, can one think through the matter of bodies as a kind of materialization governed by regulatory norms in order to ascertain the workings of heterosexual hegemony in the formation of what qualifies as a viable body? How does that materialization of the norm in bodily formation produce a domain of abjected bodies, a field of deformation, which, in failing to qualify as the fully human, fortifies those regulatory norms?" (16). In Butler's interest in "materialization," materiality is attached to the production of "viable bodies." The norm comes to occupy the celebrated mantle of the term "body," and the abnormal is excluded from full access to the term. If we were to try to populate the category of abject bodies, however, it seems as though its candidates are more appropriately conceived as those with an excess of materiality, as those with too much body. Corporeality is not distributed evenly across the normal and the abnormal. Instead, the materialization of the viable body, in as much as it relies upon abjected bodies, allows for a kind of escape from the physical body that is only possible for the unremarkable norm. The material body becomes a sticky, thick property that attaches itself to those conceived as different and becomes the over-determining force of their formation as subjects.

Embodiment is not a raw or universal property. The burden of corporeality[11] assigned to deviant bodies acts as a socially determining factor, but is obscured and naturalized as solely a product of inescapable realities. One of the barbs hiding in this burden of materiality is that its ideological effects are made invisible by its very construction as that which is outside ideology. While I argue that all acts of U.S. citizenship presume bodily ownership, it is particularly figures of bodily difference whose civic participation is understood as inescapably "embodied citizenship."

This burden of materiality includes a paradox: the anomalous characteristics that exclude individuals from full access to the political imaginary become the same features that structure their participation. When a citizen with an embodied difference enters the public sphere, that body becomes the determining force of their belonging.

* * *

Although "citizenship" can be most broadly understood as the category that organizes the relation of the individual to the state, its centrality to my project deserves a more focused articulation of what practices and identifications constitute the term. Writing in the mid-twentieth century, T. H. Marshall offers an enduring summary of the three elements that make up citizenship. He argues for a civil element, made up of individual freedoms; the political element, entailing participation in government; and a social element, requiring an equitable distribution of goods. Even as a starting point, Marshall's definition of citizenship holds together both a point of identification—a legal belonging—and a series of performative political acts, like voting or jury duty. *Reading Embodied Citizenship* works from the premise that citizenship entails not just a fixed juridical status, but also a more flexible sense of national identity that shifts in its significance. As Lauren Berlant argues, citizenship is not necessarily the central or true definitional frame according to which Americans understand themselves (10). In fact, the correct observations that "America" most properly designates a continental politic or that individuals are increasingly organized under a transnational frame both cast studies of the national as potentially passé, if not jingoistic.[12] While acknowledging these important interventions in the tradition of exceptionalism in American studies, I argue that national citizenship still carries an ideological weight that can profoundly structure how embodied subjects understand their connection to the social body.

The category of the political deserves a similar unseating; instead of seeing the state as the privileged object of political struggle, I follow Kirstie McClure's formulation of a more extended category of "quotidian politics." McClure argues for the "diffusion of political sites across the surface of the social itself, to the elaboration of 'the political' beyond its modernist enclosure within the territorially-bounded juridical institutions of the state into the far more fluid and shifting domain of cultural representation and social practices" (123). By arguing for cultural production as political practice, this more capacious model draws literary and critical work into the sphere of citizenship. Political theorists like McClure, Ernesto Laclau, and Chantal Mouffe allow for a project that can read for citizenship in such seemingly disparate forms as the literary grotesque genre and autobiographical accounts of Vietnam War protests.

As a work of literary analysis, this project assumes the centrality of aesthetic forms and strategies as constitutive forces that shape embodied citizenship. Again, Mark Twain offers a vivid example of the imaginative link between bodies and texts. In his introduction to *Those Extraordinary Twins*, Twain claims that the story was inspired after he "had seen a picture of a youthful Italian 'freak'—or 'freaks'—which was—or which were—on exhibition in our cities" (119). The linguistic ambivalence between the singular and plural here offers an emblematic instance of the destabilizing effect these characters have upon their introduction to sleepy Dawson's Landing. Writing almost a century later, novelist Katherine Dunn demonstrates the endurance of our linguistic struggle to adequately address physical anomaly. Speaking of her conjoined daughters, the mother of *Geek Love*'s carnival family instructs, "We use the plural form . . . whenever we refer to Electra and Iphigenia. We do not say, 'Where is Elly and Iphy?' We say 'Where *are* Elly and Iphy?'" (51). In both of these examples, the social apprehension of difference cannot be extricated from the linguistic tools used to process these visual encounters. Unfamiliarity makes visible the acts of reading that constitute the social sphere, exposing the often-masked requirement of corporeal legibility. Unfamiliarity also sparks the turn to narrative as the community looks for the story behind the disability. Literature carries with it an etiological impulse, and the presence of unusual bodies requires the emergence of new forms of sense-making narratives. Often, as in the work of Mark Twain or David Foster Wallace, the bodies at the heart of the story will offer a model for the textual body itself. Twain, for example, in 1894 published the fragments of *Those Extraordinary Twins* conjoined in a single volume with *Pudd'nhead Wilson*, and in *Infinite Jest*, Wallace offers a collection of disjointed bodies within a novel that is similarly piecemeal and episodic. These slips between unfamiliar bodies and new textual forms are not simply an author's attempt to make literature match reality, but demonstrations of the embedded relation in the homology of physical, social, and textual bodies.

As I've hinted at above, this work casts a wide historical net that spans from Mark Twain's work in the late nineteenth century to postmodern literature of the late twentieth. While the chapters proceed along a chronological trajectory, my organizing logic is not one of historical development. Many foundational works in disability studies have accounted for a similarly broad historical period, but take the general form of a qualified progress narrative. In *Extraordinary Bodies*, Rosemarie Garland-Thomson begins with sentimental fiction of the nineteenth century and closes with a hopeful turn to "Disabled Women as Powerful Women" in works by Toni Morrison and Audre Lorde. Both *Narrative Prosthesis* and Rachel Adams's *Sideshow U.S.A.* end with readings of Katherine Dunn's *Geek Love*, celebrated by Mitchell and Snyder as the move from "modernist freaks" to "postmodern geeks." Following these examples, one might assume a book charting citizenship and disability in the twentieth century would proceed according to a development model that finds its peak in the triumphant passing of the Americans with Disabilities Act of 1990. Instead, I set aside this linear model and draw from broad historical contexts to argue that while the terms and effects play out differently, the relation of anomalous bodies to the state has been an enduring problem in American literature. Such a wide span also represents a departure from the work done on citizenship by Lauren Berlant in which she emphatically locates her analysis in the post–Reagan-Bush era to offer a historical claim about the enmeshed relations of the public and private spheres. Rather than making a case for a newly emergent historical moment, I argue for a mobile formation, which claims that while all U.S. citizenship is embodied, only the political acts of those with extraordinary bodies are marked as such.

In the following chapters, I focus on flashpoints in the history of twentieth-century American embodiment, choosing literary works that both reflect and enact crisis moments in the enduring connection between physical, textual, and national bodies. Each text under examination stages an encounter between a disabled individual and the body politic and explores a series of narrative strategies for making sense of this destabilizing moment of contact. My first chapter, "Domesticating the Exceptional," examines the figure of conjoined twins as an embodied challenge to the ideology of American individualism. Focusing on Mark Twain's often-overlooked 1894 text, *Those Extraordinary Twins*, this analysis shows how Twain's disabled heroes demonstrate the tension between social- and self-government at the heart of liberal democracy. If liberal individualism in the United States has been a consistent push and pull between the demands of the self and the demands of the community, conjoined twins embody this dilemma in which the other man is constantly at one's side.

Where Twain exploits the comic elements of exotic conjoined twins and their encounter with a small Missouri town, in my second chapter, I demonstrate the ways in which Carson McCullers and Flannery O'Connor set their encounters with physical difference on the larger stage of a growing urban demographic. If Reconstruction and its immediate aftermath marked a crisis in American definitions of citizenship and the face of the body politic, the massive growth of American cities in the twentieth century marks a similar reconsideration of the individual in contrast to the urban crowd. Whereas by and large the modernist writers of the early twentieth century tended to locate their sense of alienation in visions of a fragmented psyche, writers of the mid-century situated their anxieties about a changing social body in a striking proliferation of disabled figures often grouped under the literary grotesque. Carson McCullers's *The Heart Is a Lonely Hunter* (1940) and Flannery O'Connor's *Wise Blood* (1952) use physical difference to represent an alienating modern state. Not just metaphors for a chaotic world, however, these disabled characters suggest a vexed position of critique stemming from the alignment of the anomalous body with a truth not corrupted by national interests. In the encounter between McCullers's John Singer and the public spaces of the café and the boardinghouse, for example, Singer's disability serves as a lightning rod for communal fantasies of a more "real" existence outside the corrupted veneer of normative, modern life. This identification between the disabled body and an abstract reality prompts a different set of imaginative strategies for managing physical difference, including reverent fantasies of exclusive, disabled wisdom.

Chapter 3, "The Uniform Body: Spectacles of Disability and the Vietnam War," locates the disabled Vietnam veteran as an embodiment of the national struggle to recuperate the ideals of militarized masculinity after the loss of the war. Corporeal incoherence emerges during this era both physically, in constant threats of death and injury, and conceptually, as the patriotic message of the nation breaks down in a failed and unpopular war. In reading Ron Kovic's memoir *Born on the Fourth of July* (1976) and Larry Heinemann's novel *Paco's Story* (1979), I argue that each author uses narrative strategies to capture an overwhelming national desire to shore up a reliably meaningful body in the face of these disintegrations. Relocating the urban crowds of chapter 2 to the patriotic spheres of parades and protests, this chapter explores the public stage of this national reconsideration.

In chapter 4, Ruth Ozeki's *My Year of Meats* (1998) and Katherine Dunn's *Geek Love* (1983) portray disabilities that are the effect of chemical or hormonal intervention during gestation or early childhood. While the authors take strikingly different positions toward these disabilities—Ozeki uses disability as a warning sign against corporate excesses, whereas Dunn's carnival world celebrates anomaly as a valuable gift—both authors see physical difference as the grounds for critiquing dominant ideology and economic practices. Like the disabled Vietnam veteran narratives of chapter 3, Ozeki and Dunn expose dominant norms through figures of disability. In "Conceiving the Freakish Body," I argue that along with this critique, however, the novels move beyond the oppositional signs and chants of political protest to demonstrate the ways in which the contemporary body necessarily incorporates the very systems the authors critique. This assimilation of dominant values does not mark the failure of the novels' progressive politics, but instead enacts a disability-inspired model, which allows for the inevitable presence of harmful or difficult elements as the grounds for necessary reconfiguration, especially in the face of a world increasingly mediated by technology and global capitalism.

My fifth chapter returns to the problem of individualism set up by Twain's conjoined twins to explore a hyperbolic vision of the unique body at the end of the twentieth century. I turn to David Foster Wallace's *Infinite Jest* (1996) in order to reject the contradictory tenets of individualism in favor of a model of interdependence—a model suggested by the physical demands and theoretical possibilities of disability. This emphasis on mutual reliance is the political component of a broader model of assemblage, which, as I argue in "Some Assembly Required," holds together Wallace's vision of nation, bodies, and texts. Promoting explicitly the model of reading that undergirds this book as a whole, this final chapter offers a theorization of these three categories in which each is legible only as a complex of interlocking parts that defer completion or unity. Like the disability-inspired model of political dissent I develop in chapter 4, the theoretical insights and material demands of disability offer a method for reading the notoriously unruly strands of *Infinite Jest*.

Each of the following chapters unfolds along two intertwined threads, first, by exploring the stakes of encounter between the body politic and the embodied citizen and, second, by using disability as a conceptual frame through which to read the ensuing reimaginations. The course of the book charts a series of expanding social encounter, from the intimate life of a small Missouri town to Wallace's vision of competing continental interests. Covering historical and literary ground between the 1890s and the 1950s, chapters 1 and 2 demonstrate how the disabled figures that are subject to scrutiny by the crowd prompt a reexamination of dominant assumptions, including the priority of the individual, the "naturalness" of the political formation, and popular fantasies of the wise, disabled guru. As suggested by my preceding discussions of the necessary connections between metaphor and materiality, or embodiment and subjectivity, this book asks about the subjective costs for citizens living according to these ideologies, but also considers disability as a productive conceptual model. Chapter 3, for example, describes the nation's insistence on reliable signs of military strength from its soldiers and then follows the tradition of spectacle in visible disability to demonstrate the ways in which the national stage of parades and protests unmakes this uniform body.

The concluding chapters consider the preoccupations surrounding the nation and embodiment at the close of the twentieth century: international paths of consumption and production, excess, waste, media saturation, infertility, and population growth. Both chapters, then, take disability seriously as the ground for a productive reconfiguration of the ideologies underlying these anxieties. In chapter 4, the acknowledgment of discomfort and difficulty inevitable in disability argues that the incorporation of critiqued elements into the body—such as reimagining human reproduction according to the genetic and hormonal interventions critiqued in agribusiness—is not failure, but marks the possibility, in fact the necessity, of accommodation and realignment. To demonstrate the influence of corporate logic on contemporary accounts of embodiment does not signal acquiescence, but instead offers a holistic account of the world, enacting the connections among person, place, and thing. Similarly, in chapter 5, the physical demands of the disabled body suggest that individualism is not only an unreachable but also an undesirable goal. Interdependence, by contrast, provides an ethical model that can reshape the contours of physical, political, and textual forms.

From the boardinghouses of Twain, McCullers, and Heinemann, to the streetside crowds of O'Connor and Kovic, to the spectacles of sideshows, documentary commercials, and AA speakers meetings, each narrative explored in this book emphasizes the social dynamics of disability. If the conflicting interests of the individual and the community lie at the heart of liberal democracy, striking physical difference exposes this tension, calling out the lie of sameness of condition. In the fantasy of equality, heterogeneous populations settle into faceless crowds. The encounter between visibly disabled individuals and that crowd prompts mutual reconsideration. In the petty trials and elections of *Those Extraordinary*

Twins, conjoined brothers require new meditations on rights and justice. In *My Year of Meats*, Jane Takagi-Little's footage of a pretty girl paralyzed by a Wal-Mart delivery truck pushes viewers by an obvious corporeal metaphor to critique the crushing impact of the superstore's pricing structures on local businesses. These spectacles of physical difference unfortunately do not chart an easy historical progression of expanded rights and understanding, but they do speak to a string of national anxieties about the changing shape of the nation.

The shifts and revisions that emerge as the political and the embodied intersect call upon narrative strategies to make sense of troubling encounters. At times, as I argue in chapter 1, this narrative process becomes a form of domestication, wherein exceptional bodies are forced into order and legibility. Other encounters lead to more progressive ends, as symbols of wisdom, political protest, and recovery. As I've suggested in my above discussion of the complexities of metaphor and materiality, the layers of meaning composing the textual body and the necessary difficulties of disability and politics require that these encounters deserve closer reading. Through this series of literary readings, I use the theoretical and material reaches of disability as a heuristic model that can open up new critiques and possibilities in understanding physical, political, and textual bodies.

The danger in seeing disability as a conceptual model lies in the potential slide from use to abuse, in which these models become merely static forms. An alignment of disability with difficulty inevitably resonates with the contemporary vogue for complexity and heterogeneity.[13] While at some level I believe this slip into reified categories is a constant threat in scholarly endeavor, I also credit embodiment, again, in providing an antidote against this trend. Whether in confronting the gaps in foundational national promises or in the handicapping ubiquity of stairs and high curbs, difficulty registers in the body and takes a physical toll. This physicality, in turn, lays out a material ground for heterogeneity, re-membering the stakes of these conceptual reconfigurations. By their difference, anomalous figures call out the naturalized assumptions that legitimate their exclusion. People seen as bad managers of their unruly bodies, those who bear the burden of an overdetermining materiality, enact a contradiction in the national imaginary that can reinscribe the conditions of citizenship. These moments of imaginative political address create a point of friction in national logic that may not enact revolution, but can momentarily make strange America's familiar categories of citizenship.

1 / Domesticating the Exceptional: *Those Extraordinary Twins* and the Limits of American Individualism

One of the richest moments in Mark Twain's fiction comes in the opening pages of *Pudd'nhead Wilson* with the "fatal" half-a-dog joke. On his first day in Dawson's Landing, David Wilson joins a "group of citizens" and offers the remark that will transform him instantly and for twenty years into a pudd'nhead. While standing together, the group hears "an invisible dog" barking, yelping, and disrupting the sleepy peace of the town. Wilson remarks, "I wished I owned half of that dog." Why? "Because, I would kill my half" (6). This early scene resonates with many of the major thematic concerns of the novel as a whole, such that the joke and its aftermath stand as a symbol for anxieties about personal and racial identity, local governance, and violence. In addition to discovering Twain's most explicit concerns in the scene, critics have bound the joke to more subtle readings of the novel, linking the desire to own half a dog to a critique of the nineteenth-century economy of speculation or seeing the joke as an exposure of reified and arbitrary social conventions.[1] In my own analysis, this scene encapsulates a trio of enmeshed problems at the center of embodied citizenship: a challenge to conventional identity categories, the management of strangeness among a citizenry, and the reliance upon legibility for ideological classification.

Like the half-a-dog joke, *Pudd'nhead Wilson* and *Those Extraordinary Twins* undermine and reveal the slips of any ideological security attached to individuality. The excessively literal mind-set of the townspeople prompts confusion over Wilson's statement—"What did he reckon would become of the other half if he killed his half?" (6). While they congratulate themselves on locating the ridiculous in Wilson alone, the townspeople mask the fact that their economy and citizenry rely upon asserting equally impossible divisions. The action of *Pudd'nhead Wilson* is set into motion by Roxy, the engineer of the novel's baby-switching plot. We are introduced to Roxy first through her use of black dialect, visually and orally marked off in the text with truncated letters, and repeated terms like "dat" or "sho." The narrative eye then follows Wilson's perspective, peering out the window with him to discover the source of this speech. The narrative interest in the problem of parts and division emerges in Twain's description of this first vision of Roxy's light skin: "Only one-sixteenth of her was black, and that sixteenth did not show" (9). As a parallel to the "invisible dog" that offers no optic proof of its identity but announces itself through barking, Roxy's "invisible" blackness becomes manifest in her language. According to the narrator's logic, Roxy both is and is not black. In the slave economy of Dawson's Landing and its antebellum setting, however, the complexities of racial identity must be collapsed into the extensively legislated fiction of a uniform black subject. Following the "one-drop" rule of American racial classification, Dawson's Landing enacts Wilson's now-tragic joke, asserting its repressive ownership of Roxy's black "part."

Where *Pudd'nhead Wilson* centers on Roxy and the problems of locating racial identity in the body, its companion text, *Those Extraordinary Twins*, showcases conjoined twins as an embodied failure of individualism. Instead of the minute focus on locating identity in ever-retreating "parts," Angelo and Luigi Cappello embody the challenge to unity residing in an excess of parts—in this case, two heads, four arms, one body, and two legs (130). The two texts themselves form a kind of conjoined pair, published together in a single volume, each revealing traces of or dependencies upon the other. Although Twain began writing the story of the twins first, he tells readers in the preface that he performed "a kind of literary Caesarian operation" (125), pulling *Those Extraordinary Twins* out of the now complete novel. Twain followed his serial publication of *Pudd'nhead Wilson* with an 1894 volume that included both stories. Bracketed asides in the twins' text offer instructions for how the action of that story weaves into the plot of *Pudd'nhead*, in which the Italian twins have been domesticated as separated brothers. The novels' meditation on parts and wholes permeates everything from moments like the half-a-dog joke, to Roxy and the twins, to the form of the text itself.

This anxiety over unity extends to the preface of *Those Extraordinary Twins*, where Twain describes the work's creative spark: "I had seen a picture of a youthful Italian 'freak'—or 'freaks'—which was—or which were—on exhibition in our cities" (119). Twain switches from "freak" to "freaks" within a single breath in a written form of the baffling simultaneity that the twins embody as seemingly both one and two people. Figures of conjoined twins embody the structure of a dialectic as it serves to undo the split between seemingly discrete categories. The categories of self and other are fundamentally disrupted by conjoined twins, a structure that reverses the divisive impulse of the half-a-dog joke, but that parallels its unsettling effect.

Twain's move from "freak" to "freaks" attempts to re-create a viewing experience in which the combination of familiar elements in an unfamiliar configuration denies easy understanding. This linguistic ambivalence between the singular and plural demonstrates language's role in making sense of or holding in suspense any assimilation of the anomalous. The struggle to find language that will appropriately describe the brothers becomes a recurring joke in *Those Extraordinary Twins*. It is a problem that, not surprisingly, is figured first in Wilson's comment about the dog. After Wilson claims that he would kill his half, "the group searched his face with curiosity, with anxiety even, but found no light there, no expression they could read" (6). As I contend through this book, the social requirement of legibility—the public need to find an "expression they can read"—acts as a repressive force that excludes people who are marked as different or disabled from normalcy, but directs anxious attention to their bodies nonetheless. For Twain's conjoined protagonists, and for the physically anomalous figures studied here more broadly, their participation in the social body depends upon a set of linguistic and figurative strategies according to which they manage and are managed by the citizenry.

The foundational assumption of legibility in Dawson's Landing masks the violence necessary to force what seems unassimilable into familiar categories. The social effects of Wilson's joke offer a condensed version of the revision that emerges in the aftermath of social and somatic illegibility. After finding in Wilson "no expression they could read,"

> They fell away from him as from something uncanny, and went into privacy to discuss him. One said—
> "'Pears to be a fool."
> "'Pears?" said another. "*Is*, I'd reckon you better say." (6)

While at first the town's social illiteracy seems to suspend Wilson in the alien position of the uncanny, the category of foolish pudd'nhead rises up to meet their needs. Emphasized by Twain's italics, the move from "'pears" to "*is*" demonstrates the depth of the townspeople's desire for appearance to align with reality. While "'pears" first seems to locate Wilson's strangeness in the town's perception—insisting at least on the relational structure of the assessment—"*is*" relocates the anomaly as identical to Wilson himself. By denying the social element of their claims, the town forgets its initial illiteracy and again reasserts the reliability of signs. There is no mediating distance between reading and reality for the townspeople. Both Roxy's white appearance and the twins' simultaneity betray the fiction of this system, but these excluded figures then become the target of ideological and political work that seeks to reseat the reliability of so-called natural distinctions.

Writing after the Civil War and the failures of Reconstruction, Twain's preoccupation with the problems of parts, wholes, and politics extends beyond the fictional community of Dawson's Landing to resonate on an allegorical level. The text imagines split dogs, multiracial slaves, and conjoined twins as figures for the nation itself. The metaphorical correspondence between physical bodies and the body politic creates effects in which each impacts the other in the national imagination. For people with anomalous bodies, this alignment with the nation complicates both the possibilities and limits of identification with national categories, undermining the fixity of positions such as individual, alien, and representative. Their figurative association with the nation also serves as another register through which they manage or are managed by the social body in a process I call "domestication." In the inverse direction of national symbolism, this association with freakish bodies produces a destabilizing effect, asking citizens to reconsider the legacy of the nation's foundational assumptions and to press the logics of individualism and American exceptionalism to their limits.

The Paradox of the Exceptional Representative

Twain's first sustained attention to the figure of conjoined twins came with his 1868 essay "The Siamese Twins." Twain's piece pretends to be an exposé into the private histories of the world's most famous pair of conjoined twins: Chang and Eng. The source of the enduring popular name for conjoined twins, Chang and Eng were born to Chinese parents in Siam in 1811 and sold to a merchant for international exhibition in 1824.[2] Despite their double exclusion from representative democracy as both foreign and disabled, Twain imagines the twins as the representative ideal of the nation. The American studies critic Cynthia Wu reads Twain's essay along with Thomas Nast's cartoon "The American Twins" to reveal both Twain's and Nast's sense of ambiguity about their use of the twins as figures of national unity, especially in the face of national concerns over "containing racial difference" (30). Wu situates her analysis against a changing history of Asians in the United States from exotic import and spectacle to exploited noncitizen labor through the nineteenth century. In my own reading, I focus on how Twain's essay reenvisions personal traits as national models, moving between the intimate body and the national body. I argue that these threads are necessarily interwoven in the national imagination of anomalous figures. "The Siamese Twins" opens, "I do not wish to write of the personal *habits* of these strange creatures solely, but also of certain curious details of various kinds concerning them, which, belonging only to their private life, have never crept into print. Knowing the Twins intimately, I feel that I am peculiarly well qualified for the task I have taken upon myself" (248). Twain's voice in this paragraph takes on the timbre of the carnival barker's as he advertises secret intimacies and authorizes his own knowledge. The language of anomaly becomes promiscuous across the text, first attached (properly) to "these strange creatures," then moving to the "curious details" of their lives, and finally infecting the author as one "peculiarly well qualified." By reseating strangeness within himself, Twain demonstrates the necessarily relational structure of embodied difference.[3] While conventionally this relation takes the comforting form of firmly locating freaks in the "not me" category, Twain's essay opens by questioning this reassurance and radically expanding the distribution of peculiarity. My understanding of his language as promiscuous calls upon the centrality of sexual fascination in the writing of and encounter with conjoined twins. Twain's turn to intimacy here is not simply his search for a hook, but is inextricable from the ways in which we understand unusual bodies. Part of the ideological burden of abnormality carries with it a sense of having too much body. This extra flesh and its seemingly attendant excess of intimate details and habits spark a persistent curiosity that determines, or overdetermines, the experiences of people with extraordinary bodies. Among the few details that circulate commonly about Chang and Eng Bunker's lives are their marriage in 1843 to two sisters, their fathering twenty-two children, and their eventually having more than two hundred grandchildren. These details carry with them the desire to peek behind the curtain—of both the bedroom and the freak exhibit—to discover the intimacies and physical intricacies that are simultaneously evoked and obscured by the sexualized anomalous body.[4] This intimate focus similarly demonstrates the relational structure of physical difference by recalling that curiosity about an unusual other can always have the effect of turning back on the norm; their habits are always like or unlike one's own.

Drawing from these particulars of private life, Twain constructs an allegory of the twins as national representatives. The first gesture toward national identity comes with the essay's title, "The Siamese Twins." The alignment between "alien" and "freak" is so close that one ideological figure seems to fall inevitably into the other. Indeed, this identification of the unusual body as exotic, foreign other—and of national difference as necessarily embodied—is so persistent that the phrase "Siamese Twins" loses the specificity of its national referent and becomes the common name for conjoined twins. This collapse from specific to general, however, requires imaginative labor not unlike the violent domestication experienced by Roxy and the "uncanny" Wilson. The ease with which Twain relocates Chang and Eng from a sign of the radical alien to the embodiment of the nation requires closer reading as it opens up the correspondence between the excepted and the exceptional.

The logic of Twain's essay trades on the paradoxical tie between the twins' exclusion from national belonging and their position as the exceptional model. If exceptionalism demands uniqueness, then Twain's metaphor suggests that there could be no better candidates than the twins. Much of the humor in Twain's piece relies upon his willful misreading of the twins' extraordinary closeness: "The Siamese Twins are naturally tender and affectionate in disposition, and have clung to each other with singular fidelity throughout a long and eventful life" (248). Their connection to each other functions as the ideal contrast to a nation at war with itself. Instead of the conventions of the literary grotesque in which the disabled body serves as a mark of chaos in the world, Twain uses Chang and Eng as a metaphor for a proper national body. In Twain's imaginative revision, the freakish body is no longer the conjoined twins, but instead the U.S. body with "its quarrelings, its wranglings, and its separation of brothers." Twain simultaneously domesticates and naturalizes the twins, but these moves must take place through the avenue of their embodied difference. The twins become exemplary only by virtue of the physical anomalies that exclude them from participation in America's representative democracy. The valued traits—fidelity and mutual affection—that stem from their physical difference become the very qualities that elect them as the embodiment of the nation.

Chang and Eng embody a series of surprising simultaneities in Twain's imagination: they are at once self and other, alien and American. The successful domestication of the twins depends on relocating their most unusual traits as also their most exceptionally American ones. While Twain's essay may itself seem anomalous in its surprising revision of the twins from the excepted to the representative, a similar imaginative dependence on foreign others resides at the heart of the legacy of American exceptionalism. This international dependence, however, is often cloaked by the commitment to a narrative of national uniqueness. Twain's essay forestalls this obfuscation as its humor threatens to collapse his national metaphor under the weight of its own energetic conception. The potential eruption of a seemingly commonsense denial—the requirements of the conjoined body are not "preferences" or "habits of a lifetime [that] become second nature"—always suggests a freakish residue lurking alongside Twain's symbolic American ideal.

The emphatically scripted humor in Twain's essay, as it arrests the twins in this simultaneous position of freak and model, makes visible the constitutive reliance on excluded figures; his work calls out the imperial dimensions and imaginative sources so often masked in the intellectual and political history of American exceptionalism. The term "American exceptionalism" first emerges during the 1830s in the work of Alexis de Tocqueville, who insists in *Democracy in America* that "the position of the Americans is . . . entirely exceptional" (430). If Tocqueville marks the origin of American exceptionalism as a concept, Perry Miller lays down America's uniqueness as a foundational assumption in the early institutionalization of American studies.[5] In his infamous preface to *Errand into the Wilderness*, Miller recalls coming to his intellectual epiphany while standing on the banks of the Congo. Miller elaborates, "What I believe caught my imagination, among the fuel drums, was a realization of the uniqueness of American experience" (ix). This realization of American difference while casting an imperial eye over U.S. influence in Africa is not an accident, but rather, as Amy Kaplan argues, a demonstration that imperialism has been both "formative and disavowed" in American studies. Kaplan stands, along with Donald Pease, Robyn Wiegman, José David Saldívar, and Lisa Lowe, at the forefront of a decade-old movement within American studies to demonstrate the fluidity of America's conceptual and geographic borders. American exceptionalism, then, becomes not the implicit assumption, but the repressive fiction within American studies that serves to mask imperial interests and cultural interdependencies. Perry Miller's strange admission that he cast aside "the priority of Virginia" in favor of the Puritan migration as "a coherence with which I could coherently begin" (viii) betrays the constructed nature of these persistent myths of exceptional national origin and legacy. Miller's repetitive insistence on coherence in this line demonstrates that origins and linear histories can be found only in the act of creating them. Kaplan and Pease's *Cultures of United States Imperialism* offers a caution against the ease with which scholarly work can articulate and act according to national interests. This brief description of the contested history of American exceptionalism establishes the disciplinary stakes of my more specific reading of Twain's complex movement between exceptional and representative. My account of this disciplinary intervention also prompts self-reflection, challenging, how can America continue to stand as one's central category of scholarship? I proceed according to the principle that national identity is not a natural or fixed entity, but operates instead as a powerful fiction that influences both explicitly national categories like citizenship as well as less obviously related discursive processes like embodiment and subject formation. The imaginative boundaries of nation highlighted by these scholars are mapped onto citizens' bodies in a series of scripts that determine the conditions of national belonging.

Individualism and the Other Man

The enduring discursive force of American exceptionalism should not obscure the ideological contradiction between the value of uniqueness and the celebration of equality. For Tocqueville, America's essential difference from other nations was located in its egalitarianism. He also noted, however, a dangerous tendency toward individualism, an isolating instinct that requires the regulatory effect of social institutions to keep it in check (482–487). Although Tocqueville saw individualism as a threatening influence, other theorists of American life domesticated the quality as an essential national virtue and placed it at the center of America's enduring mythic figures—intrepid pioneers, loner cowboys, captains of industry, or hard-boiled detectives.[6] Even through these shifts in meaning, Tocqueville's two major conceptual contributions— exceptional egalitarianism and individualism—encompass a paradox lying at the center of democracy. Democratic individualism is founded on the premise of equality and sameness of condition, but it simultaneously privileges the rhetoric of freedom and uniqueness. In *Exceptional Bodies*, Rosemarie Garland-Thomson elaborates on this tension by locating representations of disability at the center of liberal individualism: "On the one hand, the disabled figure is a sign for a body that refuses to be governed and cannot carry out the will to self-determination. On the other hand, the extraordinary body is nonconformity incarnate" (44). Physical anomaly plays a striking role in the national imagination as both the threatening breakdown of democratic foundations and the thrilling fulfillment of its promises. Nearly thirty years after writing "The Siamese Twins," Twain turns from the figure of Chang and Eng as a surprisingly exemplary national body to explore how conjoined twins' embodied difference makes strange the central assumptions of American citizenship.

The unique protagonists of *Those Extraordinary Twins* query the boundaries of individual rights and social responsibility and expose the inflexibility of legal and political apparatuses. The action in the text typically centers on the law or politics: the twins are put on trial; Luigi participates in a duel; they run against each other for alderman; and they are finally lynched for their disruption of local government. Twain's focus on politics points to a concern with ideals of citizenship; Angelo and Luigi literally embody the relationship between social and self-government at the heart of democracy. In the case of conjoined twins, the individual body is always already the social body. In order to address *their* social body, the Cappellos have developed a system of rules in which one twin controls the legs, and therefore determines mobility, for alternating weeks. This limitation of self-determination demanded by the twins' disability is baffling to the residents of Dawson's Landing. When Angelo tells Patsy that he cannot go to his room despite being exhausted, she exclaims, "And what's to hender you, I'd like to know? Land, the room's yours, to do what you please with! The idea that you can't do what you like with your own!" (145). Patsy has no understanding of freedom beyond the model of autonomous individualism. The absent referent of "your own" in Patsy's speech points to the parallel between the body and property that C. B. Macpherson theorizes as possessive individualism.[7] Rooted in the thinking of Thomas Hobbes and John Locke, this model of political membership is predicated on inalienable property rights and assumes the body as the first instance of ownership. Angelo and Luigi question Locke's doctrine of "property in one's person" by their embodiment of shared resources. Their solution, however, conforms to conventions of individualism, but with a difference: one twin becomes master and the other slave each week.

The twins' simultaneously individual and social body introduces a philosophical tension between rights and responsibilities. The ideal of individual freedom requires limitation according to the rights of others, but for Angelo and Luigi, the other man is constantly at his side. Twain pushes the boundaries of this dilemma by making the activities of one twin a particular affront to the other: Luigi smokes and Angelo coughs; he drinks and Angelo, the temperance organizer, gets drunk; Angelo is shot as the unwilling second in his brother's duel and then Luigi is forced to take the foul medicine his ill brother cannot stomach. Twain uses the disabled body as a hyperbolic expression of the dilemma of freedom and responsibility. For the Cappellos, equal right to control their shared body is only possible through repressing the rights of one's brother every other week.

A capacity for self-determination stands as the first requirement of citizenship, but also as a metaphor for the management of the body politic. The belief in the possibility of a social body that can be governed lies in the premise of self-control of the individual.[8] For Locke, a model of government based on consent assumes an equality of capacities among the citizenry. Reason and the ability to "shift for one's self" and "manage one's life" are the central requirements of humanity at its liberal foundations (Macpherson 244). Where then do we locate disabled people? How is humanity defined for these bad managers of their unruly bodies? While historically the answer to these questions has been near total disenfranchisement, Twain inverts this legacy by locating his twins at the center of legal and political life. *Those Extraordinary Twins* dramatizes the failures of these systems to address embodied difference.

The liberal-democratic premise of equal ability extends more broadly to the naturalized standard of a uniform body. Any belief in universal rights guaranteed by the Constitution must assume a fundamentally homogenous citizenry. The failures of this faith in uniformity reach a climax in the novel's courtroom scene. Angelo and Luigi are put on trial for assault after kicking a man at a local rally. Pudd'nhead Wilson rises to their defense and proves that since they trade control of the legs, only one can be guilty. The core of their defense, however, rests on the fact that since the jury cannot tell by looking which one is the kicker, neither twin can be convicted. In the face of Wilson's logic, the jurors throw up their hands and place the twins' body under divine justice, lamenting the inability of civil jurisdiction to cover the circumstances of the case. They deliver the verdict: "We cannot convict both, for only one is guilty. We cannot acquit both, for only one is innocent. Our verdict is that justice has been defeated by the dispensation of God, and ask to be discharged from further duty" (163). In the mind of the judge, however, the twins' disability affords them a special ability to break the law: "You have set adrift, unadmonished, in this community, two men endowed with an awful and mysterious gift, a hidden and grisly power for evil—a power by which each in his turn may commit crime after crime of the most heinous character, and no man may be able to tell which is the guilty or which the innocent party in any case of them all" (164). The judge displaces a failing of the inflexible law to a hidden power of the twins'. The irony of the scene lies in the contradiction between the obvious, visible fact of the twins' difference and the failures of looking produced by that visual excess. Because the twins' anatomy obscures the optic proof the jurors require, the judge and jury call upon the supernatural to explain their failures. In this case, the body that cannot be addressed by the law is considered outside it. The recourse to lynching, however, that concludes the novel demonstrates that to be outside the law is not to escape civic punishment. In this moment, the Cappellos' tragic fate reinforces their figurative connection to freed Southern blacks who are the targets of similar scrutiny and extralegal violence.

This alignment between conjoined twins and African Americans is no accident of plot, but instead marks the intertwining of these figures in the national imagination. The failures of the political system to address the physical difference of disability extend as well to the persistent location of blacks outside the guaranteed rights of the liberal citizen. Both groups are subjected to a logic of exclusion in which the justification for alienation is naturalized as a property of the body. Twain's early description of his *Pudd'nhead Wilson* heroine uses the language of voting to expose the politicized nature of truths about the body: "To all intents and purposes Roxy was as white as anybody, but the one-sixteenth of her which was black out-voted the other fifteen parts and made her a negro" (9). Twain's call to voting in this line points to the struggles over black franchise granted with the Fifteenth Amendment in 1870. Writing from the pessimism of the 1890s, Twain reverses the compromised extension of rights to freed slaves by granting Roxy's black "part" the political power to outvote her fifteen white "parts." Many critics read this parallel between the disabled and the racially mixed protagonists as the secret theme of *Those Extraordinary Twins*.[9] For the few critics who choose to read the works together, the conjoined twins are most often seen as a symbol to introduce the anxiety around miscegenation fleshed out more fully in *Pudd'nhead Wilson*. On the opposite pole, George Marcus distinguishes himself from these readings by claiming that race serves as a "kind of allegorical vehicle . . . a story through which another more profound story of the self can be told" (198). These critical hierarchies institute a false split between race and individualism, a split in which disability serves invariably as a metaphor for these "greater" concerns. In my analysis, embodiment is not "more profound" than the racial story, but can be read, in fact, as the same story. Without eliding the historical and imaginative differences between race and disability, I argue for the shared logics of exclusion, biological law, and symbolic exemplarity in the construction of national subjects marked as physically different. The danger in exploring these alliances lies in reinstituting the same essentialist logic that constructed our notions of race and disability in the first place. By identifying these similarities as part of a shared story, however, I emphasize the discursive nature of embodied citizenship and attempt to make strange the naturalized logic of physical difference.

Laughter and Tears

The shared essentialist logic of race and disability can trace its roots, in part, to the ideological legacy of the sentimental novel.[10] While Twain's 1894 text cannot be properly included within the sentimental literary genre, the popular influence of sympathy as a moral and aesthetic virtue leaves its stamp on both works of the period and their reception. In his preface to *Those Extraordinary Twins*, Twain openly strains at the dominance of the genre in describing his "light-weight heroine" Rowena as "so nauseatingly sentimental" and unnecessary to the new story that he felt prompted to toss her down a well (126, 127). In contrast to Twain's rejection of sentimental conventions, a 1904 review in *Booklover's Magazine* demonstrates the pervasive influence of sentiment on critical approaches to literature of the period. The reviewer laments of *Pudd'nhead Wilson*, "There is no one figure in the book capable of arresting and retaining our sympathies."[11] Even though Twain fails to capture this booklover's sympathies, his work demonstrates surprising correspondences with the forms and assumptions of sentimental fiction. The notoriously slippery Twain takes on the genre's conventions by mocking the insular domestic sphere and challenging the notion of biological inheritance, but then seems to undo these objections by concluding *Pudd'nhead Wilson* with the conservative legal triumph of the infallible "natal autograph." Beyond his interest in the conventions of the genre, it is this very irresolvability that locates Twain alongside theorists of sentiment in their shared reliance on simultaneity.

Given the sentimental novel's status as the dominant form of popular fiction during the nineteenth century, it seems almost inevitable that even Twain's humorous works would have to grapple with the preoccupations of sentimental literature. As a foundational principle, comedic and sentimental fiction share an open interest in the reader's body. As Karen Sánchez-Eppler argues, "Reading sentimental fiction is thus a bodily act, and the success of a story is gauged, in part, by its ability to translate words into pulse beats or sobs" (100). The embodied response expected in sentimental literature is similarly expected in the laughs and smiles evoked by comedy. Each of these genres brings the question of physical response to the fore in order to perform work on the reader's body. Twain's themes also tread upon the conventions of sentimental literature. His mixed-race heroine, Roxy, recalls both abolitionist novels and the tragic mulatta tradition, two narrative forms steeped in the strategies of sympathy. In drawing from the sideshow circuit for his conjoined heroes, Twain also collides with the sentimental tradition, but in more subtle ways. Like the opening promise in his 1868 essay "The Siamese Twins," much of the novel's focus on Angelo and Luigi centers on their "personal habits" and "private life" (248). Twain significantly locates the action of the story in a boardinghouse, following the twins to their room at night, lingering over the breakfast table, and mapping the flirtation between Angelo and Rowena. This turn to domestic space in *Those Extraordinary Twins* enacts a dominant feature in the construction of anomalous bodies: a persistent public curiosity over intimate acts and particulars of the body. This desire for knowledge finds its narrative solution in the tradition of the domestic novel, which, like the freak show, offers its own entrance ticket into the ins and outs of daily life.

The sentimental novel, like freak shows and theaters of anatomy, insists upon observation of the body as a reliable tool to gain knowledge. Sympathy relies on the ability to read the face, citing tears or grimaces as evidence of an interior truth. As Shirley Samuels and Karen Sánchez-Eppler argue in their studies of race and sentimental fiction, this literature describes the flesh as a legible sign for individual identity, a textual analogy that is tragically extended by corporeally inscribing acts like branding and whipping.[12] The nineteenth-century fashion for phrenology, fingerprinting, and palmistry all reflect a belief in truth written upon the body and the concurrent desire to interpret that data.[13] Sarah Chinn, in her 2000 text *Technology and the Logic of American Racism*, locates Twain's use of palmistry and fingerprinting in a series of systems that place the body into "evidence." Twain's hero, David Wilson, is a practitioner of both fingerprinting and palmistry, hobbies that serve as further evidence of his pudd'nhead status among the townspeople.

In the novel's extended palm reading scene, Tom Driscoll first uses the language of textuality as a mocking and hyperbolic advertisement for Wilson's skills—"Why, he'll read your wrinkles as easy as a book" (54). After Wilson successfully reads Luigi's palm, however, an anxious Tom returns to the metaphor of inscription: "Just think of that—a man's own hand keeps a record of the deepest and fatalest secrets of his life" (57). While Twain's return to the language of reading and writing in this scene could be just an extension of the colloquial term "palm reader," circling back to the metaphor also works to defamiliarize the notion of reading the body. The more explicit language of black magic in the scene and Tom's open skepticism combine with the recurring image of textuality to make the act of reading the body not impossible, but noteworthy and impressive. Twain lingers over palm reading to set up the possibility of the legible body where he is convinced of its truth: the emerging science of fingerprinting.

The trial scene at the climax of *Pudd'nhead Wilson* plays out as a tense courtroom drama costarring David Wilson, fingerprints, and Tom Driscoll's demonstrative body. The principle of corporeal legibility that fails so spectacularly in the twins' assault trial reemerges through infallible fingerprint evidence in their second, more climactic murder trial. These parallel trial scenes rely on similar staging as the body comes to serve as the defense's primary exhibit. As in their first trial where Angelo and Luigi stand kicking in the center of the courtroom, Wilson expands this strategy of corporeal evidence to the bodies of the audience and jury. In contrast to the inscrutable body of the twins and their "hidden and grisly power for evil," Wilson offers up fingerprints as a seemingly self-evident and easily interpretable sign of individuality. Although he has brought enlarged illustrations of fingerprints to the courtroom, Wilson reserves this graphic evidence and first asks each individual to discover their own fingerprints and their essential difference from their neighbors:

> "If you will look at the balls of your fingers—you that have very sharp eyesight—you will observe that these dainty curving lines lie close together, like those that indicate the borders of oceans in many maps, and that they form various clearly defined patterns, such as arches, circles, long curves, whorls, etc., and that these patterns differ on the different fingers." [Every man in the room had his hand up to the light, now, and his head canted to one side, and was minutely scrutinizing the balls of his fingers; there were

whispered ejaculations of, "Why it's so—I never noticed that before!"] (114, brackets in original)

Wilson becomes a puppet master not just of the audience's attention, but
of their entire bodies as he presides over a roomful of identically lifted
hands and canted heads. His instructions to the jury play with scale, first
miniaturizing the fingerprint lines as "dainty" and "delicate," then expanding them to map-size and the further suggestion of oceanic depth.
In contrast to the suggestion that fingerprints are obvious, Wilson's
telescoping description demonstrates the work of language to influence
perceptions of the body. His speech and the audience's response enact
a tension in the case for the infallible body. At one level, Wilson insists
upon the self-evident and unchanging nature of the fingerprint: "These
marks are his signature, his physiological autograph, so to speak, and
this autograph cannot be counterfeited, nor can he disguise it or hide it
away, nor can it be illegible by the wear and mutations of time" (114). At
another level, the audience's very shock over the discovery of their own
fingerprints and their need for these marks to be identified and interpreted by an expert suggest that this distinguishing feature has, in fact,
been hiding in plain sight. Only in the context of Wilson's extensive system of capturing and classifying the town's fingerprints does this feature
of the body begin to take on social significance, or even public notice.
As Wilson continues, it becomes clear that it is his own training and
expertise that give the prints meaning. He engages in the parlor trick of
identifying Angelo and Luigi's fingerprints from a series of anonymous
marks on the courtroom window, a display that prompts the judge to
announce, "This certainly approaches the miraculous!" (116). Wilson
vacillates between exploiting his mastery in order to stun the audience
and surrendering his knowledge by asking the jurors to participate in
matching prints. At the level of plot, the novel offers fingerprints as reliable evidence, an indelible mark to be read upon the body. By contrast,
the scene's exaggerated attention to the study and manipulation of the
assembled bodies and its dramatization of Wilson's expertise work at
a secondary level to challenge the model of the self-evident body. Wilson invokes a new feature of the body and insists upon its unchanging
nature, but this very naming enacts a much more complex, discursive
process in the social apprehension of the corporeal.

Wilson's public courtroom narrative of fingerprint identification runs
alongside his private study of Tom Driscoll's face and body. Both forms
of examination rely on a similar belief in the legible body. With each

surprising revelation of the killer's habits and motives, Wilson turns his eye toward Tom to read his reaction. The stress of discovery becomes so plainly written on Tom's face that Wilson claims "he is flying signals of distress" (115). Finally, in a page torn from a sentimental novel, the murderer swoons at the moment of his exposure: "Tom turned his ashen face imploringly toward the speaker, made some impotent movements with his white lips, then slid limp and lifeless to the floor" (120). In this climactic moment, Tom's body becomes the only effective communicator and his speech is rendered impotent. Wilson finds Tom's collapse so demonstrative that he insists, "He has confessed" (120). In fact, Tom never speaks in this scene; he communicates exclusively through physical distress. This courtroom scene offers a series of irresolvable avenues by which to approach the body. Tom's obvious "signals" and confessional swoon conform to the sentimental logic of physically betrayed distress. As an elaboration of this point, Wilson advertises fingerprints as an infallible means of identification, but cannot avoid the need for expertise and an interpretive system to make sense of the prints. A third line of reasoning expressed in this scene centers on the courtroom's shocked discovery of their own fingerprints, a discovery that belies Wilson's claim of their self-evident nature. The final trick of the scene, then, is to keep these balls in the air, leaving each position unstable and complicated by the others.

The principle of irresolvability that prohibits a secure acceptance of any of these positions is the same structure that sustains Twain's humor throughout the text. How does the figure of conjoined twins produce epistemological instability if not through this sense of troubling irresolvability, of being simultaneously two in one? Twain exploits the failures of social classification by centering his work on figures who represent a basic form of humor in joining things that should not be joined. While the strongest, most elemental examples of this kind of humor are manifest in Roxy's mixed-race heritage and Angelo and Luigi's shared body, there are smaller moments throughout the text that exploit similarly irresolvable combinations. Tom's cross-dressing as an elderly black woman, Rowena's romantic interest in Angelo, and Chambers's final restoration as a white aristocrat with the dialect and habits of his black upbringing all depend on a destabilizing mix of strongly held categories within race, class, gender, and sexual expression. These jokes solidify fixed identity categories by making their mixture ridiculous, but the cultural effect of these transgressions does not collapse entirely into the absurd. The same irresolvability that structures the humor prevents the easy redistribution of "proper" physical attributes and practices. While Twain's humor cannot—and, perhaps does not want to—unmake the normative system that enforces these categories, the jokes suspend naturalized narratives of their assignment.[14] Simultaneity, for Twain, is inextricably bound in both the physical bodies of his characters and the textual form of his humor.

Much of Twain's explicit engagement with sentimentalism presses its values to their absolute limit for comedic effect. This excessive sympathy is rooted in human identification, collapsing the twins' absolute difference into misfortune—"you poor unfortunate cretur" (148)—and driving the "nauseatingly sentimental" Rowena into the realm of the ridiculous. The ability to overcome difference is often cited as sentimentalism's dominant political feature. In her study of early American sentimental fiction, Elizabeth Barnes argues that the sympathetic emphasis on identification supplants democratic values of diversity with the vision of a homogeneous nation modeled after the family. She writes, "The idea of the American people as a single unified body is made possible by imagining diverse individuals connected in a sympathetic chain. But, in eighteenth-century constructions of it, sympathy—the act of imagining oneself in another's position—is contingent upon familiarity. In order for the reader to engage in sympathetic identification, others must be shown to be *like* the reader. In other words, sympathy is both the expression of familiarity and the vehicle through which familiarity is created" (2). The emotional and intellectual energy extended toward identification on both the personal and national levels must proceed through the mediating force of imagination. Moral philosophers Adam Smith and David Hume argue that while sympathy bridges the gap between self and other, the sympathetic process they describe relies upon an imaginative substitution in which onlookers "are constantly considering what they themselves would feel, if they actually were the sufferers" (Smith 16). Sympathy can emerge only in the face of difference, but while theorists argue that sympathy conquers difference, it also seems to suspend simultaneous processes of differentiation and identification. The defining act of sympathy—"imagining oneself in another's position"—preserves the difference between self and other, first, in its reliance on imagination and, second, by asking spectators to speculate on their own emotions in another's situation, not on what the other person is herself feeling. The fantasy, then, centers on an imaginative trade of positions, not identities. Like Twain's humor, sympathy arrests the irresolvable mingling between two categories.[15]

Although both humor and sentiment resist resolution or firm

conclusions, that very ambiguity can serve as a starting point for denaturalizing repressive cultural norms. Despite an open skepticism over the objectifying traditions of sentimentalism and pity, many disability activists and scholars call for earnest attempts at sympathetic identification to address the marginalization of disabled people. I argue for the additional place of humor as a similarly fraught, but no less productive, way to make strange normalizing narratives. I should concede at the outset that locating even a fragmentary model for challenging the stigma of disability in Twain's text must emerge through a largely resistant reading. Twain's own attitude toward his conjoined protagonists is difficult to place. He begins his concluding remarks by writing, "As you see, it was an extravagant sort of tale, and had no purpose but to exhibit that monstrous 'freak' in all sorts of grotesque lights" (184). Against this self-conscious authorial deprecation, however, stands the vitality of Twain's story. The Cappellos cannot honestly be described as rich, interior characters, but their experiences in Dawson's Landing are more round than the "picture of a youthful Italian freak—or freaks" that inspired them. One brand of humor in the novel depends upon the reader's presumed ironic distance from the humanizing impulses of the folksy Cooper family. The hyperbolic liberal acceptance expressed by Patsy *is* ridiculous in its denial of obvious difference: "You'll find there's more about them that's wonderful than their just being made in the image of God like the rest of his creatures" (172). Less outrageous, though, is Patsy's sympathetic connection to the twins and the recognition of her own able-bodied privilege. Angelo admonishes her gently, "People who have use of their legs all the time never think what a blessing it is, of course. It never occurs to them; it's just their natural ordinary condition." To which Patsy replies tearfully, "No, you poor unfortunate cretur, but I'll never get out of my bed again without *doing* it. . . . Betsy Hale, we have learnt something, you and me" (148). The joke in this case relies upon the distance between Patsy's newfound recognition of privilege and all she has still failed to learn, as represented by the excited exclamation "you poor unfortunate cretur." Other characters see the extraordinary body in the most positive sense of the term. For Patsy's son Joe, physical anomaly allows the possibility of advantage over his own form. His brother says, "Instead of pitying it, Joe, you talk as if—" and Joe responds, "Talk as if *what*? I know one thing mighty certain: if you can fix me so I can eat for two and only have to stub toes for one, I ain't going to fool away no such chance just for sentiment" (127). In this remark Joe reverses the object of "fixing" to his own normate body. He also deflates repressive social responses to the disabled body under the denigrated rubric of "sentiment." By first embodying the principle of simultaneity in the conjoined twins and then relying on it as the foundation for his comedy, Twain offers a way to take humor seriously by arresting the effervescent quality of these moments and allowing their vitality to draw one's focus to formerly stable norms.

"Powerful Good Imitations"

For those with anomalous bodies, "performance" evokes the dual legacies of the history of display on the sideshow stage and contemporary theories of performative identity. As Judith Butler cautions, this turn to performativity should not be read as a celebratory brand of agency in which subjects don their chosen identity each morning as they would pull on an overcoat. Instead, the value of understanding subject formation through performance is that it proposes a dynamic, relational subject in place of a static essentialism. As another layer of resonance between these two legacies, the repetitive practices that constitute identity depend upon public legibility and draw upon social conventions often found in literal, staged performance. Minstrel shows, autopsy theaters, skin shows, ethnographic exhibits, and freak shows are only a smattering of the kinds of performance that exceed the boundaries of their respective theaters to shape the ideological apprehension of their subjects. Pausing briefly here over the conventions of the freak show extends the resonances between performative identity and the stage. The striking juxtapositions of the sideshow circuit demonstrate the irresolvable narratives of race, nation, gender, sexuality, and disability as they construct the marked body. Strolling along the fairway, one might find a row consisting of a "bearded lady," a giant, a dwarf, and a "painted Indian." Freak shows conflate material differences among identity categories by displaying racial others alongside disabled people, but these exhibits also demonstrate the mutually constitutive elements of interpellation: the staging of Julia Pastrana, the Ugliest Woman in the World, both tempts and repels with hints of hypersexuality, an excessive sexuality that is naturalized as the product of both her Mexican and Indian background and her hirsute body.[16] These related narratives in which the disabled body is also raced and sexualized are not the unique province of the freak show, but instead point to larger practices in the construction of marked bodies. In this section and the following, I extend the dynamics of the freak show to explore quotidian performance, arguing that imitation and performance serve as strategies according to which anomalous bodies become legible to the body politic.

This principle of somatic legibility and the textual forms that both sustain and expose it can be best understood through extended close readings in which Twain plays with identity as embodied performance. *Pudd'nhead Wilson* takes seriously the problems of managing the social body, especially where its plot is driven by Roxy's baby-switching as a strategy to protect her child from the violent threat of being "sold down the river." In the months that follow that first radical switch, Roxy continues to assert the new identities of the children according to a set of practices that take on a strikingly performative cast in the text. Twain describes the accumulation of small, daily acts that eventually remake Roxy from the mother to the slave of her child:

> By the fiction created by herself, he was become her master; the necessity of recognizing this relation outwardly and of perfecting herself in the forms required to express the recognition, had moved her to such diligence and faithfulness in practicing these forms that this exercise soon concreted itself into habit; it became automatic and unconscious; then a natural result followed: deceptions intended solely for others grew practically into self-deceptions as well; the mock reverence became real reverence, the mock obsequiousness real obsequiousness, the mock homage real homage; the little counterfeit rift of separation between imitation-slave and imitation-master widened and widened, and became an abyss, a very real one—and on one side of it stood Roxy, the dupe of her own deceptions, and on the other stood her child, no longer a usurper to her, but her accepted and recognized master. (20–21)

By describing this process of accretion in a single, staggering sentence—nearly one hundred and fifty words long—Twain produces a contradictory effect. On the one hand, the break between "mock" and "real" is so easily overcome that they cannot even be divided by a period—after all, this is a single sentence. On the other hand, the sentence is excessive, and its remarkable length holds this transition in suspension, forcing readers to acknowledge the series of acts required to translate imitation into reality. The process begins with Roxy as an actor performing her subordinate status for an audience. These outwardly directed acts, however, must affect the actor as well, and the practice soon becomes "automatic and unconscious." Then, as Twain writes, "a natural result followed." The use of the term "natural" here and the following repetitions of "real" lose

any sense of fixed definition. Rather than relying on conventional notions of "real" and "natural" as a static, original essence, Twain suggests
that reality is a discursive formation. The passage illustrates the ways
in which identity involves naturalization, a process that relies upon, as
Twain says, "recognition." The dual forms of recognition in this paragraph encapsulate the performative nature of identity. According to its
manifest use in this passage, Roxy acknowledges her own position in
relation to her owner. The phrase "recognized master" necessarily must
include Roxy's recognition of herself; neither role can be recognized
without the other. In order to come to this understanding of herself,
however, Roxy must perform "the forms required to express the recognition"; in other words, Roxy's sense of self first depends upon her legible
performance as a slave for the audience of the community. In spite of its
opening attention to audience and acting, however, the image of Roxy
standing whole on one side of an abyss suggests that the passage works
to reinstall an insurmountable racial difference in the body. The vast rift
between slave and master that reasserts itself as "very real" at the close
of this sentence demonstrates the repressive effect of language. While
the passage suggests a performative model of identity that requires the
destabilization of "natural categories," it also reminds readers that discursive construction does not make the "real" any less powerful as an
ideological category. Although the sentence opens with a troubling of
racial definitions, it closes with a reassertion of a strict racial binary. The
fact that this binary depends upon fictions and deceptions does not re-
lieve its repressive consequences.

A conservative reading of this "imitation mother" paragraph might
limit Twain's critique to the construction of social roles. After all, the
discussion centers primarily upon the positions of master and slave.
Twenty pages later, however, the word "imitation" surfaces again, this
time in direct reference to the central racial categories of the novel. In
the intervening twenty years, Roxy has experienced a series of reversals
in fortune—such that she finds herself free, but penniless, and back in
the slave kitchen to learn about the fortunes of her former master and
biological son, Tom Driscoll. When her "ostensible" son Chambers tells
her that Tom has been disinherited for his gambling, she insists, "Take it
back, you misable imitation nigger dat I bore in sorrow en tribbilation"
(39). Roxy's claim that Chambers is acting like or imitating a "nigger"
offers a vision of the category that posits it as a recognizable, performative identity outside the body. She calls upon "nigger" as an epithet
that matches bad behavior to white, racist assumptions.[17] Her subsequent

appeal to the suffering, maternal body, however, posits a model of character that resides in biological ties. Roxy's insult posits imitation as the negative opposite to a valuable, bodily identity rooted in the act of childbearing. Further complicating this textual moment, Roxy, of course, did not bear Chambers at all, and he is an "imitation nigger." These ironic facts of the novel's plot diminish the force of Roxy's appeal to the body, a limitation confirmed in Chambers's scoffing reply: "If I's imitation, what is you? Bofe of us is imitation *white*—dat's what we is—en pow'full good imitations, too . . . we don't 'mount to noth'n as imitation *niggers*" (39). Where Roxy's insult opposes "imitation" with the reality of the maternal body, Chambers's reply reverses the referent of imitation to call attention to their light skin. By insisting that they are "imitation white," Chambers locates the supposed truth of their identity—their blackness—outside the body and describes their embodied, visible whiteness as that which is imitation. Chambers's next assertion—"dat's what we is"—unmakes the security of the first formulation, however, as "is" seems to suggest that identity can be located in an "imitation." The paradox of the line itself, then, is that "imitation white" seems simultaneously to point to a reliable, disembodied black identity and to assert that the best candidate for identity—for what they are—is white. If we add to this close reading another layer of Twain's characteristic irony and acknowledge that Roxy and Chambers are not related and, as such, would seem not to share any identity, the contradiction fails to resolve itself into easy or fixed categories of racial identity. How secure can blackness be if Chambers, born the white son of Percy Driscoll, is such a successful imitation? Similarly, how can the body offer reliable evidence of identity when one can be simultaneously imitation white and imitation black? If we return again to the conservative position that opened this paragraph, it could be argued that Twain offers secure footing to his reader through the tempting path of good old common sense: "Chambers" is really white, the obvious joke is that he is an "imitation," and his assertion that "we don't 'mount to noth'n as imitation *niggers*" gestures toward the inevitable failure of this racial experiment. The exuberant layers of irony and inversion that make up these few lines, however, seem to trouble such conventional assurances. In my necessarily extended reading of these layers of textual complexity, the residual effect of this paragraph is to unmake any essential connection between the body and social identity. Roxy's appeal to the body as the source of character demonstrates that embodied identity is a discursive product, created by a series of social fictions and performative repetitions. By aligning the position of common sense with a model of identity rooted in the body, however, Twain's text participates in the naturalizing discourse that obscures the ideological underpinnings of embodiment.

Anatomies of Performance

Much of the force of embodiment as an ideological category resides in masking its constructed nature. In a structure similar to the somatic legibility I've described, the history of staged performance for disabled people turns upon a social assumption of physical difference as offering a window into realities of the body. Even as sideshow displays tested the credulity of their audiences and evoked unruly expressions of doubt, their tantalizing appeal was located in the possibility that one might become worldly by seeing a freak whose identity was identical to his or her freakish body.[18] For a Lobster Boy or Armless Wonder, the truth of the body seems to be the feature that names and scripts the exhibit, not the other way around. The tradition of the Jerry Lewis telethon offers a more obvious example of a performance whose success (as theater and as fundraiser) depends upon the ostensible truth of the stories told. Resurrecting the nineteenth-century sentimental tradition for a television public, telethons perform an economy of pity that equates truth with suffering. In developing a theory of queer, racial performance, José Muñoz captures a related phenomenon under the term "burden of liveness." Muñoz argues that "otherness" carries with it the pressure to perform for a dominant audience. This burden stems, in part, from the sense that queer or racial performance is less mediated by an external apparatus of representation like film or text. The special pressure of live performance emerges from a view that sees minoritarian subjects' staging as anti-aesthetic—camp and comedy or pain and tragedy are seen as the natural outgrowth of these identities. Muñoz argues that the live performance becomes the substitute for historical and political representation (188). The paradox of this substitution lies in the fact that the burden of liveness positions this performance as a more direct representation of minority experience, so that performed racial tragedy, for instance, is read as unmediated and real suffering, but this belief in its reality—its "liveness"—does not translate to greater political recognition. I argue that Muñoz's theory can be expanded to the sphere of everyday performance, in which the ideological burden of an embodied reality masks its own performative construction.

Within the disability studies critical canon, one of the most vivid expressions of the performative everyday resides with Tobin Siebers. In "My Withered Limb," Siebers offers a scene in which dramatic conventions and questions of audience influence the material experience of public disability. In this personal essay, Siebers relies on performance-inflected language to emphasize the role of spectacle in disabled experience: "Walking just ahead of me is another cripple, limping exactly with my trademark rhythm, rocking from side to side, like a metronome. Now we are two. Tick tock, tick tock. Into the door we go. Tick tock, tick tock. Down the hall one after the other in a row. Tick tock, tick tock. One cripple is invisible compared to two cripples. Two cripples walking in a line are a comedy act. We are today's show" (24). Here, Siebers uses repetition and parallel structure to restage through writing this moment of spectacle. The onomatopoeia in "tick tock, tick tock" emphasizes the sensual realm, fleshing out the realism of the scene. Despite this gesture toward verisimilitude, however, the rhythmic and stylized syntax in the passage draws heavily on the vaudeville conventions that structure both the experience and Siebers's description of it. The second resonance of his use of rhythm and rhyme is to call up the nursery rhymes of childhood, suggesting that these spectacles are central to cultural assimilation. In this passage Siebers demonstrates that the conventions which structure his experience in the hallway are not a quirk of his own imagination or the straightforward consequence of physical demands, but instead stem from the intertwined legacies of disability and performance in the national imagination. The acknowledgment that he and his chance companion are only "today's show" and that "one cripple is invisible compared to two cripples" suggests an extensive spectrum of potential variations to abnormality that depends on the implied audience of the "show." Just before this passage, Siebers argues for a relational model of abnormality that is similarly dependent on this notion of spectacle and spectator: "We are never more normal than when we catch sight of a cripple. This applies to the fit and unfit alike" (24). These lines rely on conventions of performance—especially the changing and relative positions of the audience—to illustrate abnormality as a socially contingent identity. Part of the complexity of the longer anecdote is that Siebers is both part of the spectacle and its observer. Siebers's moment of recognition—like Roxy's performed acknowledgement of her "recognized master"—extends this relational model of identity to self-perception. This moment challenges the principle of unique individualism implied by the personal essay genre, for here is "another cripple, limping exactly with my trademark rhythm." Instead of the sense that the physical demands of the body produce that which is unique, we are left with the conclusion that conceptions of self and others are dynamic and relational. The double-bind of the "burden of liveness" is that it contains within it a mandate to perform, but collapses the artist onstage into a body that can only convey reality. While Siebers is unwilling to relinquish a reality in the body for his theory of disability, this passage from his personal essay elaborates a complex interchange between embodiment and the performance conventions that direct our thinking about that body.[19]

If this scene of parallel walkers will evoke certain associations for readers in disability studies, it should resonate quite differently for those most familiar with *Pudd'nhead Wilson*. When Tom Driscoll returns to Missouri from a brief stint at Yale, he carries with him an "eastern polish" that rankles the citizens of Dawson's Landing. The town's young people resent the citified superiority represented by Tom's fancy suit and gloves, so they set a tailor to work. Their prank plays out on the public stage of the local street: "When Tom started out on his parade the next morning he found the old deformed negro bellringer straddling along in his wake tricked out in a flamboyant curtain-calico exaggeration of his finery, and imitating his fancy eastern graces as well as he could" (26). In a novel preoccupied with doubles and "imitation," this scene of mimicry demonstrates the complex role that people with marked bodies play in social and psychic identifications. While the town's joke trades on the seeming absolute difference between Tom, the jaunty, able-bodied, white aristocrat, and his opposite, "the old deformed negro bellringer," the novel questions this sharp divide. The imitation of Tom's suit and manner demonstrates that Tom's identity is not stable, but, in fact, portable. The correspondence of this scene with the infant costume change between Tom and Chambers extends this idea, arguing that the embodied difference that seems to uphold the distinction between these men is no more secure than a replicable suit of clothes. The destabilizing effect of this scene is made all the more striking by its public setting. Tom's personal identification against "not-me" figures of racial and physical difference reflects on an individual scale the nationalist claims of American exceptionalism. Upon a second reading, the patriotic valence of the word choice "parade" suggests an allegorical resonance of this scene. The two-figure parade of an Eastern, urban Ivy Leaguer and his newly propertied black double dramatizes white Southern and Western anxieties about their powerlessness in the reconstituted national body after the Civil War. The town's prank first challenges Tom's security as an individual, then points to the ramifications of doubling and imitation for the post–Civil War national imagination.

Domesticating the Freakish Spectacle

For people with visible disabilities, the initial moment of encounter holds the dangerous potential for verbal or physical violence. On the part of the able-bodied, an experience of visual confusion must be assimilated emotionally and by reassessing traditional etiquette. Responses can run the gamut from abhorrence to fascination, all in the space of a personal introduction. The "burden of liveness" resurfaces in these moments to cast embodied difference as the object of visual spectacle. As Rosemarie Garland-Thomson discusses in her 2009 book, *Staring: How We Look*, the complex visual exchanges of social encounters serve as the scaffolding upon which a series of dynamics including pathology, normalcy, dominance, and desire are constructed. These encounters often extend beyond the physical present as people with anomalous bodies become portable in representations through literature, cartoons, film, and photography. In the second half of the nineteenth century, *cartes de visite* offer a striking example of this portability. These popular, mass-produced photographic portraits often portrayed the famous freaks of the day—Twain credits a similar photograph for inspiring *Those Extraordinary Twins*. These portraits increased the circulation of disabled figures, but never move beyond an initial visual encounter. Twain emphasizes a similar visual spectacle in the Cappellos' introduction into Dawson's Landing, describing the twins as "a stupefying *apparition*—a double-headed human creature with four arms, one body, and a single pair of legs!" (130, emphasis added). Angelo's polite introduction leaves "poor old" Aunt Patsy "in a whirl of amazement and confusion" (131). Throughout the novel, much of Twain's humor relies on the contrasts among the ultra-mannered European twins, their shocking and "grewsome aspect" (125), and the folksy residents of Dawson's Landing.

After the moment of initial encounter, physical anomaly loses some of its power to shock and unsettle in the face of imaginative domestication by the body politic. Despite her initial amazement, Patsy reasserts her authority in the boardinghouse by exaggerating the twins' disability through hyperbolic description: "There was just a wormy squirming of arms in the air—seemed to be a couple of dozen of them, all writhing at once, and it just made me dizzy to see them go" (132). In her angry confusion, four hands become two dozen and she dehumanizes the twins as "wormy" and "writhing." In an inversion of this initial moment of exaggeration, Patsy and her daughter Rowena move increasingly toward mental dissection as a strategy for managing the twins' nonconformity.

Rowena exclaims, "There's no such wonderful faces and handsome heads in this town—none that even begin. And such hands!—especially Angelo's—so shapely and—" (132). By limiting her vision to faces, heads, and hands, Rowena dissects the confusing whole into manageable aspects that she can understand. This initial exchange captures in two pages the recurring dynamics according to which visible difference becomes managed by the social body. At the striking moment of their appearance, the twins are held in suspension as a thing that defies understanding. The pair is arrested in the position of spectacle, of "apparition," and their visible anomaly extends beyond the limits of their body to test the limits of Patsy's imagination. This movement from physical body to imagined body characterizes the most basic strategy for domesticating physical difference; the body politic regains its authority through imaginative discourse.

As the narrative progresses, the twins' physical anomaly becomes a kind of elephant in the corner, rarely cited directly as the source of their uniqueness. The women displace their fascination or horror from the body to questions of breeding or fashion. Rowena, Twain's silly and romantic young Miss (126), denies the impact of corporeal difference and focuses on their background: "They're so fine, and handsome, and high-bred, and polite, so every way superior to our gawks here in this village; why, they'll make life different from what it was—so humdrum and commonplace you know" (135). This form of displacement obviously stems from Twain's farcical treatment of his protagonists, but it could also reveal a psychic defense against the unusual. Although Patsy generally retains her fascination with the particularities of the twins' body, she, too, expresses Twain's ironic humor. Describing Angelo and Luigi simultaneously singing a sweet and bawdy song, she says, "Oh, it was well enough, but too mixed-up, seemed to me" (135). Of course, what is truly "mixed-up" is the twins' body. Patsy's hedging addition "seemed to me" calls attention to her fear of seeming unfashionable in contrast with the Continental twins. Twain mocks the family for their ability to "become tranquilized" and assimilate the twins' difference. For Twain, the joke centers on the disjunction between Patsy's complaint about their "mixed-up" singing and the screaming, obvious fact of the twins' conjoined body.

Even as they are mocked by Twain, these methods of mental dissection and displacement are strategies commonly employed by the able-bodied as a way to manage the disabled figure. Patsy develops a third strategy, the attempt to read the twins' body according to a logic of "normal" anatomy. In contemporary theories of disability, negative cultural value and the practices of isolation, fixing, and exploitation stem from a socially constructed category "disabled" that is not naturally attached to bodies. Drawing from feminist, race, and queer theory, disability studies in its strongest form holds in balance an identity politics that accounts for the material effects of ideology and an anti-essentialist model that questions the neutrality of the normate body. Cultural expectations that determine assignments of "normal" or "disabled" are drawn in part from "physiological facts about most humans—such as having two legs with which to walk or having some capacity for sight or speech" (Garland-Thomson, *Extraordinary Bodies* 7). These cultural expectations are taken for granted in most interactions among the able-bodied, but they serve as a determining and ongoing feature in the able-bodied management of disabled persons. While Rowena limits her attention to faces and hands as a way to ignore the anomalous whole body, Aunt Patsy attempts to segregate parts of the body according to a familiar schema of anatomy. She studies the twins eating and thinks to herself, "Now that hand is going to take that coffee to—no, it's gone to the other mouth; I can't understand it; and now, here is the dark-complected hand with a potatoe on its fork, I'll see what goes with it—there, the light-complected head's got it, as sure as I live!" (138). Patsy's confusion stems from the failure of expectation; food only goes to the "wrong" head according to the physiological convention of two hands for one head. For Angelo and Luigi, however, their extraordinary body allows for a distribution of tasks based on convenience, not convention.

As the period's most explicitly contained, and therefore safest, structure for understanding encounters with physical difference, the conventions of the sideshow spectacle often structure the imaginative domestication of freakish bodies. Like Twain's fiction of shared arms and alternate mastery over their legs, the necessity of innovation for disabled people is often the site of greatest fervor over their "freakishness." Freak show proprietors developed displays around the juxtaposition of extraordinary bodies performing mundane acts. Quotidian activities such as drinking or writing become freakish when performed by men or women with congenital deformities such as missing limbs. Writing with one's toes or holding a paintbrush in one's teeth was often the centerpiece of live museum displays, acts made even more striking by setting the stage in the domesticating form of a Victorian parlor. In another example that multiplies the levels of juxtaposition, an African woman with extended lip rings performed for a crowd by eating, centering the audience's attention around the most striking site of her anatomical and racial difference.[20] Aunt Patsy's breakfast table is transformed into a freak show stage in which small talk suffers from the Coopers' fascination with the twins' eating: "The weather was all finished up and disposed of, as a subject, before the simple Missourians had gotten sufficiently wonted to the spectacle of one body feeding two heads to feel composed and reconciled in the presence of so bizarre a miracle. And even after everyone's mind became tranquilized there was still one slight distraction left: the hand that picked up the biscuit carried it to the wrong head, as often as any other way, and the wrong mouth devoured it" (137). In a reversal of the freak show tradition of decorating a freak's individual exhibit as a parlor or other domestic space, Twain makes a freak show out of the boardinghouse. He removes the Cappellos from the official museum space, but transforms the kitchen to a stage and the family to an audience.

By replicating the conventions of the sideshow display in the domestic spaces of the novel, *Those Extraordinary Twins* collapses the division between privacy and spectacle in keeping with the freak show tradition. Early in the narrative, Twain carries his twins to the bedroom where they begin to undress for the night. In this scene he enflames the reader's desire for knowledge of the particulars of the anomalous body. As literary voyeurs, we want to see what the Coopers do not. The promise of nudity in a bedroom setting focuses our curiosity around two questions: What does the naked flesh look like? And, Can the twins have sex? The priority I afford to the latter question may seem startling, but I argue that Rowena's romantic fantasies initially pique the reader's interest in genitalia and Twain's language heightens it. In this scene Twain peeks around the door to the bedroom to find the twins undressing for bed:

> The Twins were wet and tired, and they proceeded to undress without any preliminary remarks. The abundance of sleeves made the partnership coat hard to get off, for it was like skinning a tarantula, but it came at last, after much tugging and perspiring. The mutual vest followed. Then the brothers stood up before the glass, and each took off his own cravat and collar. . . . Each cravat, as to color, was in perfect taste, so far as the owner's complexion was concerned— a delicate pink, in the case of the blonde brother, a violent scarlet in the case of the brunette—but as a combination they broke all the laws of taste known to civilization. Nothing more fiendish and irreconcilable than those shrieking and blaspheming colors could have been contrived. (133–134)

Twain teases his readers, breaking the climactic promise generated by the removal of clothing. Our twins are in the bedroom, perspiring, undressing—the sexual content that is both homoerotic and incestuous implicates the reader and the freak show audience in their prurient fascination with the flesh. Frustrated readers are forced to follow the attention of the narrator, who disrupts the anticipated nudity to critique the twins' combined fashion sense. Again, Twain employs the technique of displacement—the cravats are "fiendish and irreconcilable," not the naked form. This sudden movement from whole to part calls out the interrupted desire to know the specifics of the body. As with Twain's focus on "intimate habits" in his "Siamese Twins" essay, or the curiosity roused by Chang and Eng Bunker's twenty-two children, the stigma of sexual excess attached to the anomalous body is not limited to the freak show stage, but becomes a portable speculative impulse that influences the social scripts of assimilation.

The intense longing to see and to know the anomalous body creates a dynamic in which figures of physical difference seem to call for opposing and dominating positions of authority. Twain further extends the conventions of the freak show as Aunt Patsy and the Judge become replica P. T. Barnums, proprietors who can translate the twins' difference into social profit. Patsy gains social status in the village by holding a widely attended "reception in honor of the twins" (142). The party reveals her thinly veiled desire to lay claim to the unusual. She boasts, "'Oh, you'll find there's more than one thing about them that ain't commonplace" (147). The narrator describes her at this moment as having "the complacent air of a person with a property right in a novelty that is under admiring scrutiny" (147). Even after their escape from the European freak show circuit, the twins' body becomes a commodity. The Cappellos leave the reception with the Judge, ostensibly for a tour of the town. Instead, Angelo and Luigi are the objects on display and the Judge's buggy recalls the traveling freak show.

Twain's literary use of freak show conventions inscribes an accompanying obsession with classification. Authority over anatomy was handed over to both popular and medical audiences on the freak show circuit. Proprietors often collaborated with doctors who would perform autopsies on anomalous bodies for a paying public. In live exhibitions this medical authority translates to the audience, who can see the truths on the body instead of having to look inside it. The quest to determine "what is it?" describes the inquiring gaze of the show patron. Is it human or animal? Man or woman? Individual or two? White or racial other? These epistemological quandaries were so central that one of P. T. Barnum's most celebrated freaks was a microcephalic black man from New Jersey called, simply, "What is it?" Named for the act of classification his spectators were asked to perform, Barnum's freak was only the most famous in a series of disabled men given this name.[21] In these spectacles, categorizing the anomalous becomes an exhilarating act of authority, particularly in the controlled environment of the freak show.[22] Although Luigi and Angelo are not literally contained in a freak show display, the villagers of Dawson's Landing attempt to understand and control their body according to familiar physiological conventions. Aunt Patsy initially manages the twins' difference by applying a commonsense assertion of anatomy: "One arm on each shoulder belongs to each of the creatures, don't it? For a person to have two arms on one shoulder wouldn't do him any good, would it?" (126). The social need to actively assimilate the unusual reflects back on the seeming neutrality of physical norms—bodies that appear to be read without interpretation. The plot of the twins' story hinges upon the persistent dilemmas of classification and knowing in the trial when the failure to know who is in control of the body at what time forces the court to throw up its hands. With their two heads and four arms, Luigi and Angelo point to other local figures that do not conform to visual expectations. Next to conjoined twins, racially mixed residents like Roxy and Chambers are the most obvious examples of the disjunction between physical appearance and social categorization. Rather than reinscribing a fixed line between normal and abnormal, this expanding spectrum of physical difference demonstrates the acts of interpretation required to read all bodies. The failure of physiological conventions in classifying and scrutinizing abnormal bodies unseats the "natural" status of such expectations. Angelo and Luigi do not conform to Patsy's expectations about the distribution of labor among their four arms and instead demonstrate how having two arms on one shoulder can be useful. The ostensible truths of anatomy are not transparent accounts of universal bodies, but instead stem from a massive apparatus of medical, economic, and political fictions. The freak show draws these activities into the explicitly performative sphere, making an entertainment out of the daily practices that direct popular assumptions about how bodies should look and function. Freak show conventions conversely move beyond the stage as a way for the body politic to domesticate the spectacle of physical anomaly.

The Literary Caesarean Operation

The epistemological crises prompted by anomalous bodies point to a problem of conventional categories, but also make visible the process by which these categories are constructed and applied. Instead of maintaining the fiction of bodies as naturally coextensive with their social meanings, these instances of poor fit between person and identity category call attention to the imaginative pushing and pulling that identity formation entails. Despite Roxy's embodied challenge to fixed racial categories, in the social register of Dawson's Landing, she is emphatically black. This disjunction in the novel suggests the ideological work required to resolve the category dilemma among the body politic and to mask the presence of a problem in the first place. Twain begins to pull back the curtain on these discursive practices by describing Roxy and her child's black identity as "a fiction of law and custom" (9). Twain's striking word choice, "fiction," demonstrates that this imaginative process is intimately bound up in the practices of reading and writing. The imaginative and interpretive labors required in fiction are necessary practices that demonstrate how physical and social bodies are woven into the written form. In turn, the unconventional textual bodies of *Pudd'nhead Wilson* and *Those Extraordinary Twins* are not just a metaphor for the anomalous bodies they describe, but instead demonstrate that all three valences of bodily construction—physical, textual, and political—are inextricably connected to one another.

Twain's 1894 volume offers an interesting dramatization of what David Mitchell and Sharon Snyder call "the dependencies of discourse." *Those Extraordinary Twins* literally cannot be read without following Twain's instructions and turning back to chapters in *Pudd'nhead Wilson*. In turn, while *Pudd'nhead* is often read on its own, traces of Angelo and Luigi's conjoined origins persist throughout the text.[23] The texts are both twinned and entwined, each literally relying on the other for meaning. Twain personifies his texts as "not one story, but two stories tangled together; and they obstructed and interrupted each other at every turn" (125). The twin metaphor stems in part from Twain's description of the texts' composition, in which he personifies the stories as gestating fetuses. The act of removing one story has been famously called by Twain a "kind of literary Caesarian operation" (125). According to his own metaphor, Twain becomes both the gendered body birthing and the doctor's body delivering the work of fiction. The author's own body becomes extraordinary—simultaneously man and woman, creative, operated upon, and operating. These changes are prompted not just by the power of Twain's language, but by the destabilizing effect of interpreting and representing a strange body. Again, we see the breakdown of the split between viewer and viewed, or the author and his creation, in which the unusual body within the text challenges the boundaries of both the "normal" author and textual convention. The promiscuous nature of abnormality rejects the notion of absolute difference attached to unusual bodies and instead suggests that constructions of extraordinary bodies depend on a process of differentiation that must also include identification. Just two decades earlier, Twain offers a similar instance in which he imagines himself as a birthing mother, this time characterizing his relief over a favorable review as feeling "like a mother who has given birth to a white baby when she was awfully afraid it was going to be a mulatto."[24] Even in this tongue-in-cheek simile, Twain suggests the corporeal instability produced by writing. The authorial body takes on a gendered and racial cast, as writing offers Twain an avenue for identification with a figure of ostensible absolute difference. In concert with this imagined identification, the process includes differentiation as well in the distancing effect of the simile—he feels *like* a mother—and the ability to cling to authority in the earlier figure as both the doctor and the gestating body. In this pair of gestation metaphors, the neutrality of Twain's white masculine body facilitates this feminine costume while still retaining the position of privileged normalcy.

The ability of fiction to reshape the authorial body is emblematic of the discursive production of bodies on a larger scale. Circling back to my opening discussion, the half-a-dog joke offers a striking moment in which to discover the interpretive processes by which bodies are understood. The public confusion over Wilson's remark dramatizes the social requirement of legibility. As described above, in this scene the citizens search Wilson's face, but "find no expression they could read" and then "fall away from him as from something uncanny" (6). In this formulation, Twain repeats the sentimental reliance on the ability to read truth in the face and the body. A similar scene emerges at the opening of *Those Extraordinary Twins* when the Coopers are left reeling after their initial encounter with "that uncanny apparition" (131). The doubled instances of the word "uncanny" mark parallel phenomena in which these characters are described as supernatural for their failure to exhibit readable, familiar bodies. The alignment between the uncanny and the otherworldly evokes the social implications of embodied legibility; Pudd'nhead and the twins are cast out of the citizenry because the face and body do not project clearly inscribed meanings. These three uncanny figures are momentarily suspended in a position of radical difference until imaginative strategies for containing their identities emerge among the population: Wilson's illegibility promptly serves as further proof of his pudd'nhead status and the twins are domesticated by freak show conventions and imaginative strategies like displacement and mental dissection. Although Twain dwells on the term "uncanny" more than twenty years before Freud published his own meditations on the subject, Twain's text dramatizes an implicit version of the structure Freud describes. Freud's 1919 paper looks to explore the nature of the uncanny and in doing so, expand our understanding beyond more common meanings of the term. The usual, if pedestrian, definition of the uncanny links its effects to a problem of uncertainty. In Twain's case this effect applies crucially to the twins who challenge the seemingly fixed distinction between self and other. Freud pauses over the question of usage, however, and notes that the German *heimlich* can be used interchangeably with its ostensible opposite, *unheimlich*, as the meaning moves from "familiar" and "friendly" to "obscure" and "inaccessible to knowledge."[25] The simultaneous suggestion of the familiar and hidden in the uncanny leads Freud to argue that its startling effect stems from its nature as the return of the repressed. This confrontation with the once-familiar confirms Freud's psychoanalytic thesis that every affect is repressed into anxiety (241). Beyond the psychic theory Freud describes, however, his model offers insights into the social structure captured by Twain's use of the term "uncanny." Freud's insistence on locating the familiar in what once seemed to be only the effect of radical difference reseats physical abnormality as a foundational imaginative structure. The characteristic illegibility of the Eastern, urban Wilson and the conjoined, Italian twins is not, in fact, the result of their otherworldliness, but instead an effect of their central, but obscured, position in the social imaginary of Dawson's Landing. These cast-out others stand as an embodied reminder of the relational structure of identity, even as the townspeople scramble to mask this reliance through ideological strategies that attempt to fix and manage the uncanny.

Just as Wilson and the twins are alienated for their failure to conform to social standards of legibility and coherence, Twain's conjoined texts have suffered a similar fate in their critical history. In the twentieth century, *Pudd'nhead Wilson's* most strident detractor has been Hershel Parker. Holding Twain to his self-characterization as "jack-leg novelist," Parker offers a detailed history of the text's composition to challenge the New Critical impulse to find unity in every text. Parker reads the novel not for thematic meaning, but for a set of truths marked out by its hasty and jumbled composition—for example, asking critics how they can wring their hands over Tom and Rowena's mixed-race engagement when, during the time the scene was composed, Twain had not yet written the baby-switching plot. Parker then concludes, "While the published *Pudd'nhead Wilson* is thus patently unreadable, anyone who knows literary critics will know that a simple fact like that has not deterred them from trying to read the book and bragging about having done so" (136). In this essay Parker takes aim simultaneously at Twain—for being a lazy author in creating a text with little revision and no legitimate claim to aesthetic virtues such as unity, or even readability—and at Twain's "sense-making" critics, for ignoring the composition history to offer up a coherent text. Parker's 1984 essay commonly serves as an opening counterpoint for contemporary critics who argue for *Pudd'nhead*'s status as a Twain classic. If Forrest G. Robinson's 1990 coedited collection with Susan Gillman stands as the most vocal champion of the novel, his included essay, "The Sense of Disorder in *Pudd'nhead Wilson*," most directly takes Parker's position to task. Robinson's thesis reflects contemporary critical preferences as he locates meaning in the gaps and disjunctions of the work. The nodes of this critical debate—New Critical unity, the challenge leveled through the "facts" of composition, and the recovery of meaning through the text's lapses—capture a shifting history of inclusion to exclusion and back in the American literary canon. Like Twain's "Siamese Twins," the texts come back to stand as exemplary national literature through the complex ties between the excepted and the exceptional. By making sense out of the very failures that Parker claims should be grounds for the novel's rejection, contemporary critics reseat an exclusionary property as the productive source of the text's merit. Just as Twain's version of Chang and Eng embody national virtues, the quirks and fissures in his textual body reflect the complexities of the national imagination. The success of this critical recovery resides in the ability to see the productive value of failed textual unity. Toppling unity as the apex of form in the literary critical sphere provides a model for rethinking the primacy of unity in national and physical bodies. The danger of this extension, however, would be to reify difference as a fixed, even if valued, property of the body. Instead of inverting the hierarchy between normal and abnormal, finding meaning in a text's gaps can, even if only temporarily, undo the security of the normal body and reveal the discursive formations undergirding its construction.

Since this chapter began with an extended mediation on a dog, it seems only fitting to close by focusing on a cat. In the opening paragraphs of *Pudd'nhead Wilson*, Twain offers an idyllic portrait of Dawson's Landing in 1830. The town is a "snug little collection" of homes with "whitewashed exteriors," covered in tangled, flowering vines. The perfections of these front porch gardens is advertised by a blissful, sleeping cat. For, as Twain writes, "Then that home was complete and its contentment and peace were made manifest to the world by this symbol, whose testimony is infallible. A home without a cat ... may be a perfect home, perhaps, but how can it prove title?" (3). Twain's opening description offers a limited tour of the town, focusing on its whitewashed and peaceful "front" and "exteriors" without discovering the backyard domains of the town's slaves. According to the same logic by which the citizenry looks for corporeal signs to reveal the truths about Roxy, Wilson, and the twins, the town itself offers up the symbolic cat as "infallible testimony" to its tranquility. This scene demonstrates the importance of signs and legibility for the social body, as well. The need to "prove title" in this passage suggests that there is not a natural correspondence between identity—title—and reality, but argues instead that identity can only be apprehended if it matches social fictions. After all, the home "may be perfect," but that perfection can only be realized through its signification. As an added layer of complication, Twain's overstatement ("infallible") and the notorious fickleness of napping cats imply the instability of such sign systems. In *Pudd'nhead Wilson* and *Those Extraordinary Twins*, Twain imagines reading as not merely a textual but also a political process, demonstrating the need to make sense of social and physical difference by domesticating the exceptional into the representative.

2 / "Marvelous and Very Real": The Grotesque in *The Heart Is a Lonely Hunter* and *Wise Blood*

Very early in *The Heart Is a Lonely Hunter*, Carson McCullers offers a scene of domestic discord between Biff Brannon and his wife, Alice. Frustrated with his preferential treatment of an unusual customer, Alice charges, "It's a disgrace to the business. And besides, he's nothing but a bum and a freak." To which Brannon responds, "I like freaks" (14). This direct statement of Brannon's affinity for freaks—a group later elaborated to include sick people, cripples, anybody with TB or a harelip, hunchbacks, amputees, and John Singer, another central character and the local "deaf-mute" (22)—applies not only to a character in McCullers's fiction but also to the author herself, as well as to a score of authors writing novels in the mid-twentieth century. American writers of the period, including McCullers, Flannery O'Connor, Sherwood Anderson, Nathaniel West, and William Faulkner, constitute a proliferation of fiction of the grotesque. As reflected in their prose, these writers are drawn to freakish bodies as both the effect of and antidote to a modern world characterized as alienating and stifling in its embrace of homogeneity. Bodies at the margins of national norms seem to provide a conduit to the material real and, in this proximity to reality, access to exceptional insights. This quality of seeming *both* more real *and* more otherworldly than the quotidian social world suggests just one of the complexities of representing physical difference and its figural burden in novels of the mid-twentieth century. In its emphasis on materiality, contradiction, spectacle, and populism, the grotesque form provides a representational scaffold for these freakish bodies, offering the tropes by which they become legible in the national imagination.

Originally conceived to name the mingling of plant, animal, and human in visual arts, the grotesque of the twentieth century retains an emphasis on the visual and on contradictions of somatic form. While much of contemporary criticism responds in some fashion to Mikhail Bakhtin's foundational work on the grotesque, *Rabelais and His World*, there are nearly as many definitions of the grotesque as there are writers about it. Unlike Bakhtin's utopic vision of a ludic and liberatory "grotesque realism," for Wolfgang Kayser the grotesque represents alienation and mocking, satanic laughter. In an even more contemporary vein, Geoffrey Harpham sees the form as an expression of a poststructuralist crisis in language and meaning. What these and shelves of other diverse perspectives share, however, is an insistence that the grotesque is never abstract, that it constantly presents its own materiality. The grotesque, then, operates alongside the figure of the embodied citizen as each entails the body as an inescapable ideological property. And like disabled citizens, the grotesque, even in its most symbolic modes, always retains a residue of the material.

This mutual burden of embodiment shared by the grotesque and disability coincides with a shared history in the approach to physical difference in literature. Before disability studies emerged as such, the two major competing critical genres for the study of disability were split between the sentimental and the grotesque. While neither form offers an emphasis on rights or offers a theorization of disability's social formulation, both sentiment and the grotesque serve as the historical rubrics under which preceding scholars discussed illness, deformity, and physical excess. In chapter 1, I explore sentiment as an animating mode in the approach to bodies, politics, and texts. Here, I turn my focus to the grotesque as an interpretive scheme deeply influential in the representation of disability in mid-twentieth-century literature. Critics who concur on little else will agree that the grotesque is as much a form as it is an unsettling effect and that this effect expresses a social, political, or spiritual comment.[1] As Bernard McElroy argues, "To imagine a monstrosity is to imagine a world capable of producing that monstrosity" (11). It is most common, among scholars of the grotesque, to show how the grotesque body reflects a social body gone awry, but less common to find critics who wonder what this role as national symbol means for the grotesque citizen. Even at their most politically invested, studies of the grotesque offer largely static accounts of the disabled figures that populate grotesquerie. In fact, many of the gains of the disability studies movement in the humanities have come from wresting symbolic control away from the critical lenses of the grotesque and the sentimental. At its core, however, the grotesque offers more than just a slice of literary history. The unyielding emphasis on materiality that resides at the heart of grotesquerie argues that further study of these literary examples can offer insights into the likewise unevenly distributed property of embodiment, not only in literature but also among disabled citizens. Further, McElroy's observation—the monstrous body will always speak to the world capable of imagining it—offers another avenue by which to examine the homology of the body politic, the physical body, and the textual body that animates my work as a whole. Where McElroy and similar critics of the grotesque see these social metaphors as the sole meaning of the form, I argue that this irreducible mingling of the symbolic and the material demonstrates the ways in which physical anomaly, more broadly, becomes legible in the national imagination. Thus, rather than set aside decades of critical interest in the grotesque as insensible to the concerns of disabled people, I take up the grotesque's central categories—material reality, the dissolution of boundaries, the folk, and spectacle—to demonstrate how these major elements serve as the constitutive forces in the cultural construction of mid-twentieth-century embodied citizenship.

* * *

When Biff Brannon, in *The Heart Is a Lonely Hunter* (1940), tells his wife, "I like freaks," she doesn't miss a beat before replying, "I reckon you do! I just reckon you certainly ought to, Mister Brannon—being as you're one yourself" (14). Alice's rejoinder captures the socially communicable property of freakishness, the danger that in admiring a freak, you might become one.[2] In Carson McCullers's novel, this sense of freakishness as the enabling and transformative figure in social relations serves as the linchpin for the story. As the narrative eye moves among five central characters in the novel, each character, in turn, has his or her focus on John Singer, the local "deaf-mute." Each aligns disability with otherworldly wisdom and locates in Singer's physical difference an embodiment of his or her own liminal form—Biff Brannon, the café owner, and Mick Kelly, a local adolescent girl, find in Singer an expression of their unconventional gender expression; Jake Blount, the "freak" and drunken labor activist Biff's wife finds so objectionable, uses Singer as a nonverbal sponge for his excessive speeches; and Dr. Copeland, the town's African

American physician, wants to share with Singer a heightened capacity for knowledge through oppression. As the narrative focus shifts to Singer, we discover that he participates in the same logic, assigning fantastic insights to his similarly deaf and nonverbal companion, Antonapolous. While I am certainly not alone in reading McCullers under the rubric of the grotesque, my dual focus on the body politic and its construction through figures of disability illustrates the grotesque form of the social in her work. Disability, in *The Heart Is a Lonely Hunter*, serves as a necessary supplement for the creation of local community as McCullers imagines physical difference an antidote to the alienating modern world.

For critics of the Southern grotesque, Carson McCullers is rarely mentioned without turning, in the next breath, to Flannery O'Connor. *Wise Blood* (1952) considers similar themes of modern alienation through its protagonist, Hazel Motes. Called "that grotesque saint" by critic William Van O'Connor (19), Hazel animates the bankruptcy of meaning and community in mid-century America. As he enters the fictional Southern city of Taulkinham, Hazel meets a cast of grotesque characters including Asa Hawks, a blind street preacher eventually exposed as a fraud; Hawks's daughter, Sabbath Lily, a precocious and misdirected adolescent; and Enoch Emery, a lonely local zoo guard whose instinctive motivations constitute the "wise blood" of the book's title. Caught up in the profane architecture of the modern world, the novel turns to disability and the body, more broadly, as an avenue toward the obscured sphere of the real. O'Connor has said of her vexed relationship with the label "grotesque," "It is when the freak can be sensed as a figure for our essential displacement that he attains some depth in literature" (*Mystery and Manners* 45). Freakishness as a viscerally unsettling form can temporarily expose the misprision of the national imagination, forcing citizens to remember the body as they look to the otherworldly.

A consistent thread through my work is an interest in the potential for language to carry both the physical and the conceptual. The literary grotesque serves as a special case of language in which the grotesque form constantly and explicitly thrusts the excessive body into the realm of the symbolic. Most theorists of the grotesque insist on its materiality, but they also understand its effect as largely symbolic, if not allegorical. This simultaneous service as both symbol and "most real" twists bodies into the awkward position of having one foot in the abstract and one in the material. The embodied tension between the material real and a fantasy of otherworldliness becomes an animating contradiction in the representation of disability in O'Connor and McCullers. Despite its awkwardness, however, this tension speaks to the necessary interaction of the material and the figurative in imagining the body. By re-membering the physical in its turn to the symbolic, the grotesque serves as a visceral reminder of the impossibility of excising language from the material and vice versa.

The Language of the Grotesque

In her 1978 volume, *Illness as Metaphor,* Susan Sontag writes, "Illness is the night-side of life, a more onerous citizenship. Everyone who is born holds a dual citizenship in the kingdom of the well and in the kingdom of the sick" (3). This description of illness as a "more onerous citizenship" resonates with the ideological burdens of embodied citizenship that I have been describing. In the national imagination, physical difference becomes an inescapable property, and embodiment constantly shapes the political membership of disabled people. The focus of Sontag's argument lies "not in what it is really like to emigrate to the kingdom of the ill and live there" (3), but in a genealogy of this extended network of fantasies and social meanings attached to disease. In addition to the physical struggles associated with illness and disability, the "onerous" elements of this citizenship lie in the relation of disability to the social body, a relation bound up in a series of imaginative constructions. Sontag stages *Illness as Metaphor* as an ethical intervention in the symbolic use of disease, insisting that "illness is not a metaphor, and that the most truthful way of regarding illness—and the healthiest way of being ill—is one most purified of, most resistant to, metaphoric thinking" (3). These moral arguments find voice most explicitly in the opening and closing pages of Sontag's text. What lies between these ethical claims is an extensive history of the "stereotypes of national character" that structure how cancer and TB operate as metaphors. Accounts of the experience of illness and disability, both in medical psychology and more colloquially, would confirm Sontag's argument that the "punitive and sentimental fantasies" associated with physical disability make the experience of illness harder. Stereotypes, stigma, and cultural and physical inaccessibility suggest only the tip of the iceberg in the social obstacles laid out for disabled people. What the balance of pages in Sontag's text would suggest, however, is that it is easy to illustrate all the ways illness does function as a social metaphor and difficult to articulate for very long what it might look like if it did not. Certainly it would be unhelpfully conservative to suggest that Sontag's goal of a metaphor-free space for illness should be cast aside because it is difficult. In fact, her text does illustrate the way that metaphorical thinking about disease has risen and fallen, especially as figures of TB have lost ground to a more pervasive national fear of cancer. But I believe that it is difficult to talk for very long about disability without slipping into metaphor, not only because these figures are so pervasive, but also because I understand embodiment as inextricably wrapped up in both the material and the social. The body should not be reduced to symbol, but it is not entirely distinct from symbolism, either.

The figural history of the grotesque is so overburdened by symbolic turns that it lies nearly defenseless against the ethical interventions made by Sontag and others. The aesthetic category of the grotesque can focus and extend the discussion of the stakes of metaphor and materiality found in my introduction. For grotesque fiction and its critics, physical difference serves as a sign for a chaotic world and a voice for social protest, leaving little or no attention to disabled subjectivity. In William Van O'Connor's case for the grotesque as the dominant mode of fiction in the United States, he slights even those authors who would see grotesque bodies as a symptom of social or political problems and instead argues that the grotesque must always point further outward to a "backdrop of cosmic pointlessness" (13). Where a character's subjectivity is considered, critics see physical disability as a sign of psychic or spiritual troubles. Conventional readings of McCullers and O'Connor, in particular, follow this mode: an essay on McCullers's dominant themes finds her fiction populated by characters "whose physical deformities reveal outwardly the twisted, distorted spirits of their inner lives" (qtd. in Clark and Friedman 7). Similar formulations appear countless times in critical accounts of grotesque fiction. Despite this repeated turn to metaphysical problems, however, grotesque figures inevitably preserve a sense of the body. Unlike more pedestrian symbols in which the object is reduced to a vehicle by which to approach the abstract—the point of "my love is a rose" is the love, not the rose—theorists of the grotesque describe a special emphasis on the material in grotesque figures. While reams of essays on McCullers and O'Connor have ignored the social and personal effects of disability, the grotesque image, in its inescapable materiality, retains the residue of embodiment even when the stakes of physical difference lie outside the critical focus.

One of the binding elements in the fiction of McCullers and O'Connor is their shared use of metaphors of sight and blindness in ways that are dislodged from the subjective experience of disability. I open with this focused discussion of blindness as metaphor to underscore the tension between the material and abstract in what has become a very common symbolic formulation. Both novels thematize a familiar contrast between insight, vision, and blindness, especially in their focus on the eyes of a major character. In *The Heart Is a Lonely Hunter*, John Singer, made powerful by virtue of his disability, has eyes that "made a person think that he heard things nobody else had ever heard, that he knew things no one had ever guessed before" (25). And *Wise Blood*'s protagonist Hazel Motes has eyes that seem like "passages leading somewhere" (4); Sabbath Hawks, the teen daughter of the ostensibly blind preacher, observes, "I like his eyes. They don't look like they see what he's looking at but they keep on looking" (56). Each author exploits a long-standing literary tradition of literal sight as a figure for knowledge and insight, but their more extended meditations on physical disability trouble the potentially uncomplicated use of disability as metaphor in these novels.

What does it mean, for example, in a novel that includes a character who is actually deaf and nonverbal for Jake Blount to announce, "Everybody is blind, dumb, and blunt-headed—stupid and mean" (69)? Or, similarly, for Doctor Copeland to announce "I am deaf" upon hearing of his son's brutal mistreatment at the hands of racist prison guards? The universalizing impulse of these statements is deflated by McCullers's characterization of John Singer's disability. While the claims seem to suggest that blindness or deafness can be the transportable property of anyone, Singer's figure in the novel grounds these examples of disability as metaphor in a broader scheme of the social meanings of embodied difference. In a later scene where black community members temper white activist Jake Blount's desire for direct action against the violent and racist guards, they tell Blount, "Nothing us could do would make no difference. Best thing us can do is keep our mouths shut" (257). This scene understands the mute response of the black community as a social necessity in the face of threats of violent repression. While their publicly silent resignation lacks the drama of Blount's call for protest, the black community takes Singer's speechless example as a viable model of citizenship in order to preserve their physical safety. It is easy to read McCullers's novel as exploitative in its use of disability as metaphor, but it also seems possible to find moments in the novel that offer a confirmation of Singer as an enviable model of social participation.

The questions of vision and blindness in *Wise Blood* are even more difficult. O'Connor sets up a constellation of complex figures for sight and blindness in the novel where each point serves to undermine the others. The female characters in the novel, from the casual fellow passenger on the train entering Taulkinham, to Sabbath Hawks, to his landlady, Mrs. Flood, all see in Hazel's eyes a conduit to otherworldly wisdom. Hazel, similarly, for much of the novel, equates literal sight with knowledge, crying, "Don't I know what exists and what don't? Don't I have eyes in my head? Am I a blind man?" (28). One of Hazel's major failures lies in his belief in the correspondence between quotidian vision and truth.[3] In O'Connor's formulation, Hazel's fidelity to the concerns of this world demonstrates a misplaced adherence to the naturalized artifice of modernity.

The question takes on a strikingly bizarre cast, however, when the voice of spiritual vision is found in the body of Asa Hawks, a fraudulently blind preacher. Hawks tells Hazel, "I can see more than you. You got eyes and see not, ears and hear not, but you'll have to see some time" (27). The spiritual correctness of Hawks's words is undermined by his exposure several pages later as a fraud. Hawks's imitation blindness offers an interesting test case of the theory in which physical difference serves as the critical capacity to discern the real. Hawks's feigned disability reflects a thoroughly modern attempt to appropriate the knowledge of the anomalous body through the outward trappings of difference. Hawks exploits the contemporary confusion of signifier for reality, knowing that by carrying the external apparatus of his wounding—glasses, cane, and scars across his cheeks that stop short of his eyes—he can play the social role of embodied knowledge without the physical impairment. Hawks's critique of Hazel's exclusively mundane vision, a charge that seems to be rendered true by O'Connor's religious commitments, suggests that even imitation can serve as a mouthpiece for truth. For much of the novel, O'Connor seems to position the anomalous body as the last vestige of the real in a modern world consumed by mass media, mass production, and the crowd. In the figure of Asa Hawks, however, she allows that the modern zeal for the image can paradoxically offer a road back to a deeper real. At the close of the novel, Hazel's final turn toward spiritual redemption through the act of self-blinding is, in fact, another imitation of the falsely blind preacher, but Hazel succeeds in mortally wounding his body where Hawks failed. Hazel's true blindness becomes a grotesque manifestation of the trying road to Christian redemption.[4]

Among the external apparatuses of his injury, Asa Hawks carries in his pocket a newspaper clipping announcing, "EVANGELIST TO BLIND SELF" (59). In making a public appeal to the printed promotion, Hawks understands the truth status of the mass media in the contemporary moment. He constructs his identity by eschewing the actual event in favor of the arrested moment of reported anticipation and the apparent physical aftermath of the act. The hidden second clipping, reading "EVANGELIST'S NERVE FAILS" (60), exists in a kind of tense equivalency with the first—the first remains true only while the second is secret.

The alienating values of the modern social world have a deforming effect on the body and, in the proliferation of words as commodities or commercials, can make language unreliable as well. From misleading newspaper accounts to strobing neon signs, language and the body perform mutually grotesque acts. Hazel Motes's landlady, Mrs. Flood, illustrates how the modern principle of substitution and fungibility has unmoored language from O'Connor's version of spiritual reality: "She was not a woman who felt more violence in one word than in another; she took every word at its face value but all the faces were the same" (108). According to Flood's metaphor, words have become like faces in the urban crowd, characterized by homogeneity. This dominating influence of sameness compromises the ability for language to capture anything outside of the norm.

In *The Heart Is a Lonely Hunter*, the young protagonist Mick Kelly describes her sense of language's failures: "What she had to say was terrible and afraid. But what [Singer] would tell her was so true that it would make everything all right. Maybe it was a thing that couldn't be spoken with words or writing. Maybe he would have to let her understand this in a different way" (307). Mick understands that in a world where language is under the service of an economy of exchange, words may be insufficient to account for something "terrible," something outside the accepted norms of the social body. In this case Mick looks to Singer's extraordinary body as the possible site of expression that will move beyond the neutered limitations of everyday words. Singer serves as the embodiment of truth and, by the necessity of unspoken communication, seems to offer an escape from the problems of everyday language. Toward the closing pages of the novel, McCullers experiments with language in a continued quest for a new mode of communication. In a moment of optimism, Mick thinks,

> It had to be some good if anything made sense. And it was too and it was too and it was too and it was too. It was some good.
> All right!
> O.K.!
> Some good. (354)

Like the representations of physical excess that offer reassurance throughout the novel, McCullers turns here to a written form of excess in the repetition of the phrase "and it was too." At one level, the phrase serves as an expression of Mick's insistence to an imagined interlocutor that the events of the past year are both good and meaningful—she imagines the doubtful objection, "It was not," and supplies the childish rejoinder, "It was, too." While the repetition of the phrase suggests a residue of the adolescence she has left behind in her new role as store clerk, the second meaning of "too" as "too much" indicates that Mick cannot make sense of her experience except through stubborn insistence and an inarticulate appeal to excess. The linguistic experimentation in the passage, with its truncated exclamations and trailing fragment ("some good"), calls into question the premise of the opening sentence that "it had to be some good if anything made sense." The converse proposition suggested by the word "if" and the strange language that follows is, of course, that nothing makes sense. The tone of the passage concludes in an unsteady belief in good, but it also understands that McCullers must go outside the norms of expression to arrest this optimistic possibility.

The tension that McCullers captures—between language as the overdetermining force of interpellation and as a site of strangeness and potential incompletion—speaks to the need to open up our treatment of metaphors of disability. Imaginative and ideological structures infuse the material body so thoroughly that language serves an indispensable role in studies of embodiment. In our social imagination, metaphor structures both studies of the grotesque and popular approaches to disability. Many disability theorists have called out the ways in which metaphor can serve as a distorting lens in the often far-sighted use of physical difference as a sign for universal crises. The limitations of metaphor in these cases, however, should not obscure an inevitable grappling with language in understanding disability. In this way, close readings of literary texts can serve as the ground on which to discover the complexities of disability and its cultural meanings.

Grotesque Realism

In the decades before disability studies emerged as a coherent field, treatment of physical difference in literature often collapsed under the rubric of the literary grotesque. Rather than turn away from these critical antecedents and their neglect or open dismissal of disability as lived experience, I hope to construct a genealogy in which their dominant category can speak to contemporary questions of identity and social formation. This move to the past begins with Mikhail Bakhtin and a reclamation of the often-lost second half of his complete term: "grotesque realism." In his repeated emphasis on realism, Bakhtin encodes the grotesque as a simultaneous movement toward the real and the abstract. Although her own approach is usually more spiritual than political, Flannery O'Connor shares with Bakhtin a commitment to the transformative possibilities of realist fiction.[5] She argues that fiction is essentially realist, writing, "All novels are fundamentally seekers and describers of the real, but the realism of each novelist will depend on his view of the ultimate reaches of reality" (*Mystery and Manners* 40–41). O'Connor sees a sharp disjunction between reality as she understands it and the quotidian practices and culture of the social world. The grotesque body emerges in literature to address this break, serving to both bridge and illuminate the distance between modern life and "the ultimate reaches of reality." O'Connor argues for the grotesque as a required tool for the "realist of distances" because its jarring and disorienting nature is necessary to unmask the pervasive fictions of modernity. For O'Connor and McCullers, modern life consists of a vast and convincing architecture that obscures its own construction. In response, these writers frequently turn toward the grotesque body as a conduit to reality. And while reality often remains out of reach, the anomalous body consistently becomes cast as its approximation, exposing the fictions of modern life. When the lived world is detached from reality, even that which is understood as most real will take on an otherworldly quality. Modernity may be artifice, but its masking effects are not only made natural, they also serve as the architecture of the lived reality of the social body. In contrast, striking physical anomaly seems to be the site of mystery, omniscience, and fantasy.

O'Connor suggests her belief in the connection between the grotesque and reality in the maxim "It is the extreme situation that reveals best what we are essentially" (58). This alignment of margin with essence articulates a guiding belief about embodiment among these writers: pain, disfigurement, and disability are the exceptional cases that uncover the center. In *The Heart Is a Lonely Hunter*, Carson McCullers twice dramatizes scenes in which Mick, her adolescent protagonist, turns to pain as an antidote for the alienating effects of modern life:[6] "She thought a long time and kept hitting her thighs with her fists. Her face felt like it was scattered in pieces and she could not keep it straight. The feeling was a whole lot worse than being hungry for any dinner, yet it was like that. I want—I want—I want—was all that she could think about—but just what this real want was she did not know" (52). In these lines McCullers seems almost self-conscious in her deployment of the stylistic hallmarks of high modernism here, most notably in the turn to fragmentation and repetition. Mick's sense of her face as disordered and "scattered in pieces" evokes Picasso's visual representation of the same condition. Repetition as the textual evocation of desire—"I want, I want, I want"—infects even Mick's attempt to express this drive through repeated violence to her body. Fists, thighs, and pain counter the sense of disintegration with a grounding vision of the material body. If the modern condition is to be estranged from one's self, McCullers suggests that one route toward this elusive "real want" is through the body in its most demanding and elemental state: pain. In the second version of this scene, Mick hits her thighs again with all her strength, "but she could not feel this hard enough." She grabs a handful of sharp stones and begins to drag them over her legs, scraping on the same spot until she draws blood and "with the fiery hurt in her legs she felt better" (119). In these scenes, Mick embodies the adolescent battle with a mundane world she finds anesthetizing. The slightly odd syntax in the phrase "feel this hard enough" seeks to associate a new adverb with the act of feeling and, in the process, to reanimate the notion of what it might mean to feel. The twist in this earlier description of feeling calls attention to the more pedestrian phrase "felt better," suggesting not only that Mick is relieved by the pain but that it has also improved her very ability to feel. The appearance of blood in McCullers's second scene of self-mutilation plays a significant role, as it signals for Mick the temporary success of discovering the elemental body. Blood, in its association with pain, death, and the internal, serves in these novels as a sign of the real. Flannery O'Connor, of course, is most explicit in her deployment of blood in opposition to the anesthetizing norms of the social world. In her characterization of Enoch Emery, O'Connor locates his wise blood as an inherited quality—"He had wise blood. Just like his daddy" (40)—offering an archaic mode in conflict with the modern experience.

The reliance on pain and blood in this model of approaching reality signals the unsustainable nature of the endeavor. Like O'Connor's belief in the revelatory but rare and unsustainable "extreme situation," McCullers's scenes of self-inflicted pain present only an ephemeral moment in the quest for the "real want." My interest in these novels is not to point out their persistent failure to discover the real, especially because I already find this impossibility articulated in the books themselves. I am interested, however, in the framing of the body as the conduit toward the unattainable real and in how this perceived proximity shapes notions of physical difference within the modern social body. The extreme circumstances and moments of pain described by these authors are necessarily fleeting, reflecting a model of embodied difference that depends on its own impermanence. These writers understand these insights as temporary, whether they emerge from acute physical conditions or depend on the movement of a more permanently disabled figure in and out of the narrative frame.[7]

The use of the grotesque as a conduit to an obscured reality extends our notion of realism beyond the historical limits of literary production. O'Connor is careful to establish the distinction between her understanding of realism as the essence of fiction writing and Realism as a literary genre. In contrast to the literary movement of the late nineteenth century, which in its broadest strokes advocated the accumulation of details in fiction writing, writers of the mid-twentieth century express open skepticism about the nature of parts and wholes. Carson McCullers articulates this skepticism in *The Heart Is a Lonely Hunter.* In defending his affinity for freaks—for the spectacle and the circus of life—Biff Brannon tells his wife, "But you don't know what it is to store up a whole lot of details and then come upon something real" (16). The fantastic leap from the collection of details to "coming upon" the real depends entirely on the fact that the details Biff describes are freakish. These authors move through abnormality to approach reality. The lack of symmetry between parts and whole are a necessary component in this endeavor. A few pages later, Biff allows, "Blount was not a freak, although when you first saw him he gave you that impression. It was like something was deformed about him—but when you looked at him closely each part of him was normal and as it ought to be" (21). In contrast to the approach of the social scientist, the careful study of each part does not yield a more thorough understanding of the whole, but instead demonstrates the sharp disjunction between the macro and micro views. Although Biff comes to conclude that if he cannot isolate Blount's difference in his body then it must be in his mind, this solution seems naïvely attached to both the split between mind and body and the premise that freakishness can be definitely pinned down. The realist goals of mid-twentieth-century fiction allow for the asymmetry between details and wholes, and between the body and its perception, because they understand modernity and reality in a lop-sided relationship. The hope of "coming upon something real" lies in turning to the grotesque body as so weighted with materiality and weirdness that it can undo some of the unevenness in this relation.

These shifts among the "real," the body, and a vision of the world as constructed tease out the Möbius strip–style interplay between the meta-phoric and the material that I began to explore in my introduction. Dis-ability theorist Tobin Siebers's work illustrates the political stakes of the simultaneity of the grotesque as I've described it—the constant balance and tension between the body, aligned with the real, and the symbolic, understood as the force of culture and abstraction. In his chapter "Body Theory: From Social Constructionism to the New Realism of the Body," Siebers outlines realism as an artistic movement that "[does] not hesitate to represent the ragged edges and blunt angles of the disabled body . . . [,] as if [these artists] are trying to get people to see something that is right before their eyes and yet invisible to most" (*Disability Theory* 65). Siebers advocates an out-of-fashion turn to the terms "real" and "reality" be-cause he argues that the emphasis on discourse in social construction-ism empties out the corporeal experiences of disability. Siebers argues that while representations of the body may depend on social attitudes and institutions, the physical and political inequality faced by disabled people is so entrenched in expectations about the body that even radical shifts in attitudes seem inadequate to changing these expectations. To demonstrate his argument, Siebers quotes Cheryl Marie Wade's descrip-tion of "these blunt, crude realities":

> To put it bluntly—because this need is as blunt as it gets—we must have our asses cleaned after we shit and pee. Or we have others' fin-gers inserted into our rectums to assist shitting. Or we have tubes of plastic inserted inside us to assist peeing or we have re-routed anuses and pissers so we do it all into bags attached to our bod-ies. . . . The difference between those of us who need attendants and those of us who don't is the difference between those who know privacy and those who don't. We rarely talk about these things, and when we do the realities are usually disguised in generic language or gimp humor. Because, let's face it: we have great shame about this need. (65)

If the inequality and shame shaping these experiences stems in part from the social expectation that people of a certain age can attend to their own hygiene, Siebers wonders, "What sea change in social attitudes about the body could bring an end to this expectation?" (66). For Siebers, this turn to realism sparks a mobilizing ethic that can lay the groundwork for new perspectives in civic debates. In considering potential costs, however, aesthetic questions that dovetail with problems in literature demonstrate that reality in representation is not an unmediated category. In the above quote, Wade immediately marks the self-described "reality" of the blunt needs of the body by attempting to mirror them through blunt, crude language. This reliance on an aesthetic notion of crude elements as being more real similarly informs her closing lines, in which realities are "disguised" by language and humor is a distilling force that does not match bodily experience. In this case Wade self-consciously draws on crude language to confirm the reality of what she describes while at the same time critiquing the power of humor or euphemism in speech to mask these realities of the body. Each strategy gestures toward the debt that notions of reality owe to language.

Siebers makes a similar point when he acknowledges the risks of his call to realism and, in the process, implicitly indicts writers like O'Connor and McCullers for their belief in the disabled body as "more real":

> Somehow, today, a photograph of a daisy in a garden seems less real than a photograph of garbage blowing down an alley. Incidentally, literary and cultural theorists often obey the same rules. A closer look at many of the major concepts of current theory—hybridity, heterogeneity, difference, performativity—would reveal that each works as a substitute for the real, countering the notion that reality is sound, smooth, and simple with the claim that it is in fact sick, ragged, and complex. The disabled body is no more real than the able body—and no less real. (67)

Siebers assures us that the body is not more real than the things of culture; he also wants to establish a space for the forces of the body that are not merely subject to "manipulation by social representation" (68). While I agree that the disabled body is no more real than the able body, the force of the above paragraph for me rests in the observation that disabled bodies carry a burden of being *conceived* as more real. If we return to Wade's claims that language can mark or mask realities, the important element in this argument is not that language is some neutral, universal mediator between real experience and its representation, but that the ideological presumption of greater access to the real distributes itself differentially and with weighted political effects. While Siebers argues for a new realism that will open up representations of disabled experience where few have existed, this realism operates through the aesthetic and theoretical construction Siebers critiques above—these claims to the real don't come without a price. Reality in its uneven distribution becomes a burden, potentially casting its subjects as apolitical, timeless, and inactive. When experiences located in the body are viewed as the most real, then identities located in the body—such as disability, age, race, or gender—will be read as essential. The demands of representation placed upon these subjects will seem possible as no other than the "blunt, crude realities" Siebers champions, because the body's construction as that which is more real makes it an overdetermining force.

Cheryl Marie Wade's description of crude, material truths about the disabled body captures one effect of the perceived reality attached to physical anomaly in which the body is seen as limited to its basest functions. There remains another side, however, in which embodied difference serves as a sign of mystery and knowledge. The disjunct between the disabled body and the expressed norms of the modern world can be startling and disorienting—for example, Wade's daily confrontation with excrement is at odds with a modernity that prides itself on obscuring the perceived indelicacies of bodily waste and its storage. The disabled body that seems to escape or contradict the standards of the normalized social body—even in ways that seem unpleasant or undesirable—becomes the site of insight and fantasy. The driving force of *The Heart Is a Lonely Hunter* resides in its representation of disability as the heart of social connection and knowledge. The four major characters of the novel gravitate to the fifth, John Singer. Singer can read lips and communicates with notes, but the bulk of his interaction with each of the other characters consists of them speaking to Singer and believing that he has perfect knowledge of their problems—"they felt that the mute would always understand whatever they wanted to say to him. And maybe even more than that" (94). Perhaps the most interesting element of this dynamic is that Singer himself has a deaf friend who serves the same function for him. Even as we understand that Mick, Jake, Dr. Copeland, and Biff each have a relationship with Singer centered on fantasy, we watch Singer duplicate this fantasy of disability as knowledge in his friend, Antonapolous. In the following description, offered from Singer's perspective, Antonapolous's inscrutability is the condition for his apparent wisdom: "He saw Antonapolous sitting in a large chair before him. He sat tranquil and unmoving. His mad face was inscrutable. His mouth was wise and smiling. And his eyes were profound. He watched the things that were said to him. And in his wisdom he understood" (204). Given McCullers's broader characterization of Antonapolous as greedy and foul and our exposure to Singer's side of his interactions with other characters, it is clear that these relationships depend only on the narrowest sense of relation. These characters, including Singer, find in the physical difference of the other a blank slate upon which to project their fantasies of being understood. The disabled body seems so outside the norms of social life that the characters discover in its excessive materiality an apparent escape from the constraints of modern life. That Singer and Antonapolous clearly do not have special insight assigns the mysterious property of knowledge even more strongly to physical difference, as though wisdom exists independently of embodiment. Although the social structure disintegrates with Antonapolous's and Singer's deaths, the closest approximation of interpersonal connection in the novel depends upon the notion of disability as the fantastic site of knowledge and the real. The veracity of embodied wisdom becomes less important than the social role of disability as the opposition to an alienating modern world.

Singer's lack of verbal communication and Antonapolous's "inscrutable face" produce a perceived flexibility and openness—an underdetermination—in bodies that are simultaneously overdetermined by the cultural and material demands of their disabilities.[8] The same feature of the body that makes it an ideological burden becomes the very feature that allows for variable interpretations of that body. McCullers's novel demonstrates that while Singer's physical embodiment is identical to his disability—he is "the deaf-mute"—his role in the social body is endlessly flexible:

> So the rumors about the mute were rich and varied. The Jews said that he was a Jew. The merchants along the main street claimed he had received a large legacy and was a very rich man. It was whispered in one browbeaten textile union that the mute was an organizer for the C.I.O. A lone Turk who roamed into the town years ago and languished with his family behind the little store where they sold linens claimed passionately to his wife that the mute was Turkish. He said that when he spoke his language the mute understood. And as he claimed this his voice grew warm and he forgot to squabble with his children and he was full of plans and activity. One old man from the country said that the mute had come from somewhere near his home and that the mute's father had the finest tobacco crop in all the county. All these things were said about him. (200)

In an earlier scene, this time from Dr. Copeland's perspective, the African American doctor similarly discovers racial affinity in Singer's infinitely flexible appearance: "[Singer] listened, and in his face there was something gentle and Jewish, the knowledge of one who belongs to a race that is oppressed" (135). Singer's ability to embody all things to all people depends on the social perception of disabled bodies as outside the limiting norms of modernity. The social body can retain their fantasies of affinity with Singer because his nonverbal communication preserves their belief in interpersonal connection beyond the limits of conventional social discourse. According to a worldview in which the major characteristic of modern life is its alienating effect, the fantasy that disability offers an escape from these forces aligns physical difference with both mysterious understanding and the obscured real. In a slightly modified version of this dynamic, as expressed by Dr. Copeland, the disabled body is seen as so thoroughly subject to repression that its very exclusion from modern life produces insight and knowledge. [9]

As Tobin Siebers acknowledges in his call for a return to realism, the representational history of the real and its alignment with physical anomaly burdens any account of disability in the United States. While Siebers feels confident that the immediate goals of the disability movement are better served by a renewed attention to the physical realities modern political and social life seek to obscure, these uncovered narratives will invariably be influenced by a long-standing ideological alliance between the real, the grotesque, and the disabled body. The turn to the body in grotesque realism casts that body as the conduit to a reality that has been hidden by the massive architecture of modern life. The jarring confrontation between modernity and the materiality it masks may temporarily disrupt dominant fictions, but this scheme relies on a notion of physical difference as unstable and flexibly underdetermined in its interaction with the social body. In the following two sections, I explore how O'Connor and McCullers attempt to extend the temporary nature of these disruptions by recasting grotesque bodies first as anachronistic holdovers, and then as a characteristic effect of modernity itself.

Disabled Relics

In the work of O'Connor and McCullers, grotesque bodies are often seen as savage holdovers or relics from a premodern past. If we return to O'Connor's maxim—"It is the extreme situation that reveals best what we are essentially"—the language of "essence" in this formulation suggests a timeless, ahistorical quality to her understanding of reality. Where modernity itself is seen as the distorted lie, figures aligned with the premodern carry an enduring symbolic importance. John Singer's alignment with the "ancient Jew" and the primitive terms used to describe Enoch Emery locate these figures not only as outside the norms of modernity, but as relics of the past. The disjunction captured by O'Connor and Mc-Cullers is both ideological and temporal.

My reading of these grotesque bodies according to a model of temporal disjunction owes much to Dipesh Chakrabarty's essay "Time of History and Times of Gods." In looking to establish a model for subaltern history, Chakrabarty argues that linear historicism can only account for events on a continuous line; where there is a simultaneous presence of things from different historical times, some things will be read as relics, survivors from dead worlds. The term "relic," both in Chakrabarty's work and in an examination of Flannery O'Connor's, should carry a spiritual connotation. Chakrabarty understands secular history as "disenchanted," a thesis that O'Connor similarly pursues in *Wise Blood*. In the following exchange between Hazel Motes, now practicing self-mutilation, and his landlady, Mrs. Flood, O'Connor demonstrates the modern sense of incommensurability between reason and faith:

> "What's that wire around you for? It's not natural," she repeated.
>
> After a second he began to button the shirt. "It's natural," he said.
>
> "Well, it's not normal. It's like one of them gory stories, it's something that people have quit doing—like boiling in oil or being a saint or walling up cats," she said. "There's no reason for it. People have quit doing it."
>
> "They ain't quit doing it as long as I'm doing it," he said. (116)

Mrs. Flood's language is charged with the disciplinary modes of contemporary life, a world that requires adherence to the "natural," the "normal," and the "reasonable." Hazel, by contrast, challenges Flood's retreat into temporal security by insisting on his own participation in the modern totality, demonstrated by extending "people" to include the practices of Hazel's lone "I." He challenges the ideological safety of what is "natural" based on the homogeneity of the masses by locating his radical difference within its set of embodied behaviors. Hazel's anomalous body then must be reconciled with this contemporary investment in universal norms.

The regulatory effect of Mrs. Flood's word choice of "natural" and "normal" speaks to the colonizing effect of dominant modes as described by Chakrabarty. The position of the relic is not neutral, but instead reflects an uneven distribution of power and social legibility. Those cast outside the norm may look to reinscribe the category, as Hazel looks to reposition himself, but "unnatural" forms often seem unrecognizable in the most profound sense. In order to reassert authority, the body politic explains away the perceived distance from modernity by comforting contemporary categories—for example, through the catchall label "crazy." Such accounts, however, are often insufficient to overcome the residue of difference attached to bodies. These normalizing efforts at categorization result in an uneasy balance between competing narratives in which physical anomaly is either the excluded category in modern norms or, conversely, the embodied form of a purportedly universal modern condition.

The ability to transgress boundaries is both the defining feature and an often-celebrated effect of the grotesque. The temporal disruption that places two elements from different times into a simultaneous existence can work by either pulling the past into the present or pushing the present into the past, but in either case, each time will contain a residue of the other. O'Connor's portrait of Enoch Emery focuses on his affinity for things out-of-time. Spurred on by his wise blood, Enoch leads Hazel on a quest through the zoo at the center of the city, ending in a small museum and a mummy display. The encased man they find there is three feet long: "He was naked and a dried yellow color and his eyes were drawn almost shut as if a giant block of steel were falling down on top of him" (51). The museum display operates as a fusion of the modern and the primitive: bowls and blunt weapons lie beside the man under the safe boundary of the glass case, and a typewritten card collapses lived specificity into a generalized history. The dominating effect of the present is so strong in this scene that the mummy's expression seems to be an effect of modernity, represented in the impression of "a giant block of steel" falling toward him.

Enoch Emery's wise blood operates in a similarly archaic mode, privileging an instinctive body over the cerebral alienation of his time. Enoch's primitivism surfaces as well in his mixed feelings of anger and identity with monkeys, apes, and gorillas. In addition to his daily taunting of the primates at the zoo where he works as a guard, Enoch becomes obsessed with a visiting film star, "Gongo the Gorilla." Surprised to learn that the gorilla is in fact a man in costume there to promote the opening of a film by the same name, Enoch nevertheless remains fixated on the gorilla, finally sneaking into the back of a van to attack the actor and steal away with the costume. Escaping into a pine grove, Enoch buries his own clothes and dons the gorilla suit: "In the uncertain light, one of his lean white legs could be seen to disappear and then the other, one arm and then the other: a black heavier shaggier figure replaced his. For an instant it had two heads, one light and one dark, but after a second, it pulled the dark back head over the other and corrected this. It busied itself with certain hidden fastenings and what appeared to be minor adjustments of its hide" (101). This scene acts out the racial fantasies of primitivism. Enoch sheds the insubstantiality of his relatively normal white body for a racialized form—a "black, heavier, shaggier figure"—whose burden of materiality conforms to Enoch's previously unseen embodied difference. The gorilla suit addresses the problem of Enoch's wise blood by offering an absurd, but nevertheless appropriate, outward form. Racial primitivism emerges in this scene as the means of externalizing and therefore making sense of Enoch's embodied, but hidden, difference. Along with this turn to a primitive past, however, the mention of "certain hidden fastenings" captures the residue of the modern in the transformation. The pronoun shift from "he" to "it" continues through the remaining two paragraphs in the chapter, the last two paragraphs in which Enoch appears in the novel. In transforming from "he" to "it," Enoch has become the gorilla, but even as he takes up the primitive, O'Connor offers reminders of the modernity that makes the suit possible. The gorilla's final act is to sit and contemplate the city from a distance in a spatial representation of his exclusion from, but necessary confrontation with, the urban social body.

In the above passages, modern elements linger in otherwise archaic modes, taking form as a threatening block of steel or the nagging reminder of hidden fastenings. In these scenes, largely consistent with the model of grotesque realism outlined in the previous section, Hazel's ascetic practices and Enoch's primitivist instincts do not emerge from modernity but instead point to an excluded reality at its margins that can jostle unified notions of the contemporary social body. In this ideological grappling between modern norms and the grotesque, however, the grotesque body is sometimes co-opted into dominant narratives such that its monstrous elements become seen as the effects of modernity instead of its excluded margin.[10] The use of the grotesque to illustrate the effects of modernity is still a mode of critique, but it differs in its logic from the alignment of the grotesque body with the real. In the following section, I pursue a complicating feature of the grotesque, in which the very features that push figures of disability out of time are seen as characteristically modern. This second mode also uses the central features of the grotesque—an emphasis on the material, boundary crossing, the masses, and visual spectacle—but these elements emerge directly from the modern rather than serving as an avenue toward an obscured past or lost reality.

Grotesque Modernity

In the preceding sections, I hope to have demonstrated how grotesque figures typically serve as a conduit to an obscured or lost reality. The turn to the body in pain, to blood, or to disabled others opens up a proximity to the real and produces special knowledge, offering a temporary antidote to the alienating modern world. The jarring impact of the grotesque can illustrate the distance between the normalized narratives of modern life and the author's sense of an obscured real, whether that notion of reality is spiritual, political, or psychic. Even as the grotesque body serves as an approximation of an excluded material reality, there remains a residue of dominant fictions in these characterizations. The grotesque, then, becomes characteristic of bodies out-of-time, but paradoxically also serves as a sign of the somatic effects of modernity itself. In the latter formulation, the proximity to material reality becomes compromised in bodies that are read as physical evidence of modernity's alienation. In the repeated scenes of Mick's self-mutilation described above, Carson McCullers captures this dual dynamic in which the body is both the sign of and the antidote to modernity's alienating effects. When Mick feels her face "scattered in pieces" as an embodied form of modern fragmentation, she does not reject the body but, in fact, attempts to push the body to more grotesque extremes; she treats a psychic and social pain that manifests itself in the body with an attempt to discover a more real body that can feel "hard enough" and "better."

Both O'Connor and McCullers cite alienation—from self or others—as the most dominant grotesque effect of modernity.[11] In *The Heart Is a Lonely Hunter*, Carson McCullers largely uses disability as a bridge to overcome the social alienation and loneliness of the modern world. John Singer embodies wisdom and proximity to reality for the other major characters, and Antonapolous plays that role, in turn, for Singer himself. In one scene, however, where McCullers chronicles Singer's increasing unhappiness and distance from his friend, she offers a version of the grotesque body as an effect of the modern social world, not its antidote:

His hands were a torment to him. They would not rest. They twitched in his sleep, and sometimes he awoke to find them shaping the words in his dreams before his face. . . . When he walked up and down the floor of his room he would crack the joints of his fingers and jerk at them until they ached. Or he would strike the palm of one hand with the fist of the other. And then sometimes when he was alone and his thoughts were with his friend his hands would begin to shape the words before he knew about it. Then when he realized he was like a man caught talking aloud to himself, it was almost as though he had done some moral wrong. The shame and the sorrow mixed together and he doubled his hands and put them behind him. But they would not let him rest. (206)

The conceit of hands with a mind of their own would eventually become fodder for horror films, but it plays a similarly destabilizing role in the literature of the modernist period. In *The Day of the Locust* (1939), Nathaniel West offers Homer Simpson, whose outsize hands are similarly restless and symbolize the desires Simpson has repressed. Sherwood Anderson, writing self-consciously on "grotesques," is perhaps most famous for the story "Hands," published in *Winesburg, Ohio* (1919). In this story Wing Biddlebaum fears that the excessive animation of his constantly moving hands will betray his queer desire. For both Simpson and Biddlebaum, their unruly hands serve as a sign of unconventional sexuality. While the characters retreat into shyness and passivity, their hands represent the social threat of acting on desire even when that desire is sympathetically rendered. McCullers's portrait of John Singer shares the implication of same-sex desire with Anderson's "Hands." Singer's love for Antonapolous here finds embodied expression in his restless hands. Specifically, his hands betray Singer's desire for communication with one who shares his language and experiences. His role as deaf and nonverbal audience for the community requires that Singer's body serve as a blank slate for others' projections. His physical difference is the condition for their feeling of connection, but this scene represents Singer's body as an active force in his subjectivity, not as the passive receptacle for the fantasies of the social body. The hands become a torment to Singer because they insist on the disjunction between his prescribed role in the community and his desires, both for his friend and for mutual communication.

Singer experiences the alienation of the modern world as estrangement from his body and desires, but the response offered in the novel falls back on the anomalous body as the site of self-assurance. McCullers chronicles two central problems in the novel; one is loneliness and distance from others and the second extends that sense of alienation to the self. According to the logic of the novel, the answer to both problems lies in their projection onto the screen of physical difference. This form of projection both allows the character to imagine connection with the other and serves as a form of reflection, shoring up the character's own identity. In Singer's vision of Antonapolous, his friend serves as a mirror for the self—"The eyes of his friend were moist and dark, and in them he saw the little rectangled pictures of himself that he had watched a thousand times" (220). The image of "watching little rectangled pictures" suggests a cinematic logic to this relation, offering a metaphor for the above language of projection. Biff Brannon calls out the other characters for a similar practice, even as he too looks to reflection to secure his identity: "And why did everyone persist in thinking the mute was exactly as they wanted him to be—when most likely it was all a very queer mistake. . . . He exchanged a deadly secret glance with himself in the mirror" (224). The reflexive process by which each character finds what he or she needs in the disabled other is not unlike the "secret" confirmation of Brannon's gendered difference in the mirror. Queerness here is imagined as a kind of self-love, one that the characters might find literally in the mirror or more figuratively in their projections upon disabled others.

Brannon understands that Singer's disability is the central characteristic that makes him into a kind of embodied screen. He thinks, "The thing that mattered was the way Blount and Mick made of him a sort of home-made God. Owing to the fact that he was a mute they were able to give him all the qualities they wanted him to have" (232). In these lines, McCullers articulates the social role of disability as the embodiment of understanding and the possibility for retreat from the modern world. Unlike the scene in which Singer experiences the estrangement from his hands as an effect of modern alienation, his function throughout the bulk of the book is to serve as this "home-made God," and to offer an antidote to others' struggles with the social body.

This search for a new and homespun deity resonates with Flannery O'Connor's description of "the new jesus" in *Wise Blood*. Enoch Emery eventually returns to the museum to steal the encased mummy, bringing it to Hazel and Sabbath as the fulfillment of his blood's instructions. Sabbath studies the unconventional gift:

> Two days out of the glass case had not improved the new jesus' condition. One side of his face had been partly mashed in and on the other side, his eyelid had split and a pale dust was seeping out of it. For a while her face had an empty look, as if she didn't know what

she thought about him or didn't think anything. She might have
sat there for ten minutes, without a thought, held by whatever was
familiar about him. She had never known anyone who looked like
him before, but there was something in him of everyone she had
ever known, as if they had all been rolled into one person and killed
and shrunk and died. (94)

This "new jesus"—the ancient relic that Enoch imagines earlier as cringing away from a giant, modern block of steel—once again serves as a
bridge between the contemporary and a lost social body. This paragraph dramatizes a scene of self-recognition in which Sabbath locates
the obscured humanity of the modern world in the grotesque body. The
mashed and leaking face of the mummy parallels the "empty look" on
Sabbath's face, staging the feeling of acknowledgment first in the body.
Like John Singer's disability, the mummy's physical difference—"she had
never known anyone who looked like him before"—becomes the screen
onto which she can project familiarity. He becomes the embodiment of
a universal sense of recognition, including self-recognition. The passage
represents this moment of identification as both hopeful in its ability to
overcome modern alienation and cynical in placing this universal body
in the emphatically dead form of the relic. Sabbath's realization is in the
here and now, but the vehicle for her awareness is necessarily located in
the excluded body of the past.

These novels focus on physical difference as the site of projection,
whether as the threatening end of social and economic conditions or as
the screen for an imagined sense of identity and connection. Grotesque
bodies, paradoxically because of their extraordinary physicality, lose
much of the property of distinction that comes with subjectivity and
instead become placeholders for a modern emphasis on substitution.
Despite all his seeming uniqueness and loneliness as a disabled man in
a small town, John Singer's difference actually serves as the condition
for his many roles in the social imagination. His community with Antonapolous and the other deaf and nonverbal characters they confront
throughout the novel continues the theme of duplication, multiplying
the site of embodied projection. In *Wise Blood*, Hazel Motes's temporary
answer to his problems lies in a similarly modern philosophy of substitution: "He would get another room [in a new city] and another woman
and make a new start with nothing on his mind. The entire possibility
of this came from the advantage of having a car—of having something
that moved fast, in privacy, to the place you wanted to be" (95). As Hazel

notes, the car, the very symbol of modern America, offers the possibility of substitution that extends to the city, and the body, and the mind. Although the grotesque body can stand for either the exception or the effect of modernity, the premise of the body as a site of imagination reflects the twentieth-century principles of interchangeability and an ideology of mass production and mass culture. The folk spirit of the masses that resides at the heart of Bakhtin's grotesque transforms over time into the dominating force of the urban crowd.

The Body Politic as Crowd

Hazel Motes's belief in the possible substitution of city for city and woman for woman relies upon the early-twentieth-century economy and culture of mass production and mass media. Written in the 1940s and 1950s, *The Heart Is a Lonely Hunter* and *Wise Blood* demonstrate that era's preoccupation with the crowd. For mid-century America, the crowd suggests the broadest possible consumer base and reflects the national demographic shift from agricultural centers into cities, manifested most strikingly in the Great Migration of rural Southern African Americans to the urban centers of the North. The critical histories of O'Connor and McCullers share an immediate association with place; each author is nearly synonymous with the setting of her fiction. Among these authors, regionalism and urbanism are inextricably woven together.[12] Each novel finds characters living in crowded boardinghouses; taking meals in cafés; and navigating the sidewalks, trains, and highways of the mid-twentieth-century cityscape. The city becomes the contemporary site of the body politic and, in turn, these authors interrogate how this social body impacts its citizens. In *Rabelais and His World*, Mikhail Bakhtin's theory of grotesque realism celebrates the folk population and the possibility for the excessive body to invert repressive norms. Instead of Bakhtin's utopic folk values, O'Connor and McCullers translate this populist impulse into the modern crowd and the crowd, in turn, shapes and is shaped by the often-excluded grotesque bodies at its margins. Whether as the object of spectacle or as screens for projected fantasies of wisdom, disabled citizens in these novels serve as a vehicle for commenting on the dominant narratives of the social world. As Bakhtin's medieval folk shifts to the modern crowd, these novelists demonstrate the centrality of the regional city in the construction of the contemporary body politic.

The reception and marketing of the novels themselves reflect a national reading public centered on best sellers and the Book-of-the-Month Club (founded in 1923). Itself a surprise best seller, David Riesman's 1950 sociological study *The Lonely Crowd* connects these economic and cultural trends toward mass consumption with an emerging social character.[13] According to Riesman, the new middle class in America is profoundly bureaucratic and managerial. These organization-men find personal direction externally, whether from their immediate peers or from the vision of their contemporaries represented in the mass media. The mid-century American is "shallower, freer with his money, friendlier, more uncertain of himself and his values, more demanding of approval" (19). The term "crowd" in Riesman's title seems especially appropriate to this twentieth-century approach to the social body. "Crowd" connotes the bustle of urban streets and department stores. It can also suggest sexual menace and the violence of the lynch mob. As I argue in the following section, for individuals whose bodies are marked by disability, gender, or race, the crowd constantly threatens to isolate them as spectacle. In both of these novels, characters struggle with the crowd as it defines and limits their role in the social body. In its collapse of internal differences and constant turn outward for definition, "the crowd" signals the deforming effect of standardization on the national body. Citizenship, according to this model of collapsed boundaries and public spectacle, falls under the rubric of the grotesque. Perhaps Riesman sums up this problem best in saying, "The problem for people in America today is other people" (xxi).

The priority of the crowd, both in the literally changing demography of urban spaces and as a psychic category, cannot exist independently from the principles of mass production and public marketing. In this economy, unspecialized products and services meet purportedly universal needs. From the moment Hazel Motes steps into the city, he confronts an urban street constructed by commercial interests: "When he got to Taulkinham, as soon as he stepped off the train, he began to see signs and lights. PEANUTS, WESTERN UNION, AJAX, TAXI, HOTEL, CANDY. Most of them were electric and moved up and down or blinked frantically" (14). Such strikingly simple advertisements rely on the notion of a crowd, constructing their public as an indiscriminate mass with common desires. These signs hail the citizenry, drawing together a public defined by their mutual need for clean counters, or transportation, or speedy communication over a distance. The most aggressive campaigns, like those listed in capitals in the passage above, are quintessentially contemporary. They solve modern fears over bacteria with industrial cleansers or satisfy privileges like increased leisure time for snacking or tourism among the middle class.

The twentieth-century economy of unspecialized goods requires a universal body as its market. Standardization serves as the dominant principle in an economy and culture defined by mass production: from the unskilled, interchangeable laborer, to the goods rolling off an assembly line, to the advertising campaign and its vision of a universal public body. In *Wise Blood*, Flannery O'Connor dramatizes the cult of consumerism and its requirement of standardization in a scene where a man tries to sell potato peelers on a crowded street. He stands before an "altar" of boxes and demonstrates the process by which a raw potato enters a tin box and, with a few turns of the crank, emerges on the other side, peeled and white. In the explicitly religious language of this scene, commerce becomes sacred. The mystery of the closed box, which obscures the mechanism for turning out uniform, white potatoes, alienates the cook from the raw materials of the meal. Typically a classic symbol for homely, simple food, the potato in this scene becomes complicated, the object of mechanization, homogenization, and marketing.

The bodies in *Wise Blood* serve as evidence of a similar process of standardization. Like workers coming and going during the shift change on a Fordist assembly line, characters in O'Connor's novel frequently confront their own doubles. Hazel Motes has the uncanny repetition of his grandfather's face (10);[14] Enoch Emery's "daddy looks just like Jesus" (26); a boy and his father at a local used car lot resemble one another almost exactly (29); and, at the climax of the novel, Hazel kills a preacher-for-hire who copies his suit, car, and physical likeness (85). Simple family resemblance evolves in the twentieth-century culture of mass production into a disturbing form of somatic repetition. Individuals in the crowd become fungible, easily exchanged for a newer model as in the case of cross-generational resemblance or replicated for greater profits as in Onnie Jay Holy's discovery of a more pliable mouthpiece that looks like Hazel but lacks his intractable nature. When Enoch Emery insists upon meeting Hazel, saying, "I seen you sommers before. I know I seen you sommers before" (29), even his repetitive speech demonstrates the modern principle of universal familiarity. Hazel seems "familer" because his body is subject to a culture of standardization, one that values substitution and conformity. Despite the eccentricities in O'Connor's characterizations, no individual is safe from this grotesque form of embodied repetition. In fact, the qualities in Hazel that seem to make him most exceptional and distinct from the crowd—his fanaticism and his outmoded style—are the very elements that are most subject to commodification and imitation. This redeployment of unusual characteristics repeats the logic of embodied citizenship, in which the qualities that exclude disabled people from the full rights of citizenship become the foundation for any recognized expression of national belonging.

The proliferation of somatic repetition and co-optation of difference is not merely a signal for cultural standardization, but also speaks to the impact of such desired uniformity among disabled people. The social history of disability captures the often violent practices that emerge to protect the fantasy of a universal embodied norm. Institutionalization, prosthetics, and, at its most violent, eugenics contribute to a public sphere that excludes or attempts to obscure physical difference. These attempts to cast out, substitute, or supplement the disabled body, however, contain an inevitable exposure of difference. Even as the crowd seeks formal homogeneity, the processes that seek to reject difference and replicate sameness produce an alienating effect.

Carson McCullers employs the crowd as a social category with similarly alienating ends. The settings in *The Heart Is a Lonely Hunter* are almost invariably public: Biff Brannon lives above and manages the New York Café, Dr. Copeland's home is also a medical practice and gathering space for the black community, Jake Blount works at the busy local carnival, and Mick Kelly shares her room with siblings in the family's congested boardinghouse. The constant presence of often anonymous others works as an oppressive psychic force in Mick's life, shaping her imaginative world nearly as much as the music she loves:

> This is a funny thing—the dreams I've been having lately. It's like I'm swimming. But instead of water I'm pushing out my arms and swimming through great big crowds of people. The crowd is a hundred times bigger than in Kresses' store on Saturday afternoon. The biggest crowd in the world. And sometimes I'm yelling and swimming through people, knocking them down wherever I go—and other times I'm on the ground and people are trompling all over me and my insides are oozing out on the sidewalk. I guess it's more a nightmare than a plain dream—. (39–40)

In using the department store as the foundation for comparison, McCullers's passage expresses the link between commerce and the crowd. The literal crowds in the public settings of the novel expand in Mick's imagination to the level of ecosystem; in this all-encompassing crowd, the mass of people takes on the proportion of enveloping water. The passage dramatizes the central conflict between the crowd and the individual in American democracy. Mick offers two outcomes in what is invariably a struggle: triumph through yelling and knocking down others or personal obliteration at the foot of a mass "trompling." Mick offers a version of individuality that crucially depends on the crowd as the locus against which it must be defined. As a dominant metaphor for the social body, the crowd becomes a fundamental category in the twentieth-century imagination.

In contrast to Mick Kelly's anxiety over the consuming crowd, John Singer's room in *The Heart Is a Lonely Hunter* becomes a utopian space of imagined community. McCullers once again represents fantasy as the crucial binding force in interpersonal connections: "One by one they would come to Singer's room to spend the evening with him. . . . Mick Kelly and Jake Blount and Doctor Copeland would come and talk in the silent room—for they felt that the mute would always understand whatever they wanted to say to him. And maybe even more than that" (94). Imagination in the form of vague feelings and fantastic "maybes" attempts to close gaps between individuals. The community of the novel sees receptiveness both in Singer's disability and in his room as the extension of his body. Singer's lack of speech forms a necessary vacuum into which the other characters can insert their fantasies of sympathetic comprehension. In the phrase "one by one" and the parade of individual names, this passage emphasizes the novel's repeated contention that links can only be formed between Singer and each of the other major characters, never all together. On those accidental occasions when all four characters do find themselves in Singer's room together, the presence of hearing, speaking others disintegrates the imagined bond of the space and its occupant. McCullers represents community, in contrast to the ever-present crowd, as essentially ephemeral, dependent on physical difference as the site of projected connection. These personal alliances, furthermore, are no less grotesque than the crowd from which they seek escape. Disability forms the necessary center around which the social body coheres, and this reliance on the body as the animating force of the abstract connection parallels exactly the operation of the grotesque.

In contrast to Bakhtin's utopian vision of the ludic and bawdy folk, the twentieth-century model of community offered in these novels has degenerated into the crowd.[15] Whereas Bakhtin finds liberatory values and destabilizing practices among the masses, "mass" in contemporary terms seems to almost inextricably modify "production" or "media." The crowd typifies the grotesque form of the social body as it collapses distinctions among individuals and depends on physically anomalous others as its constitutive outside. This is not to say, however, that the populist impulses of Bakhtin's vision have gone missing entirely from the twentieth-century imagination. Certainly, a similar kind of nostalgia for folk practices and folk wisdom drives versions of American history. Furthermore, this typically nostalgic mode should not suggest that communal values are an exclusively lost property. What these novels demonstrate, however, is that community and interpersonal connection are necessarily compromised in a twentieth-century economy of mass production that constructs interchangeable normative bodies among its workers and consumers. The simultaneous cultural and political turn to standardization imagines the social body as the crowd, crucially altering the liberatory potential of a plea for the masses.

Embodied Spectacle

In the opening sentence of her biography of Carson McCullers, Virginia Spenser Carr offers an anecdote about McCullers's excitement over the annual visit of a traveling freak show. Carr's *The Lonely Hunter* begins with a slice of dialogue recalled by McCullers's childhood best friend: "Let's skip the cotton candy and hot dogs and save our dimes for the Rubber Man and all the freak shows this year. The Pin Head, the Cigarette Man, the Lady with the Lizard Skin . . . I don't want to miss a single one" (1, ellipses in original). For her biographer, this fascination with freak shows encapsulates McCullers's lifelong preoccupation with physical difference and spiritual isolation. As in most approaches to the grotesque, Carr moves from the material body to its function as an "exaggerated symbol of . . . everyman's . . . condition" (1). *The Lonely Hunter*, as a whole, engages in this persistent sleight of hand, exchanging physical conditions for spiritual concerns. Tennessee Williams's brief foreword to the biography dwells on this problem of the physical most explicitly. In describing his hesitation before speaking with Carr, he cites another author's recently printed posthumous critique of McCullers's work "which had placed its main emphasis on the physical illnesses which had beset her" and which "had somehow contrived" to connect those illnesses to her place as an artist (xvii). He proceeds, however, with both the interview and the written endorsement of the project because of his hope that a "true appreciation" of Carson's work will be written, one that understands the difference between vague "physical catastrophes" on one hand and "purity of spirit" and "genius" on the other (xvii–xviii). Williams returns to this question more than once in the space of his very brief foreword, expressing his open anxiety over the public discussion of McCullers's illnesses.[16] The source of his trust in Carr stems largely from her position as a "lady of Georgia," one who would be bound by the sense of propriety indicated by her gender and heritage not to engage in the messy confusion of public and private. Of course, as a biography, Carr's work will inevitably open the doors of McCullers's private life, exposing her excessive drinking, her frequent struggles with illness, her bisexual practices, and her open marriage. Williams trusts Carr, however, to expose the body in the service of appreciating the art and not to collapse McCullers, as other reviewers have done, into the freak-show-like epitaph of the "Queer, Disabled Writer." The form of embodied spectacle that the young Lula Carson Smith clamors for is the same dynamic that Williams and Carr hope to protect her from after death. What Tennessee Williams understands, in his desire to erect a wall preventing the exposure of McCullers's disability and its conflation with her work, is that any approach to the embodied author, especially one whose life was characterized by illness and unconventional expressions of gender and sexuality, will proceed by way of spectacle.

The term "spectacle" best captures the intersection between the crowd as social body and the freak as anomalous physical body. Throughout the first half of the twentieth century, the freak show serves as the most literal point on a broadly existing continuum of embodied spectacles.[17] In chapter 1, I describe the everyday use of freak staging conventions that can emerge when physical difference prompts a series of reading and narrative strategies to domesticate anomalous bodies. Here, these performative elements similarly function to make bodily difference legible. In *Wise Blood*, Flannery O'Connor turns to the sideshow as the site of knowledge about the body. For O'Connor, the modern primal scene is crucially public. At a local fair, the young Hazel Motes becomes bored with the main thoroughfare and sneaks over to the darkened tents of the sideshow after his father. Unsure of what he will find behind the flap, Hazel bargains with the ticket taker to let him in:

> "I got fifteen cents," he said. "Whyn't you lemme in and I could see half of it?" It's something about a privy, he was thinking. It's some men in a privy. Then he thought, maybe it's a man and a woman in a privy. She wouldn't want me in there. "I got fifteen cents," he said.
> "It's more than half over," the man said, fanning with his straw hat. "You run along."
> "That'll be fifteen cents worth then," Haze said.
> "Scram," the man said.

"Is it a nigger?" Haze asked. "Are they doing something to a nigger?"

The man leaned off his platform and his dried-up face drew into a glare. "Where'd you get that idear?" he said.

"I don't know," Haze said.

"How old are you?" the man asked.

"Twelve," Haze said. He was ten.

"Gimme that fifteen cents," the man said, "and get in there."

Like all the sexual experiences in his lifetime, Hazel's first window into sexuality comes with an admission charge. The repetition of the word "privy" in the opening lines of this exchange captures exactly Hazel's youthful sense of danger and excitement, but it also emphasizes the turn from the private to public display. Once the tent has been erected—seeming to obscure that which it draws into the spotlight of the imagination—the mere promise of spectacle brings the intimate body into the social body. At ten years old, Hazel does not understand entirely what he will find inside, but the path of his imagination from excretion to vague sexual practices to racial violence is a fascinating illustration of the influence of spectacle upon social definitions of the body. The man becomes startled and angry at Hazel's guess that they are assaulting a black man, demonstrating that the explicit conflation of sexual desire and lynching that comes so easily into Hazel's mind cannot be openly acknowledged. The scene dramatizes two related forms of social indoctrination. The first is that Hazel must not announce the persistent cultural connections between homosocial masculinity ("*men* in a privy"), heterosexual practices, physical secretions, and racial violence. That he does take these immediate associative steps, however, demonstrates the constitutive force of these categories for embodied subjects and the formation of the social body.

The second indoctrination that Hazel experiences comes when he steps behind the curtain and joins the crowd of men. In fact, once Hazel lifts the flap of the first tent, he discovers a second tent inside it and must enter into a further interior space. The overcompensation of multiple layers of obscuring fabric suggests an inadequacy in the cultural architecture that would represent the show behind the curtain as distinct from the world outside. Once inside this tent-within-a-tent, O'Connor domesticates the extraordinary elements of the sex show through the mundane imagery she uses to describe it. In his initiation into the homosocial bonds of objectifying masculine desire, Hazel peeks around the crowded backs of the men to find a naked woman lying squirming in a coffin. Hazel again processes the scene according to the familiar experiences available to him: initially he mistakes the white, squirming figure for a skinned animal, then he recognizes her as "fat" and with "a face like an ordinary woman" (32). The scene serves as a nearly archetypical illustration of the central elements of the Bakhtinian grotesque; it combines fertility, death, excess, sex, spectacle, and humor and it centers on the body. Capped off by Hazel's father's deflating joke—"Had one of them ther built into ever' casket . . . be a heap ready to go sooner" (32)—the scene suggests that in contrast to the doubled attempt to circumscribe the spectacle from the rest of the world, it is merely a more open dramatization of the quotidian experiences of the body. Hazel's imaginative turn from sex to race to violence binds each of these elements to the modern embodied spectacle.

This sense of bringing the private into the public—of sneaking behind the sex show curtain—is one of the central, animating features of embodied spectacle. For bodies marked by physical difference, spectacle becomes a portable quality, carrying the private constantly into the public. The excessive body is both too intimate, in its suggestion of unusual sexual and hygienic practices, and too public, seeming to call constantly for widespread social scrutiny. In *Publics and Counterpublics*, Michael Warner introduces the useful term "intimate vulnerability" for the conflation of male desire with the visibility of public space. Intimate vulnerability also seems appropriate in these cases where physical difference makes individuals the target of public examination, a scrutiny that may be motivated by sexual desire, but that is often complicated by revulsion or pity.

Gendered norms confirm the racial and somatic characteristics of monstrosity as well. As Mary Russo argues in her essay "Female Grotesques: Carnival and Theory," the visual dynamics of grotesquerie distribute differently among men and women. Where woman "make a spectacle of themselves," men are guilty of "exposing themselves." As Russo elaborates, whereas exposing oneself carries with it a sense of volition, for women, making a spectacle of oneself suggests loss of control and a lack of boundaries; women are considered blameworthy as "the possessors of large, aging, and dimpled thighs displayed at the public beach, of overly roughed cheeks, of a voice shrill in laughter, or of a sliding bra strap—a loose, dingy bra strap especially" (213). The spectacle Russo describes enumerates the many ways in which the social categories of class, sexuality, and gender become somatic properties. The focus on boundary crossing in studies of the grotesque resonates in feminist theory with the notion of excess and gendered spectacle examined here.

In *The Heart Is a Lonely Hunter*, McCullers locates Mick Kelly's adolescent growth spurt as another threatening female body. Mick tells Harry Minowitz, "I grew three and a fourth inches just in the last year." In citing the measurement down to the quarter of an inch, Mick tries to discipline her own uncontainable body according to the reassuring standards of exact figures and science. In his response Harry deflates Mick's attempts to manage her immoderate growth, telling her, "Once I saw a lady at the fair who was eight and a half feet tall. But you probably won't grow that big" (111). Harry both raises the alarming suggestion of the continuation of her growth and asserts an absurd authority in the process by then dismissing the possibility. The fact that he allows for a lingering "probably" in his assurance, however, evokes the specter of social ostracism like that experienced by the freaks at the fair. Mick and Harry's exchange captures the boastful and hyperbolic qualities of adolescent speech, but their use of excessive language does not undo the threats to the social body they discuss. Mick's description of her height suggests both pride and anxiety; she knows exactly how much she has grown in how long and she's aware that it makes her different, more like the sideshow lady than not.

Across her fiction, Carson McCullers focuses on the adolescent female body as a special case of the embodied spectacle of gender and sexuality.[18] For a tomboy like Mick Kelly, gender and youth exist in a liminal state. Mick is "at the age when she looked as much like an overgrown boy as a girl" (132). This visual indeterminacy shapes Mick's introduction in the novel, where she first appears as a "gangling, towheaded youngster, a girl of about twelve . . . that at first glance was like a very young boy" (18). The transitional body of the adolescent is no less threatening to social norms than the excessive body marked by fat, extreme height, or promiscuity. Both flaunt the unstable properties of the body in contrast to ideals of static homogeneity. For Biff Brannon, Mick's publicly visible ambiguity serves as an avenue to ruminate over the universal extension of dual sexuality. Upon seeing Mick, he thinks, "By nature all people are of both sexes. So that marriage and the bed is not all by any means. The proof? Real youth and old age. Because often old men's voices grow high and reedy and they take on a mincing walk. And old women sometimes grow fat and their voices get rough and deep and they grow dark little mustaches. And he even proved it himself—the part of him that sometimes almost wished he was a mother and that Mick and Baby were his kids" (132–133). Biff moves from the socially acceptable spectacle of liminal adolescent gender across the spectrum to old age before returning to a more transgressive statement about his own identity. By first proceeding through observations about bodies that are typically neutered in the social imagination, Biff can recast himself in a maternal role. Unfortunately, Biff's desire to normalize his fantasies does little to chip away at the idealized social monument to sex and gender.

Even while we might align McCullers's own attitudes about sex and gender with Biff's arguments above, she is careful to demonstrate how insidious more conventional models can be. While Mick's boyish costume of khakis and a denim shirt might be more socially acceptable than a public appearance by Biff in his wife's robe, McCullers doesn't paint adolescence as an entirely free space of gendered indeterminacy. Awareness of the feminine self as a sexual spectacle reaches back even into very young childhood, as demonstrated in the characterization of Biff's niece, Baby. Pushed by her mother into pageants, song-and-dance routines, and hair permanents, the preschool-aged child serves as a performing miniature of the sexual pressures on women. Baby's sense of self as the object of admiring scrutiny extends to the way she carries her body—"There was a certain way Baby always held her head when people looked at her, and it was turned that way now" (126). Always the tiny coquette, Baby offers a perverse counterpoint to Mick's youthful resistance to gendered norms. In contrast to the party scene in which Mick casts off her fancy, hand-me-down dress in order to chase after the neighborhood children in pants and sneakers, Baby suggests a new vision of gendered identity in which sexuality extends appropriately into earliest childhood. An object of persistent fascination for adults and other children alike, Baby becomes wounded by Mick's obsessed younger brother because he finds Baby "just so little and cute" (169). After her injury, Baby becomes a more obviously grotesque manifestation of sexual pageantry, listless and scarred, but still performing under the direction of her fanatical mother. McCullers suggests that while the extreme manifestations of gendered identity are unstable, the pressures that produce these figures are very real.

Mick's transition by the end of the novel into the woman's world of heels and dresses as a department store clerk illustrates the triumph of traditional gender roles. In place of the individual ambitions that drove her in adolescence, Mick conforms to the expectations of her role as an extension of the spectacle of commerce. Even in earlier scenes, gendered ideology constrains Mick's vision of her place in the world. Sneaking into a house under construction, Mick scrawls a series of words that illustrate her sense of dominant hierarchies: "Mick drew the big block letters very slowly. At the top she wrote EDISON, and under that she drew the names of DICK TRACY and MUSSOLINI. Then in each corner with the largest letters of all, made with green and outlined in red, she wrote her initials—M.K. When that was done she crossed over to the opposite wall and wrote a very bad word—PUSSY, and beneath that she put her initials, too" (37). Mick struggles to assert her own identity in the face of the all-consuming world of men represented by an inventor, an animated detective, and a fascist dictator. Later, she adds her personal hero, "MOTSART," and casts artistry under similarly male control. She places her own initials in the corners of the room, an ambiguous signal of marginalization or a desire to encompass and consume masculine success. Placing her initials under the sexual obscenity is no more straightforward. In her study of gendered identity in McCullers's novels, Sarah Gleeson-White reads the above scene and concludes, "It is no wonder the young girls fearfully consider their changing bodies as freakish, for femaleness frequently loses any capacity for alternative conceptualization beyond (male) obscenity" (15). Clearly, Gleeson-White's reading is at one level appropriate; Mick subordinates herself to a vulgar synecdoche where genitalia becomes totalizing. The graffiti can also stand, however, as an act of reclamation, one that does not undo the discursive force of the word, but that reanimates the body of its writer.

* * *

Mick's desire to make a written spectacle out of a "very bad word" brings us to the power of language in representations of the grotesque body. In the opening to this section on embodied spectacle, I dwell on a reference to Carson McCullers's affinity for freak shows, arguing that her biographer places this anecdote at the opening of the book to serve as a symbol for McCullers's understanding of universal alienation. This symbolism works so effectively—and emerges so repeatedly across genres of writing—because the contrast between the excessively material freakish body and the abstract nature of a spiritual condition seems so extreme. The grotesque body, despite—or, in fact, because of—its inescapable burden of materiality, becomes the paradoxically ephemeral part of the metaphor, lending its weight to the seemingly more significant, but intangible, problems of abstraction. In conventional approaches to the literary grotesque, the body serves as the vehicle for universal concerns. But even in this tradition of inattention to the anomalous body, a residue of materiality attaches to abstract categories, suggesting that disability cannot be cast aside so easily.

McCullers's turn to unusual forms of language in order to speak back to dominant principles reflects a linguistic version of the formal strategies of the embodied grotesque. Grotesquerie evokes bodies marked by contradiction, spectacle, and striking anomaly as excluded figures that can call out the failed assumptions of a society predicated on the principle of interchangeable parts. Driven by a sense that the mainstream world is shaped by a set of fictions that are profoundly false or repressive to those that lie outside the norm, these authors imagine grotesque bodies as the approximation of an excluded condition that must be more real. At the same time, however, their position at the margins of modernity seems to imbue these characters with an otherworldly access to knowledge. Like Hazel Motes's literally blind but spiritually seeing eyes or Singer's wise and inscrutable face, anomalous bodies serve as the seat for others' fantasies of truth and connection beyond the alienating modern world. The tricky position for embodied citizens, then, lies in this demand to be most real, often defined as the most of-the-body, and at the same time to be the site of otherworldly imaginative fantasy. The grotesque body carries with it a constant tension between the turn to the abstract and the turn to the material. Unlike more pedestrian symbols in which the vehicle is easily forgotten, the striking physicality that defines the grotesque image always leaves a residue of the material in the abstract. The insistent nature of this residue offers a model for our attention to literature as a shaping force in embodiment more broadly; our avenues of approach to physical difference cannot be wholly abstract or wholly material, because the body itself carries the burden and potential of both forms.

3 / The Uniform Body: Spectacles of Disability and the Vietnam War

In the months leading up to the 2004 presidential election, media coverage of political life in the United States grappled with the tangle of disability and citizenship in the figure of Max Cleland. The former senator, who lost three limbs in the Vietnam War, took the national stage most emblematically in his introduction of John Kerry at the Democratic National Convention. A *Los Angeles Times Magazine* profile captures the veteran's iconic status: "In many ways, Cleland is more powerful as a symbol than he ever was as a senator" (Barabak). This casually expressed belief in the symbolic potential of embodied difference deserves closer scrutiny. This statement, locating a political figure's power in his role as symbol rather than in his legislative acts, serves as a fulcrum between the discussion of individualism in my first chapter and the public desire to find meaning in the disabled body explored in both chapters 1 and 2. Cleland's role in American political theater prolongs the tradition of the disabled "poster boy," in which the one-dimensional figure collapses the complexities of policy or background into a symbolic, rallying image. His power as a symbol offers a striking example of the ways in which physical difference serves as the determining force of political participation for disabled people. Never granted the luxury of invisible neutrality, individuals perceived as different take their place among the body politic constantly bearing the mantle of that difference. As Max Cleland's role in the 2004 presidential campaign suggests, our national ideologies of physical difference do not only cast the subject positions of disabled people into a fixed mold, but also allow for moments in which the body itself seems to speak. This chapter explores the embodied spectacles surrounding the Vietnam War to discover those moments in which the disabled body itself becomes politically eloquent.

As a central strategy of the Vietnam War, U.S. commanders relied upon soldiers' bodies as signifiers of American strength and superiority. In a logic similar to the homogenizing force of the urban crowd described in chapter 2, the spectacle of soldiers together in uniform serves as powerful symbol. For individual soldiers the gun—part of an elaborate system of corporeal supplementation—prosthetically extends the soldier's body into a terrifying fighting machine. U.S. commanders understood the Vietnam War as a limited "war of attrition," in which success is not defined by taking territory, but by convincing the enemy that he is unable to win. With the goal of forcing a treaty on favorable terms, commanders wanted the perception of U.S. strength as much as its execution. Noisy helicopters, spooky illumination rounds, and fast fighter planes all served a dual psychological purpose to shock and demoralize enemy troops. In *The Perfect War: Technowar in Vietnam*, James Gibson argues that the escalation of bombing campaigns in the north followed the logic of advertising, with military managers hoping to sell the U.S. war machine as inescapably superior.

Foundational to both disability studies and the doctrine of limited warfare is the belief in the body as a striking communicator. The exact form this communication will take, however, loses any reliability as the notion of bodily coherence breaks down in war, specifically, and disability more broadly. Within the sphere of the Vietnam War, bodily boundaries were increasingly subject to expansion (with guns, gear, and flight suits) or reduction (amputation and death). As one veteran argues, "You put on that flight suit, man, and it's like you're getting a whole new body" (Horne 174). Although U.S. strategy relied in part on the dramatic presentation of "new," hybrid bodies, it could not separate this technophilic phenomenon from a broader, and often disturbing, sense of the dissolution of corporeal borders and human flesh. Shifting definitions of the body emerge at every level of military service through the open prioritization of enemy body count in U.S. war policy. In order to reflect success, counts were often manipulated from the grunt counting squads, through the reporting officers, to cabinet level statistics. James Gibson offers a definition of inferential counting, a practice that was widely recognized as standard operating procedure: "An inferential counting rule is a rule that a company uses to infer numbers of enemy dead according to some found object or sign—an enemy weapon, a blood trail, a dismembered body part, or other mark of enemy presence" (126).[1] Gibson reports one case in which an American officer nearly got into a fistfight with an ARVN advisor over a severed arm, because each man wanted to get credit for the "body." Making each scattered limb or pool of blood into a whole numerical integer, however, cannot erase the disintegration of the body in such violent death. The body's persistent vulnerability to expansion, reduction, wounding, and deterioration suggests a lack of bodily coherence and the unreliability of the body as a signifying system.

In the face of these corporeal contradictions and dissolutions, the Vietnam War and its domestic aftermath require a series of symbolic strategies (both ideological and literary) to make sense of diverse corporeal meanings. The unruly nature of this symbolism heightens attention to the body as a signifier, but also prompts the extensive production of spectacles and social scripts to secure that message. In his popular memoir, *Born on the Fourth of July*, Ron Kovic turns to parades and protests as parallel spectacles of the signifying body. During an antiwar rally in Los Angeles, Kovic wheels in front of a passing car on Wilshire Boulevard and demands, "Look at the war! Take a good look at the war!" (138–139). For Kovic at this moment, there is no distance between the war and his disabled body. His protest relies upon the metonymic power of disability and the body's power to make material that which occurs 8,000 miles away. Kovic's critique of the war resides in the juxtaposition between symbols of American military strength—the marine uniform, medals— and evidence of the breakdown of these symbols through the technology of disability, in this case, a wheelchair. Published as a birthday gift to his country on its bicentennial, Kovic's memoir reveals and exploits the social resonance of the disabled body in the national imagination. Anticipating prominent spectacles of protest like the Gallaudet "Deaf President Now" action or ADAPT "stair crawls" in demonstration against inaccessible public transportation, antiwar protests by visibly disabled veterans stage an embodied expression of the contradictory tenets of U.S. military policy.

In a parallel scene of national spectacle, Kovic similarly displays the symbolic force of his disability, this time inverted to the openly patriotic space of a Memorial Day parade taking place soon after his return home. Carried onto the stage with another wounded veteran, Eddie Dugan, Kovic sits silently among the town's mayor and veterans of former wars while a commander speaks about his belief in America's cause and necessary victory. Nearly crying, the commander points his finger at Kovic and Dugan and tells the crowd, "*We have to win . . . because of them!*" (106). In this instance, the commander uses the nationalist trappings of the parade and the interpellative force of his pointing to make disabled veterans the driving force of U.S. success. The wounded soldier's body substitutes for South Vietnamese interests, and the war becomes fought for and by Americans.

These two scenes of corporeal signification demonstrate the conflicting registers through which the disabled veteran's body is made nationally legible. The cultural contexts of protests or parades attempt to assert a strict split between representing the body as the war's failure and representing it as the inspiration for continued fighting. Despite the conviction in both Kovic's and the commander's speeches, the contradictory messages of the body bleed into one another. At the Memorial Day parade, Kovic's heroic function is already compromised by the lukewarm response he's received from onlookers who stare but do not wave. Similarly, when the antiwar protest prompts police violence, Kovic tries to resume the protected status of the veteran, insisting, "I'm a Vietnam veteran! Don't you know what you're doing to me?" (154). These moments of contradiction elaborate upon the simultaneity of militarism's failure and success as expressed in the figure of the disabled veteran. The juxtaposition of the wheelchair and the uniform complicate not just representations of militarism, but expressions of protest as well.

These moments of insistence upon the legibility of the disabled body—each offering no more explication than the exhortation to look—call for an examination of the discursive systems that make the body itself an effective communicator. Among the performative encounters explored through this book, the parades and protests of the Vietnam era mark the most explicitly political form of embodied spectacle. In the case of the Vietnam War and its aftermath, the body is pressed into service as a public symbol—whether of military masculinity, of American technological might, or, in the case of antiwar protest, as the mark of the breakdown of those ideals. These contradictory registers of corporeality emerge most strikingly in the face of war and its necessary crises of bodily coherence. In the context of Vietnam, the dissolution of bodies overseas corresponds to a similar disruption of the national body. In turn, both protestors and nationalists look to the disabled body as a way to shore up increasing fragmentation. Kovic's memoir and the Larry Heinemann novel *Paco's Story* dramatize corporeal dissolution in the war and chronicle the social registers of disability for the returning veteran. While perhaps less iconic than *Born on the Fourth of July*—after all, Tom Cruise has not starred in its adaptation—*Paco's Story* should be classed alongside *Coming Home* and Kovic's memoir in its complex treatment of disability and national reconciliation. At the core of my reading lies an examination of the diverse set of strategies that emerge as an attempt to secure the body as a coherent symbol. In the end, not surprisingly, each endeavor involves a return of the contradiction that provoked it, reinspiring the desire for an (impossibly) uniform body.

Corporeal Tales

Marked by both their visible status as veterans and their cane or wheelchair, Heinemann's protagonist, Paco Sullivan, and Ron Kovic are repeatedly pressed into service as spectacles. Their bodies serve as multivalent signifiers, standing alternately for the losses of the war or the reason the United States must continue to fight—*"We have to win . . . because of them"* (Kovic 106). When Kovic yells, "Look at the war," he relies upon the body's legibility as spectacle to communicate his protest. The weight attached here to visual encounter echoes Rosemarie Garland-Thomson's reformulation of "the gaze" in feminist scholarship to "the stare" in disability theory. The sense of discomfort attached to the stare suggests the burden of visibility carried by disabled people. It is these public moments of quotidian staging and staring that constitute the social meaning of disability. Visible spectacle aligns with narrative, however, as seeing the body requires an act of reading the body. The possibilities of finding meaning in the body steal a page from literary studies in imagining the body through a complex action of close reading. Disability itself sparks a narrative impulse, prompting among onlookers the desire to "know the story," often figured as curiosity about cause and prognosis.

In American accounts of the war, the illegibility of the body is most often located in racialized difference. In the opening paragraphs of *Dispatches*, Michael Herr offers the paradigmatic example of this American illiteracy, claiming that reading maps of Vietnam "was like trying to read the faces of the Vietnamese, and that was like trying to read the wind" (3). Despite Herr's articulation of a widespread belief in absolute racial difference, soldiers in the field were consistently asked to search for meaning on the body. In fact, in *Paco's Story*, the company assures itself of a local woman's Vietcong status precisely by reading her face: "No, James, she was as hard a hardcore VC as they come (by the look of the miles on her face)" (175). In military action, soldiers depended upon (or fabricated) bodily signs in order to distinguish Vietcong fighters from other Vietnamese.

James Gibson offers accounts of "reliable" marks established by ground forces, including circles under the eyes suggesting exhaustion, shoulder indentations from wearing a pack, or ankle scratches from moving in the jungle. Gibson concludes, "Pity the unfortunate man who walked in the jungle while chasing a loose pig or chicken" (132). The American perception of Vietnamese illegibility requires a system of reading that can instill belief in the possibility of finding meaning on the body. To supplement or replace their struggles at verbal communication, GIs relied upon the Vietnamese body as a communicating agent uncompromised by dishonesty or language barriers. As soldiers were asked themselves to serve as embodied symbols of U.S. force, they looked to the Vietnamese for the same external marks of national affiliation.

Larry Heinemann locates the primacy of the legible body within the larger tradition of the war story. From the opening line of the novel—"Let's begin with the first clean fact, James: This ain't no war story" (3)—Heinemann reflects on the relationship between narrative and the Vietnam veteran. The narrator of *Paco's Story* is the collective voice of the ninety-two marines of Alpha Company who did not survive an attack at Fire Base Harriette. These ghosts follow the sole survivor, Paco Sullivan: describing his movements, giving him nightmares, and, despite all initial protestations, recounting war stories. Although the action in the present of the novel takes place in the United States, *Paco's Story* combines narratives of war and homecoming. Storytelling drives the action, often breaking from the meager plotline of Paco's stay in small-town Boone to explore other characters, remembered events, and recounted dreams. The novel's opening denial of its own status as a war story mirrors a tale recounted by Michael Herr early in *Dispatches*, a story the correspondent claims took him a year to understand. A Lurp (Long Range Reconnaissance Petrol) tells Herr, "Patrol went up the mountain. One man came back. He died before he could tell us what happened" (6). This story, quoted in its entirety, describes the problems of witness and access to knowledge in narratives of war. At the most basic level, *Paco's Story* begins with its own negation because war stories are told only by the survivors. This opening denial also resonates with the narrators' report that war stories are unpopular and politically shunned. According to these opening pages, those in charge, "the people with the purse strings and the apron strings," reject war stories "as a geek-monster species of evil-ugly rumor" (3). The reference to carnival sideshows through the phrase "geek-monster," however, betrays a sense of prurient fascination among the purportedly appalled mothers (the apron strings) and economic elite (the purse strings). As the narrator acknowledges, "Any carny worth his cashbox ... will tell you that most folks will shell out hard-earned, greenback cash, every time, to see artfully performed, urgently fascinating, grisly and gruesome carnage" (4). The opening chapter of the novel, ironically titled "The First Clean Fact," shuttles between these two positions: the claim that "folks do not want to hear" and, second, the tacky lineage of widespread morbid curiosity suggested by the connection to the freak show. The link between the tales of the carnival barker and the war veteran suggest the dual impulses of shame and fascination attached to corporeality. The simultaneous need to stare and to look away introduces one model of disability's pull. From the first page of the novel, the visual force of the anomalous demonstrates the potential of the body as spectacle. Finally, the novel "ain't no war story" because of Heinemann's belief in a tacit national prohibition against coming too close to the "grisly and gruesome carnage." After describing a raucous evening of soldiers engaging in mutual masturbation at a USO performance by a Filipino jazz band/skin show, the narrators ask, "Let's tell it true, James, do you expect we'll ever see that scene in a movie?" (13). In its inclusion of brutal rape and murder, the alienation of the disabled veteran at home, widespread drug and alcohol dependencies, and a casual misogyny, *Paco's Story* overruns the standards of legible heroism established by war stories before Vietnam.

In this denial of its status as war story, *Paco's Story* challenges the role of narrative in domesticating the brutalities of warfare. As Paco, with his cane, limp, and extensive scars, travels into small-town America, however, the dual visibility of his injury and his combat experience speaks to the ways in which disability constantly prompts a social desire for stories. For people with visible disabilities, the moment of initial encounter plays out a disjunction between the physical excesses of impaired bodies and a deficiency of knowledge for the able-bodied viewer. The act of looking produces a desire to assimilate the disability into a sense-making narrative. Over and over, Paco's entry into Boone is staged as the disjunction between what his body reveals—his veteran status, his disability, his use of painkillers—and the curiosity these revelations spark. Heinemann describes Paco's encounters with others as centered on the demand for explanation. After Paco enters Mr. Elliot's store to ask for work, the second question the shopkeeper asks is "You a pretty young fella, vhy do you have that cane?" Heinemann elaborates a series of possible responses:

> How many times is it, James, that Paco has answered that? He has dwelt on it with trivial thoroughness, condensed it, told it as an

ugly fucking joke (the whole story dripping with ironic contradiction, and sarcastic and paradoxical bitterness): he's told it stone
drunk to other drunks; to high school buddies met by the merest
chance . . . ; to women waiting patiently for him to finish his telling
so they could get him into bed, and see and touch all those scars
for themselves. [Paco] immediately distills all that down to a single,
simple sentence, squares himself (standing as straight as he can),
looks the old man full in the face, and says bluntly, "I was wounded
in the war." (72–73)

In this passage the resentful energy of the long, descriptive list of moments of encounter collapses in the anticlimactic response, "I was
wounded in the war." Like the cane and scars themselves, this laconic
sentence points to the unknown even as it includes the narrative elements of character, action, and setting. Paco speaks to the narrative desire prompted by his visible disability, but the sharp distinction between
the rambling description of possible responses and their distillation to "a
single, simple sentence" leaves this desire unfulfilled.

In Kovic's concise demand, "Look at the war," the figurative impact of
metonymy expands the meaning of his injuries to this nearly encyclope-
dic category, the war. By contrast, Paco's statement foregrounds his individual identity, locating himself as the singular subject, placing the event
solidly in the past tense, and avoiding any potential politicized critique.
In the space of the novel, Paco's reply, "I was wounded in the war," evokes
two pages of Mr. Elliot's recollection of his own war story, in 1917 Russia.
In the emotional experience of remembering his own war wounds, Elliot
can only think to ask, "Which war was that, young man?" (75). Paco's
vague phrase "the war" prompts a shared memory of military trauma
but also displays ignorance about current events on the part of uninter-
ested Americans—"as if not one word of the fucking thing had made the
papers" (76). By opening his statement to multiple identifications, Paco
reproduces the narrative interest in establishing male collectivity. Paco's
visible status as a wounded veteran becomes the focus of identification
for a series of veterans in the novel who locate their own war experiences
in Paco's scars.

Still in search of work, Paco leaves Mr. Elliott and finds Ernest Monroe, a World War II marine and owner of a local diner. Paco's entry into
the Texas Lunch sparks another moment of identification, this time in
Monroe's successful reading of Paco's body: "He fully recognizes Paco's
1,000 meter stare, that pale and exhausted, graven look from head to toe"

(95). Monroe offers Paco chili, bottomless water and coffee, and a job as a dishwasher at the diner. Finally, he asks about the cane and Paco answers again, "I was wounded in the war." Monroe replies, "'Me too' . . . and points to the dark, crescent-shaped scar on his right chest under his T-shirt" (103). While Monroe's injury lacks the more visible status of Paco's limp and cane, the two share embodied reminders of warfare. Although Paco's injury serves to mark his alienated status as a survivor of the war (literally the lone survivor among his marine company), the gaps in knowledge evoked by the spectacle of disability serve as the avenue toward a renewal of the masculine community of wartime. For Paco, national reconciliation is only possible by dehistoricizing his experience so as to allow identification with a larger subset of military servicemen. As Monroe insists, "Once a goddamned United States Marine, always a fucking Marine" (97). Each of the veterans described in the novel slips into an extended recollection of their experience of combat, experiences contained under the umbrella sentence, "I was wounded in the war." The lack of personal details and historical or political context from this line suggests that where this redemptive masculine community is possible, it relies upon a universalizing move away from political specifics. In order to locate himself among a larger sector of the American citizenry, the novel suggests that Paco align himself with a collection of veterans from historically disparate wars.

Paco's connection with Elliot, Monroe, and Jesse (the loquacious drifter veteran), however, never blossoms into an entirely redemptive force in the space of the novel. After all, by the end of the novel, Paco has abruptly left Boone and the Texas Lunch with the note saying, "Thanks for the work. Got to go. See you around. Paco" (209). Despite seeming to abandon his community in leaving, the tempered optimism suggested in the line "See you around" suggests that Paco travels in order to circulate his wounded body as the signifying catalyst for a specific national male collectivity.

This masculine community relies on its capacious inclusivity of physical injury, in which the general categories "wounded" and "the war" can elide differences not only in the disparate cultural and political meanings attached to specific military campaigns but also among the disabled. In this case, disability serves as a flexible banner under which similarly wounded veterans can collect and discover a coherent social body. The list of alternate responses that Paco considers and discards, however, points to the discursive work required in settling on *this* sense of the injury. Even as the body performs as an emphatic signifier, the

social body relies on an extensive and competing set of strategies to secure its meaning.

Eloquent Symbols

Whereas Larry Heinemann's masculine community relies on flexible
and underdetermined readings of the body, Ron Kovic's expressions of
both patriotism and protest call for a body that is markedly uncomplicated. *Born on the Fourth of July* captures Kovic's belief in the power of
the body as spectacle, but in contrast to the excessively discursive nature
of Heinemann's work, the story that Kovic hopes to embody condenses
into the simplified terms demanded by the genres of his public performances. Kovic's body, of course, is no less multivalent than Paco's, but
the memoir imagines the "wounded American veteran" as a galvaniz-
ing and straightforward symbol for public consumption. Buoyed by
the supplementary visual apparatus of the parade or the protest, Kovic
represents his body as a thoroughly reliable communicator of a specific
message.

Throughout the memoir, Kovic contrasts the failure of speech with the
power of visual symbols. He imagines his body as an antidote to military
and political rhetoric. In the dramatic spectacles of protest, the visual elements of encounter eclipse Kovic's need to verbalize a sustained critique
of U.S. policy: "I think I honestly believed that if only I could speak out
to enough people I could stop the war myself. I honestly believed people
would listen to me because of who I was, a wounded American veteran.
They would have to listen. Every chance I had to get my broken body on
the tube or in front of an audience I went hog wild. Yes, let them get a
look at me. . . . One look would be enough—worth more than a thousand
speeches" (136).

Although Kovic begins this reflection by expressing his desire for
public speech, he concludes with an assertion of the symbolic value of
his visibly "broken body." The phrase "wounded American veteran"
marks a break in the passage, translating the focus from speaking out to
relying on the body itself as communicating visually. Kovic understands
that this phrase, as it encapsulates both his disability and his war record,
names his embodied authority. The passage expresses a belief that to see
his impaired body is to know the trauma of war, and his faith that to
know is to join in protest. Of his successful recruitment into the army,
Kovic wonders, *"What if I had seen someone like me that day, a guy in a
wheelchair, just sitting there in front of the senior class not saying a word?*

Maybe things would have been different. Maybe that's all it would have taken" (127, italics in original). Kovic imagines his own drama in which the juxtaposition of his broken body with the erect marine recruiters is sufficient to derail the military effort. By "not saying a word," Kovic contrasts the symbolic force of his wounds with the charged rhetoric of discipline, loyalty, and patriotism pronounced in martial yells by the recruiters. He puts on a miniature drama in which the spectacle of disability deflates the spectacle of war.[2]

Parades and protests serve as the centerpieces of performative citizenship in *Born on the Fourth of July*. Both events are collective spectacles of citizenship that appeal to a form of political identity in the viewer. Parades and protests draw on slogans, songs, and symbols of national identity to build a sense of community among the participants. As spectacles, both confuse the divisions between audience and participant, a confusion that seeks to construct a coherent social body around shared symbols. Soon after he returns to his childhood home from the military hospital, Kovic participates in a Memorial Day parade. He cannot understand why the crowd does not respond to him as they do in his fantasies of past wars:

> But it was different. He couldn't tell at first exactly what it was, but something was not the same, they weren't waving. . . . Maybe, he thought, the banners, the ones the boy scouts and their fathers had put up, the ones telling the whole town who Eddie Dugan and he were, maybe, he thought, they had dropped off into the street and no one knew who they were and that's why no one was waving. . . . If the signs were there . . . they'd have been swelling into the streets, trying to shake their hands just like in the movies, when the boys had come home from other wars and everyone went crazy throwing streamers of paper and confetti and hugging their sweethearts, sweeping them off their feet and kissing them for what seemed like forever. (90)

In this passage, Kovic's disillusionment describes a temporal break in which the values of the past fail to reclaim the veterans of the present. Kovic is a failed symbol in this parade because the heroic role he is asked to play contrasts with the spectacle of his disabled body. Parades require the uncomplicated visual representation of abstract notions of loyalty, military strength, and patriotism. The hybrid elements of Kovic's physical display include militarism and weakness, incommensurable elements in the world of the parade. Here, in contrast to Kovic's fantasy of social embrace, the body's meaning cannot be straightforwardly read, even with the supplementary banners instructing the crowd that these boys be seen as heroes. Just as the audience cannot read Kovic easily, he in turn cannot read the crowd according to familiar scripts of a thankful citizenry. By corporeally exceeding the spectators' expectations, Kovic finds there is no room for him in the earnest performance of ideals of military patriotism.

As he later discovers, however, the spectacle of the disabled veteran can be redeployed by the protest movement as a more complicated symbol of the broken promises of the state. Like the flags, uniforms, and marching bands of the parade spectacle, protests draw on similar visual elements of nation. In Kovic's first demonstration experience he witnesses the possibility for revision of national symbols: "One part of me was upset that people were swimming naked in the national monument and the other part of me completely understood that now it was their pool, and what good is a pool if you can't swim in it" (123). Successful protests rely on this kind of juxtaposition between the rectilinear Reflecting Pool and the amorphous, unrestricted sight of a naked crowd. The stakes of this visual metaphor lie in taking up the values of the state—freedom and democracy—and drastically changing the referent according to the principles of critique.

This moment provides the intellectual key for Kovic to express criticism without rethinking his youthful ideals. Consistently and without irony, Kovic reclaims the principles of military patriotism in the name of an antiwar movement. He describes a later protest: "It is a historic event like the Bonus March of thousands of veterans upon the Capitol in the thirties. And now it is we who are marching, the boys of the fifties. We are going to the Republican National Convention to reclaim America and a bit of ourselves. It is war and we are soldiers again, as tight as we ever have been, a whole lost generation of dope-smoking kids in worn jungle boots coming from all over the country to tell Nixon a thing or two" (158). Kovic does not seem troubled by the paradox of protestors becoming soldiers of the antiwar war. Instead, these renewed martial metaphors represent resolution of the traumas of alienation, expressed through the text's experimental chronology. By understanding his own disillusionment in terms of the past, Kovic finds a place for himself in a transhistorical tradition of veterans in protest. In the second, more unconventional chronology along which the novel is written, Kovic presents his experiences according to a narrative of trauma that withholds resolution. The book ends in the scene of Kovic's injury, circling back to its opening. Although this repetition and nonlinear chronology reinscribes the trauma of disability, Kovic finds resolution to his position as an alienated citizen by finding a place for himself in history. Success, for Kovic, lies in re-creating the masculine community of the war and in finding a contemporary expression of its promise from his youth. The circular structure of the book as a whole prompts a second form of return, this time in the reconfigured signs of patriotism and brotherhood.

In the closing page of *Born on the Fourth of July*, Ron Kovic concludes a last look at his idyllic childhood with the lines "It was all sort of easy / It had all come and gone" (224). This sentiment encapsulates Kovic's nostalgia for lost American ideals and prompts the major structure of his activist work: revision. When his body can no longer signify the uncomplicated virtues of military strength, Kovic employs the protest strategy of using symbols of the nation—his own uniformed body—to unsettle a watching public's convictions. This spectacle serves to disrupt the familiar associations of political icons, but can remain ambiguous in the depth of its critique. In the Last March protest described above, the veterans suggest an essentially liberal strategy in making Nixon the direct audience of their complaint. The charge of a promise broken can still express faith in the past glory of the nation and hope in its ability to follow Kovic's model of return. Thus, Kovic achieves national reconciliation by revising the ideals of his youth to the form of his antiwar convictions.

Kovic, finally, in his emphasis on revision in the interest of similarly singular messages, shares his methodology with the U.S. command in Vietnam. Like Kovic, these commanders understand the value of the body as a symbol and, also like Kovic, exploit a series of visual supplements to remake that body into an emphatically straightforward symbol. While their messages are in direct opposition, both sides hope to shore up the body as a singular entity in the face of its increasing dissolution, both overseas and at home.

Wheelchairs and Fighting Machines

In the context of combat, U.S. militarism must work against two expressions of corporeal differentiation: first, in the pull of individual self-interest that would lead soldiers away from dangerous situations and, second, the return of corporeal delineation that emerges in death and injury. Subordinating the goals of self-preservation to the specter of nationalism, the military embraces a model in which the personal body is identical to the body politic. In order to achieve this leap from the personal to the uniform—and uniformed—body, the military employs an extensive system of homogenization. Metaphors of technology emerge as a central tool in this reconstruction, casting U.S. marines as parts in the "green machine" (Heinemann). Rehabilitation for the wounded veteran is no less subject to the national desire for a uniform body. The homogenizing approach of treatment unfolds according to a similar literal and conceptual dependence on technology. As corporeal prosthetics, the wheelchair and the gun operate in very different registers, but each technology remakes its attendant body. Hoping to consolidate increasingly incoherent physical and social bodies in the context of the war and its aftermath, the national military and civilian command embrace linguistic and procedural metaphors of technology, replacing dissent and injury with a fantasy of structure and functionality.

Of course, the desire for a uniform body of men is not unique to the Vietnam War—the logic of military campaigns in most wars does not include concern for the survival of individual soldiers. In the Vietnam War, however, the command's thinking was so strongly shaped by managerial and technological systems that soldiers occupied an increasingly dehumanized position. James Gibson describes this phenomenon in his book *The Perfect War: Technowar in Vietnam*. Gibson makes an epistemological argument about how information was understood by U.S. policymakers given their bias toward technology:

> Limited war fought as a war of attrition means that only information about technological-production systems will count as valid knowledge about the enemy. For the military as well as civilian policy makers, the enemy becomes a mirror image of ourselves, only "less" so. Military strategy becomes a one-factor question about technical forces; success or failure is measured quantitatively. Machine-system meets machine-system and the largest, fastest, most technologically advanced system will win. Any other outcome becomes *unthinkable*. Such is the logic of *Technowar*. (23)

As the divisions among politics, business, and technology became increasingly nonexistent, policy makers developed a view of the world in which political and social power were measured solely through a nation's ability to produce high-technology warfare (Gibson 19). Military officers became "military managers." The language of debits and credits and statistical models of efficiency took over the Pentagon. In a comparative assessment of Vietnam's military strength, analysts placed Vietnam behind the United States on a universalized scale of development. Following Gibson's schema, strategists wondered, how could a nation of peasants with bicycles defeat the United States (16–17)?

The logic of business and industrialization that infused U.S. military strategy from the Cold War to Vietnam similarly reimagines the soldier's body as an expression of the "war machine." Mechanical metaphors of the male body overwhelm Vietnam discourse. In press interviews for the film, Sylvester Stallone describes Rambo as a "fighting machine" (qtd. in Jeffords, *Remasculinization* 12). Citing an earlier iconic American hero, the young Kovic is fascinated by Superman comics, looking to "transform his body into a hulk of fighting steel," with each push-up becoming "more and more determined to build a strong and healthy body" (61). In *Born on the Fourth of July*, Kovic describes his early experiences at boot camp in eerily mechanized terms: the men are forced through "a barbershop that was more like a factory" and encounter other "young bodies tense and twisted naked together . . . through the long metal hallways of the hangar" (67). In Kovic's imagination, induction into the Corps is an assembly-line process of homogenization. To further distill personal identity, drill instructors play pranks, including switching the uniforms of the recruits, and giving tall men short trousers and fat men tiny shirts. These marine commanders imagine a future when men are interchangeable parts of a military machine.

Any representation of the disabled veteran's experience will reflect the diverse technologies surrounding the body in the twentieth century, including rescue choppers, hospitals, painkillers and antibiotics, surgical tools, wheelchairs, catheters, prosthetics, and machines for physical therapy. The use of technology in the management of disability overlaps into technology's impact on the imagination. In the national idiom, the marines "build men," and the body, like the best appliance, is "a beautiful and remarkable machine that will last you a lifetime if you care for it properly" (Kovic 49, 62). Once home, however, Kovic's experience of rehabilitation in the United States is one of alienation, represented most strikingly in the technology-dependent and machine-like atmosphere of the VA hospitals. In a scene early in the novel, Kovic is in a long line of men waiting to be given their enemas, a process described as routine bodily maintenance, administered every third day in a room much like a car wash. Crossing the threshold into this room enacts the change from "I" and "myself"—"I watch the dead bodies being pushed into the enema room, then finally myself"—to language that ranks Kovic among these "dead bodies." In his writing Kovic marks this transition with both the jump to a new paragraph and a change in narrative perspective. The point of view now follows Tommy, the attendant, "running to each body . . . squirting the tube of lubricant onto his fingers, ramming his hands up into the rear ends, checking each of the bodies out" (34). This objectification of men into bodies is made possible by a logic of industry that suggests an assembly-line model of care. Later in this chapter, Kovic describes the failure of the therapy machines that are supposed to celebrate American ingenuity and advancement: "There are newly invented machines sold to the hospital by the government to make the men well . . . to fix the broken bodies. There are machines that make you stand again and machines that fix your hands again, but the only thing is that when it's all over, when the guys are pulled down from the machines, unstrapped from them, it's the same body, the same shattered broken man that went up on the rack moments before" (43). The economic interests made explicit in the complicity of the government selling to its own VA hospital are conveyed implicitly by the advertising jingle rhythm in the lines "make you stand again / fix your hands again." Despite the shared recognition among the veterans that the machines can never remake them in the image of health and coherence, the hospital staff radiates optimism. Forced to perform for his visiting mother and sister during physical therapy, Kovic stands with the aid of a machine, but his legs shake in spasms, his pants drop to his knees, and he vomits explosively from the exertion. His attendant insists to the family, "He's standing," and offers, "It's a really great machine. We have a couple more coming in real soon" (44).

The Erotic Script of National Reunion

In the masculinist arena of Vietnam, erotic and mechanical metaphors intersect to overdetermine the soldiers' encounter with the landscape and people. As the narrator of *Paco's Story* complains, "Now according to some people, folks do not want to hear about Alpha Company—us grunts—busting jungle and busting cherries from Landing Zone Skator-Gator to Scat Man Do (wherever *that* is), humping and *hauling ass* all the way" (5). The marine idiom captured in this passage evokes a sexualized worldview: "grunts," "busting cherries," "humping," "hauling ass."[3] Frequently, the dominant registers of sex and technology fuse together to indoctrinate marines with a new vision of what their body might become. In a roundtable discussion on "The War and Race," Carlos Campbell describes how the eroticization of weaponry reimagines killing as inevitable sexual climax:

You put on that flight suit, man, and it's like you're getting a whole
new body. You're getting rid of those 15 pounds you don't need.
You put on that anti-G suit. Then, all of a sudden, take your .38 and
you slip it up here and get your bullets and your tracer bullets sliding across your chest. Get your little life vest coming down here.
Get this great big, beautiful helmet going to protect you, right. Get
your great big flight boots. And all this shit. Step out to that airplane, and you might as well be getting into bed with Denise Nichols or Pam Grier. Because you just go *Oooooo*. You just gotta get it
off now. You are in the preorgasmic mindset of the military person.
And when you're in the airplane, and you fire a rocket, and you
hear that whoosh leave your wing, then all of a sudden it hits. POW.
It's like an orgasm. (Horne 174)

These sexual and technological metaphors find their archetype in the
marine chant, "this is my rifle this is my gun this is for fighting this is
for fun" (Kovic 76). As the gun metonymically replaces the penis, the
rifle becomes an extension of the human body. The distinction between
fighting and fun is blurred by the figurative impulse to draw the tools of
warfare into the human body. The metaphorical energy of this erotic language creates soldiers who are themselves an extension of the spectacle
of American technological might. Each grunt's body is a hybrid display
of weapons and erotic masculinity.

The heightened eroticism of the soldier's body at war, in turn, structures the veteran's homecoming. In the context of the war, the perceived
absence of appropriate sexual partners leads to an inversion of asexuality
into hypersexuality in which the landscape and fighting itself become
objects or expressions of masculine potency. At home, American women
hold the place of the proper sexual object and their accepting interaction
with men serves as a mark of successful return. Films and literature of
the soldier's homecoming consistently offer positive sexual relationships
as the dominant metaphor for national reconciliation. The war acts as a
figurative drain on domestic masculinity, relocating the "real men" to
Vietnam and leaving America to the women.[4] The subsequent encounter between the returning veteran and his nation becomes analogous to
heterosexual courtship.

The national stakes of these erotic reunions recur throughout twentieth-century war narratives. As the paradigmatic example of the period,
1978's *Coming Home* charges Jane Fonda's character with the emotional
rehabilitation of a bitter paraplegic veteran, a healing dramatized by his

sexual prowess in giving his nurse and lover her first orgasm. In *Paco's Story*, the protagonist's stay in Boone seems to be a reference to Boone City, the hometown setting of the World War II film *The Best Years of Our Lives*. This 1946 drama is often credited as offering a tempered vision of return, translating ticker-tape parades and ecstatic kisses into a more anxious reunion with ill-fitting former clothes, alienating bureaucracies, or the low ceilings on working-class upward mobility. Despite the dramatization of a rocky transition, many critics read *The Best Years of Our Lives* as a hopeful narrative in which the closing emphasis on marriage and love shores up American family values and the successful assimilation of struggling veterans.[5] In this common heteronormative scheme, relationships between women and veterans take on a charged significance and women stand in for the home nation. In her analysis of marginal male subjectivity, Kaja Silverman challenges this vision of reconciliation in the film, arguing that *The Best Years of Our Lives* breaks with the dominant fiction of masculine wholeness to repeatedly dramatize women's need to witness and accept male lack. This acceptance, however, is insufficient to repair the castrated male subject, and the movie rests on its own disbelief in patriarchal ideology. These divided readings of the potential for sexual reconciliation offer a critical frame for closer readings of gender and sexuality in Heinemann's and Kovic's work. As Silverman suggests, it may be that any recuperation of masculine sexual identity for these disabled veterans takes the form of disavowal, obscuring physical and emotional impotence in order to create new narratives of sexual success. Rather than essentializing lack to the position of disability, these disavowing moments of "yes, I know, but . . ." can demonstrate the socially contingent fiction of masculine wholeness more broadly.

In *Paco's Story*, nostalgia and patriotism figure as feminized sexual attraction among viewers at an imagined Vietnam memorial. These patriots, both women and feminized men, "get a lump in their throats and all creamy between the thighs, feeling sad and sorrowful, remembering and admiring the old days" (158). In the context of the Vietnam era, the veteran's failure of reconciliation is already determined by the public's nostalgia for "the good old days." When female sexual response is conditioned according to this anachronistic model of patriotism and masculinity, veterans face both sexual and social rejection. The perceived temporal break between the heroic past and the dishonorable present provides the first hurdle to successful national reunion.

In the case of disabled veterans, for some of whom intercourse may be impossible, the conditions of national alienation are further represented as rooted in physical limitations. In *Born on the Fourth of July*, Ron Kovic imagines joining a young couple on the beach and asking, "'Excuse me, would you like to pull my chair across the sand? Or maybe you'd like to carry me over your shoulders and I could hold your hand laughing . . .' NO NO NO NO, that's not right!" (97, ellipses in original). These physically awkward scenarios capture Kovic's inability to include himself in the romantic cliché of the stroll on the sand. The inaccessible sand and grotesque image of a third lover carried on one's back emphasize the embodied source of Kovic's alienation. The final cry, "that's not right," describes a profound sense of disconnect between the disabled veteran and the possibility of integration into the social and sexual landscape of the nation.

Paco's Story and *Born on the Fourth of July* both describe physical impotence as a metaphor for alienation. For Ron Kovic, the relationship between impotence, masculinity, and homecoming is more complex. Through the course of the memoir, Kovic comes to center his experience of disability in his compromised masculinity. He writes, "Everything that is going to heal has healed already and now I am left with the corpse, the living dead man, the man with the numb legs, the man in the wheelchair, the Easter Seal boy, the cripple, the sexlessman, the sexlessman, the man with the numb dick, the man who can't make children, the man who can't stand, the man who can't walk, the angry lonely man, the bitter man with the nightmares, the murder man, the man who cries in the shower" (27). The constant repetition of "man" in these lines calls into question Kovic's relationship to his own masculinity. He uses repetition in an anxious assertion that, while he is a man, he cannot be so without modifiers that question his alignment with conventions of manliness, including his inability to have sex, father children, manage his emotions, and walk. The passage points to the social foundation of masculinity by evoking a public persona, "the __ man," and relying on public images like the Easter Seal boy. This focus on public image bleeds into intensely personal description—"the man who cries in the shower." Kovic's wheelchair collapses any possible refuge within the private sphere for sexuality. Instead, his disabled body becomes a public mark for questions about his sexual potency and by extension, his masculinity.[6] Within this litany of "man," Kovic repeats the neologism "the sexlessman." By pressing the two terms into one, Kovic emphasizes the relationship between impotence and masculinity; he cannot have sex and is therefore "sexless" in the double meaning of impotence and failed gender expression.

The force of the paragraph leaves the impression that if Kovic can be considered a man, it is only through a series of compromises. For Kovic, the possibility of reconciliation with America as a sexual relationship is precluded by his injuries.

In the masculine world of *Paco's Story*, we are assured that Paco can and has had sex since his injury, but he fails to make a sexual connection with any of the women in the novel. This scenario reassures readers of Paco's intact masculinity while pushing the limits of the failed sexual reconciliation metaphor. The figurative assignment of femininity to the United States requires a complex play between women as the object of both desire and resentment. In his analysis of sexual dynamics in *Coming Home, In Country,* and *Paco's Story,* James Campbell writes, "The veteran desires to reintegrate himself with society or, in terms of the metaphor, to develop a sexual relationship with the woman, yet the woman herself is also the object of his anger at his alienation; she is both what enables and prevents his reconciliation" (204). In *Paco's Story,* Jesse, a drifter veteran, characterizes American antiwar sentiment through a performance of his imagined encounter with a female college student. He tells Paco and Ernest,

> "Been waiting for one of those mouthy, snappy-looking little girlies from some rinky-dink college to waltz up and say"—and his voice rises into a fey falsetto, squeaking as though he's rehearsed it— "'You one of them *vet'rans,* ain'cha? Killed all them mothers and babies. Raped all them women, di'n'cha'—*I only got two hands, lady!*—'Don't touch me, *so* nasty,' as the fella says, 'I ain't putting out for you, *buster,* not so much as a handshake!' Okay by me girlie," Jesse says, looking straight up, "'cause I got sixteen different kinds of social diseases—runny sores and all swoll up and everything dripping smelly green pus all the time, no telling what and all. And when this happens—this conversation with this here girlie—I'm gonna grab her by the collar of her sailor suit (or whatever the fuck they're parading around in these days), slap her around a couple of times, flip her a goddamned dime—got the fuckin' money right here," he says and leans back so he can pat his pants pockets, "and say, 'Here, Sweet Chips, give me a ring in a couple of years when you grow up.'" (156)

In Jesse's imagination, the rejection he has faced from the public as a whole is condensed into the hyperbolic naïveté of a college coed. He responds with a triumphant fantasy of violence, base witticism, and reverse rejection. If America is a woman for the alienated veteran, she is college educated but still ungrammatical; she assumes the worst of the returning soldier; and she is sexually fickle, tempting men with her "snappy-looking sailor suit," rejecting them, but finally open to future advances. In contrast to Heinemann's vision of male solidarity across national and historical lines, differences between U.S. and Vietnamese women are emphasized in each sphere of cultural encounter. In *Paco's Story*, the rape of a young Vietnamese girl that forms the climax of the combat scenes locates her in the position of victim, but in the home context, white U.S. women are the victimizers through the power of sexual rejection (Jeffords, "Tattoos").

Figured as a woman, America taunts the disabled veteran by being available but sexually withholding. In the masculine world of *Paco's Story*, women offer one path to national reintegration. The narrator asserts the healing potential of sex: "And he's a man like the rest of us, James, who wants to fuck away all that pain and redeem his body. By fucking he wants to ameliorate the stinging ache of those dozens and dozens of swirled-up and curled-round, purple scars" (173–174). Relief in the novel is a transitive act, requiring a woman's participation. For men "like the rest of us," the grotesque body can be redeemed through sexual proximity to the female body. Women's participation may be necessary to enact sexual healing, but their sexual consent in the novel occupies a more ambiguous place. Paco never has sex in the space of the story, but in his and other characters' fantasies, consent is either nonverbal, misunderstood, or won in a physical contest. A description of the gang rape of the Vietnamese girl follows immediately from Paco's desire for redemptive sex. This violent rape in turn destabilizes the meaning of consent in the rest of the novel. In the second narrative climax, Paco steals into Cathy's room and reads fantasies about him in her diary. In one entry Cathy writes, "[I] urge him off me with my hips—but I think now that he must have thought I wanted to fuck more" (208). Unlike the raped Vietnamese girl's physical struggle, Cathy's imagined rape occupies the ambiguous register of miscommunication, undermined further by Cathy's past-tense reflection and the multiply mediating registers in the phrase "I think he must have thought." A terrifying encounter for Cathy acts out Paco's desire to ameliorate his pain through a woman's body: "[He] begins to peel the scars off as if they were a mask. . . . I think I hear *screams*, as if each scar is a scream. . . . He's laying strings of those scars on my face, and I'm beginning to suffocate" (208). Cathy focuses originally on the signs of Paco's disability—the phallic cane and "livid" scars—as demonstrations of virility. Then his disabled body quickly degenerates into a memorial of screams and pain as each scar becomes contagious. By locating the scene of domestic rape in the female imagination, Paco and the masculine community of the novel have another opportunity to identify with a female subject. In this case Heinemann's doubled narrative ventriloquism through Cathy's diary presents a revision of the narrators' earlier belief in the redemptive possibilities of sex. By the end of the novel, the potential for reconciliation has been completely closed off for Paco, who feels like "a piece of meat on the slab" (209) after reading Cathy's account. In line with the feminized metaphor for America, Paco expands his sense of rejection by Cathy to Boone: "Whatever it is I want, it ain't in this town" (209). Paco's confused desire—"whatever it is I want"—suggests the breakdown of the sexual redemption model and enacts a search for another avenue of reconciliation.[7]

In her article "Tattoos, Scars, Diaries, and Writing Masculinity," Susan Jeffords comes to the opposite conclusion about the ending of Heinemann's novel. Instead of reading the diary entry and Paco's response as a confirmation of alienation, Jeffords argues that Paco has achieved a form of homecoming: "Paco's departure is not so much one of fear and self-repulsion as of completion. Paco leaves Cathy, not with his scars literally placed upon her, but with his signature inscribed upon her through her diary. . . . Paco's 'story' has been told, heard, and recorded, now by a U.S. rather than a Vietnamese woman's body, solidifying its participation in U.S. dominant culture. Through Cathy, the war and the masculinity it inscribes have truly come 'home'" (223). In the action of the novel, Cathy's position is indistinguishable from Jesse's snappy-looking college girl. Her initial fascination with Paco's scars turns to disgust and terror when she imagines those scars as a residue of greater pain and screaming. As an alternative to Jeffords's reading, I argue that the masculine point of view in the novel rejects the version of Paco's story that Cathy records. Within the novel's structure of direct narrative address, Paco's story *has* been told and heard, but not by the female body. Instead, the more striking audience of his tale is the imagined masculine reader, "James." Like Jesse's reverse rejection of the college girl or Paco's leaving Boone, women's rejection of men shores up the boundaries of male collectivity, and this emergent homosocial collective serves as a substitute for an impossible heterosexuality in the performance of national reconciliation.

Imagining the Uniform Reader

Just as boot camp for marines serves as an elaborate homogenizing technology, turning a motley collection of young men into standardized fighting machines, both Heinemann and Kovic employ a striking form of narrative positioning that seeks to produce a similarly uniform readership. In *Born on the Fourth of July*, the encounter with the memoir is manipulated by unconventional narrative choices and Ron Kovic's autobiographical voice. Instead of openly assigning a role to the reader, Kovic develops his own position as a naïve subject in order to appeal to the critical faculties of a general readership. In a more open ploy for sympathy, Heinemann uses direct narrative address and the name "James" to induct readers into the masculine collective of the novel. Bridging the space between the particular and the universal, "James" embodies Heinemann's fantasy of broad masculine identification, a process threatened and enabled by the war as it stages clashes between nations and genders but insists on connections among men. As social scripts, military strategy, and rehabilitation techniques proliferate in an extensive technology looking to repair the incoherent body at war, Kovic and Heinemann are no less deliberate in their narrative pursuit of a reliably signifying body.

Underlying Kovic's description of his transition from marine to antiwar activist is his intense desire to recuperate the promises of the nation. The recurring tropes of patriotism—military service, parades, and the Fourth of July—suggest Kovic's desire for a revision, not rejection, of American ideals. Although Kovic's memoir describes a kind of break with the patriotic militarism of his childhood, the moment of disillusionment is hard to find in the text. Consider, for example, Kovic's account of a letter home to his parents, written after killing Vietnamese women and children, after killing the corporal from Georgia, and after being paralyzed: "I am telling Mom and Dad that I am hurt pretty bad but I have done it for America and that it is worth it" (14). Kovic writes with simple diction, choosing one- or two-syllable words and no punctuation that would suggest a complication or elaboration of the straightforward idea that he has been wounded for America. In this instance, the present-tense description limits the mediating impact of Kovic's position as an author writing at a later period. At this moment in the memoir, despite his experiences and brutal violence, it *is* worth it.

The plot of *Born on the Fourth of July* is punctuated by events that would seem to produce Kovic's disillusionment with American ideals. Each break, however, is simultaneously tempered by his retreat into wistful hope or bewilderment. Kovic insists just over halfway through the book that "the hospital had changed all that [a sense of betrayal by antiwar protesters]. It was the end of whatever belief I'd still had in what I'd done in Vietnam" (134). But even after this claim of disillusionment with the Vietnam War, Kovic continually expresses hurt and confusion about the lack of support he finds from others. As the patriotic emblem in a Memorial Day parade, Kovic wonders why the crowd won't wave to him (103). In his first protest experience in Washington, DC, Kovic is baffled by violent police response to the demonstrators—"I couldn't understand why this was happening, why the police would attack the people" (139). This confusion is particularly ironic given that the demonstration is part of the response to four students killed by National Guardsmen at Kent State on May 4, 1970. When Kovic is himself the target of police brutality at a protest in Los Angeles, he cries, "I'm a Vietnam veteran! Don't you know what you're doing to me? Oh God, what's happening. . . . Don't you understand? My body's paralyzed. I can't move my body, I can't feel my body" (154). Kovic's retreat into the status of the Vietnam veteran at this moment of crisis reveals his earnest desire for his uniform and visible disability to express the fulfillment of military patriotism and bravery, even as he openly protests the war.

Kovic's persistent dramatization of shock and confusion at the broken promises of the nation reflects a naïveté that is itself shocking. The voice of the memoir consistently displays a childlike faith in the state to address its own faults. The force of this narrative perspective can be best understood by Lauren Berlant's theory of infantile citizenship. Berlant addresses the perceived limitations of this form of citizenship, but also argues that the childlike relation is a powerful position from which to make claims upon the state:

> The infantile citizen's ingenuousness frequently seems a bad thing, a political subjectivity based on the suppression of critical knowledge and a resulting contraction of citizenship to something smaller than agency: patriotic inclination, default social membership, or simple possession of a normal national character. But the infantile citizen's faith in the nation, which is based on a belief in the state's commitment to representing the best interests of ordinary people, is also said to be what vitalizes a person's patriotic and practical attachment to the nation and other citizens. (27–28)

By locating attachment to the state in a childlike perspective, Berlant offers a new valence through which to read Kovic's description of his youth in suburban Long Island. As children, Kovic and his friends play-act the masculinist national culture of baseball, military campaigns, athletics, and parades. This pastoral section of the memoir recounts how Kovic comes into national subjectivity as a "Yankee Doodle Dandy," one literally born on the Fourth of July. He develops a filmic montage of coming-of-age clichés: "And during the summer nights we were all over the neighborhood, from Bobby's house to Kenny's, throwing glid-ers, doing handstands and backflips off fences, riding to the woods at the end of the block on our bikes, making rafts, building tree forts, jumping across the streams with tree branches, walking and balancing along the back fence like Houdini, hopping along the slate path all around the back yard seeing how far we could get on one foot" (37). This long sentence offers a sense of the tone and movement of the chapter as a whole. The series of gerunds suggests a childhood of constant activity centered in the healthy body. Kovic uses the perspective of youth to paint a portrait of able-bodied masculine camaraderie, stable working-class family life, and dependable cultural heroes. As he describes it in the book, there is no ironic distance between the nostalgic recollection and childhood as he experienced it.

Structurally, Kovic sets aside a linear movement from childhood in-nocence to adult realization in favor of a circular narrative structure.[8] Although Kovic's work distinguishes itself as the only explicitly nonfic-tion text under examination here, *Born on the Fourth of July* is emblem-atic of the shifting textual body that emerges in the face of confrontation between the public and a striking figure of disability. Like David Foster Wallace's excessive and episodic *Infinite Jest*, discussed in chapter 5, or Mark Twain's conjoining of one fragmented and one fleshed-out novel, Kovic's work demonstrates the experimental textual forms required to account for the physical realities and subjective experience of disabil-ity. Kovic's text opens and closes with a description of his injury in the field. The second chapter describes the brutality of the hospital, the third recalls his childhood and enlistment, and the fourth jumps past the war and recovery to a longer strand describing Kovic's life in the United States as a wounded veteran. By beginning and ending with his experience overseas, Kovic arrests the sense of progress suggested by the increasing commitment to activism described in the rest of the mem-oir. The text circles back to its opening questions, enacting suspension around the moment of trauma. Kovic produces, then, not a story of heal-ing, but a narrative that searches for etiology, looking past the obvious cause of the wound—the moment of injury—back toward the "causes" located in childhood and the formation of the nascent soldier. While the most manifest cause of the wound would seem to be addressed and "cured" in the hospital scenes, the memoir suspends resolution of the narrative because the ideological source of the disability—the demands of patriotism—have not been cured.

At one level, starting the memoir with his injury and rehabilitation colors the following childhood reflections with the knowledge of Kovic's mistreatment. And certainly, Kovic's faith in childhood heroes and the promises of masculine authority takes on a threatening cast in these sections. According to the narrative voice, however, the ideals of childhood were not bankrupt at the time. Like Berlant's infantile citizen, Kovic reminds his readers of the joy and potential in youthful idealism. For the Catholic Kovic family, their relationship to John Kennedy and his claims for a New Frontier carry special significance. Kovic describes his reaction to President Kennedy's assassination: "I was deeply hurt for a long time afterward. . . . The pain stuck with me a long time after he died. I still remember Oswald being shot and screaming to my mother to come into the living room. It all seemed wild and crazy like some Texas shoot-out, but it was real for all of us back then, it was very real" (59). Repeated phrases within the passage—"a long time after" and "it was very real"— describe the residual traumatic effect of the assassination. Nonetheless, Kovic's antiwar convictions in the seventies do not lead him to an openly critical reassessment of his youth. His disillusionment occupies a temporal disjunction between two equally "real" moments: the patriotic ideals of childhood and his adult revision of those ideals. The narrative voice in the memoir does not change dramatically as Kovic ages; he is suspended in an infantile position. The same patterns of simple vocabulary, bewildered misunderstanding of political complexities, and nostalgic faith in the promises of his youth continue throughout the memoir.

As an extension of Berlant's theory, I'd like to propose a reciprocal position to infantile citizenship: the savvy citizen who can identify naïveté and provide political critique. Kovic describes the disjunction between his movie/military heroes and his actual experience, but his disenchantment does not lead him to a deeper analysis of cultural indoctrination. For some critics, Kovic's infantile citizenship is the limit of his activism. Peter McInerney finds in Kovic's memoir a single "thesis": the "cultural manipulation" of American children and soldiers (199). He condemns Kovic's narrative choices, claiming, "Kovic is not in control of some of the secret history of his text, not even aware of it, and his lack of awareness, the absence of an ironic self-consciousness, limits the effectiveness of his account" (197). McInerney ignores the fact that the text has prompted *his* awareness of this "secret history" even if Kovic does not voice it. In light of this critical tendency to cite Kovic's naïveté as the failure of the work, I suggest the external position of the savvy citizen as a way to reread his tone as a productive device. It seems possible that Kovic performs naïveté as an activist strategy. Intentional or not, the narrative voice presses the reader into the role of savvy citizen. Kovic's ingenuous voice positions his readers as smarter and more critical. The critical effectiveness of the memoir relies on this extratextual response from the reader.[9] Lauren Berlant argues, "The infantile citizen's stubborn naïveté gives him/her enormous power to unsettle, expose, and reframe the machinery of national life" (29). In Kovic's case this power relies on an external position that will pull together an argument the infantile citizen does not present himself. This savvy reader can apply an etiological logic to the memoir, discovering the ideological source of Kovic's injury.

Both Kovic and Heinemann address the formal problems of writing about the Vietnam War, in part, by constructing their own readers. These texts reflect their authors' desire not just to control how the war is represented on the page, but to manage the external experience of reading. In the more striking case, Heinemann's direct narrative address, James, does not simply hope for a sympathetic (and complicit) reader, but instead calls him out by name. The position of savvy citizenship, which I argue emerges from Kovic's infantile point of view, is less explicitly a feature of Heinemann's work, but offers the possibility for political analysis where other critics typically locate failure. Both forms of narrative positioning foreground the constructed nature of legibility more broadly. By naming or using tone to produce a reader, these texts call attention to the mediating force of language in political critique.

Heinemann's opening sentence—"Let's begin with the first clean fact, James. This ain't no war story" (3)—also marks the inaugural moment of explicit narrative positioning, a strategy that initiates a process of male bonding between his reader and the masculine community of the novel. These stories are all told to a reader named by the direct address, "James." A sense of intimacy develops between the narrator and reader, whom the novel figures as male and sympathetic. As Heinemann describes in the foreword to the paperback edition, "James" is a broad referent encompassing everything from jive street talk—"hey, Jack,"—through a series of literary and outlaw Jameses, Heinemann's oldest brother, and a possible nickname for his recently deceased father. [10] "James" becomes the stand-in for a male American brotherhood that finds its heightened expression in all-male companies in combat. As Susan Jeffords describes in her foundational analysis of masculinity and the Vietnam War, *The Remasculinization of America*, "Although Vietnam narratives show the bonding of soldiers from diverse and often antagonistic backgrounds, those bonds are always and already masculine. At no point are women to be included as part of this collectivity. And, given American prohibitions against women in combat, prohibitions based largely on sexual difference, such exclusions take on the appearance of the 'natural' rather than the social" (59).[11] The narrative voice of *Paco's Story* shores up identification among men—even civilians like James—by constructing and naturalizing masculine identity. In this collective, combat experience and nationality are secondary to gender.

Storytelling, with its illusion of orality, further inducts the reader into a male collective. After all, as Heinemann has said in an interview, "*Paco's Story* is meant to be read out loud."[12] The narrator's sentence structure and vocabulary conform to the style of a tale told among male intimates, most emphatically in his use of slang, profanity, and sexualized language. Each moment of strikingly exuberant diction acts as a wink or a nudge to envelope the listener. The first page offers a paradigmatic instance of Heinemann's style: "War stories are out—one, two, three, and a heave-ho, into the lake you go. . . . Just isn't it a pity, because here and there and yonder among the corpses are some prize-winning, leg-pulling daisies—some real pop-in-the-oven muffins, so to speak, some real softly lobbed, easy-out line drives" (3). Heinemann achieves the fast-paced cadences of speech through rhyme, hyphenated phrases, and interjection. These lines move between metaphors of sex and sports, reflecting and drawing the boundaries of proper masculine speech. Seemingly feminized, innocuous words like "daisies" and "muffins" instead showcase a hard masculinity by their resignification as death and sex. The narrator's aside, "so to speak," furthers an illusion of orality that draws the reader into an American brotherhood. As Grant Scott argues, in the value system of the novel "the oral form of representation is more true, is harder, coarser, grittier, more manly than writing" (74). Through this illusion the novel produces its own masculine readership in order to manage the encounter between the reader and the book.

The reader's engagement with this male collective meets its potential breaking point in one of the climaxes of the novel, a twelve-page description of the gang rape of a fourteen-year-old Vietnamese girl by our narrators and protagonist. The memory, prompted by Paco overhearing consensual sex between an American man and woman, unfolds through description that is both "beautiful and terrible" (177). The victim is a captured VC soldier and the rapists are the entire Alpha Company we have come to identify with throughout the novel: Gallagher, "Jonsey and Paco and the rest of us" (178). The nature of gang rape blurs the distinction between spectator and participant in the same way that the first-person plural and direct address of the narrator reject the possibility of a passive reader. Violence in this case extends from physical penetration to the encouraging or coercive behavior of the group as a whole.[13] According to Jeffords, "Gang-rape combines collectivity and display as the masculine bond performs as a group, with itself as audience" (69). Heinemann illustrates this dynamic through the recollection that "dudes still ambled over to the doorway to watch, to call out coaching, taking their turns, hanging around the side of the building after—some getting back in line" (181). The total conflation of spectator and rapist in the space of the story forces the reader into complicity. Grant Scott describes this coerced participation as a "sinister sleight of hand" and outlines how "other features of the description, particularly the analogies to common activities—zipping up a parka, wringing out a rag, standing in line—force us to see the rape in ordinary terms, through the vocabulary of everyday experience" (77). Gang rape lies at the extreme of performative models of gender because both rapist and onlooker enact the masculine alliance. Although Gallagher clearly emerges as the leader of the group, each of the other actors blurs into "the rest of us," creating a fluid movement between rapist, spectator, and reader.

The Vietnamese girl's subaltern role makes her vulnerable to both rape and literary exploitation through metaphor and narrative positioning. Her race, gender, and death open her victim status to habitation by men. According to Jeffords's article on *Paco's Story*, "Tattoos, Scars, Diaries, and Writing Masculinity," the effect of the rape scene is to emphasize the pain of the Vietnam veteran through identification with another victim. The parallels between Paco and the girl—outlined by both Grant Scott and Susan Jeffords—are achieved through description of their physical injuries and narrative point of view. Paco's frequent recollection of Gallagher's red and black dragon tattoo mirrors the VC soldier's experience as her glances at the tattoo become a refrain throughout the scene. Unlike Paco, however, the girl is not a survivor and her death leaves him in the uncontested position of surviving victim of the war. By positioning male figures as the victims of rape, the act becomes desexualized and metaphorical. Jeffords writes, "Heinemann constructs then a deliberate parallel between the experience of the Vietnamese girl and Paco, both 'raped' by the war and scarred by its tiny, relentless injuries. To enhance this analogy, Heinemann has Paco see the dragon as she sees it, narrating from her point of view" ("Tattoos" 212). More explicit in the narrative, however, is Heinemann's manipulation of the *reader* into the simultaneous positions of victim and rapist: "(Take your hand, James, and reach around the top of your head, grab as much hair as you can grab in one hand and *yank*, then press that arm tight against the side of your head and look over, hard, at your arm out of the corners of your eyes. That's as much of Gallagher's arm as the girl saw)" (176). We may be asked to recognize a parallel between Paco and the girl as victims of the war, but the commanding repetition of "you" insists that the stronger identification demanded in the passage is between the reader and the girl. This identification is further complicated, however, because the narrator asks the reader—again reinforced as the masculine James—to be both the hand that grabs the hair and the eyes that see the tattoo. Extending the point of view of the victim to the reader offers the same elision of the gendered dynamics of violence that Jeffords finds in the alignment of the veteran and the raped soldier. Difference reemerges in these lines, however, in the reminder of the dual positions of attacker and victim. The awkward position described and its placement in parentheses demands a pause on the part of the reader. The lines engage the reader's body with the text, twisting and contorting the arm to create a sense of corporeal immediacy. This awkwardness re-members the body of the reader in order to insist on embodiment as an organizing form of masculinity. While the narrators of the novel may be disembodied ghosts, their masculine identity, like that of men more broadly, depends on a persistent reimagining of the male body. Paco's present-day recollections of Gallagher's tattooed forearm—a phallic substitute—speak to the novel's belief in an enduring masculine body, one sustained by the fearful looking of the gendered sexual target. While women are one explicit vehicle for shoring up masculine embodiment, the dynamics of gang rape and these striking parenthetical lines demonstrate the ways in which men mutually reinforce each other's masculine identity.

The sexual violence of gang rape is a perverse manifestation of the brutality demanded in the Vietnam context and encoded as masculinity. The other side of female abjection is a transcendent male collectivity. As Jeffords describes in her chapter "That Men without Women Trip," "Combat can thus yield bonds not only between races who fight together but between races who are enemies. The collectivity of war, we are to understand, encompasses all men who engage in battle on any battlefield

and overcomes all barriers between races" (57). While the barrier of racial difference is never entirely overcome, Heinemann does illustrate the
international bond among men through two passages that contrast female and male Vietnamese speech. In the gang-rape scene, the Vietnamese girl cannot achieve her own salvation because she lacks the language
to appeal to the men's "humanity": "She screamed in Viet that no one
understood but could figure out pretty well, 'Pig. You pig. GI beaucoup
number ten goddamned shit-eating fucking pig. I spit on you!' ... He
pulled her—arms flailing, legs kicking, screaming that hysterical gibberish at the top of her lungs" (178). Although they admit they could "pretty
well figure out" her meaning, the masculine interest in sexual violence
reduces her language to "hysterical gibberish." Compare her vulgar and
ungrammatical speech to the language allowed to a Vietnamese male
soldier in a similarly imperiled position: "Paco pushed the clean carbon
blade. The man gasped as if the wind were knocked out of him and he
was trying to recover, but he whispered distinctly in up-country Viet,
'Lạy ông xin đừng giết tôi. Trời ơi! Xin đừng làm vây.' ('I pray you, please
don't kill me. Oh, God! Please do not do this, I beg you' is a decent translation, James.) He looked up at Paco man-to-man—the overpowering,
stinging pain welling up in him, overwhelming him; Please, he said, as
if talking to his older brother and relying on a lifetime's blood relations,
please do not do this" (195). For the dying male soldier, pleas are spiritual
and spoken in a language that looks to eclipse national boundaries even
as the passage preserves difference by presenting both the Vietnamese
and the English characters. The vulgar and imagined translation of the
girl's speech is replaced in the latter case by an explicit and "decent"
translation with its double meaning of correct and humane. The male
soldier has recourse to "brotherhood" and "blood relationship" while the
female is disowned from the human family. In these parallel scenes of
death, the enemy male soldier whispers and looks "man-to-man" whereas the enemy female soldier is a screaming hysteric.

The narrative address in Paco's Story enacts the collapse of the individual into the social body, a collapse that is central to both warfare and
gang rape. For Heinemann, the imperiled bodies of the soldier and the
disabled veteran find a fragile coherence in the collective body of the
marine company and the scarred community of veterans. Scenes like
the gang rape and the death of the male Vietnamese soldier demonstrate
the violence and extensive ideological labor required to hold together
masculine collectivity. The constantly reiterated narrative address,
"James," enacts the compulsory social dynamic of army organization

and group sexual assault. Despite demonstrating the permeability of the line between self and community and allowing for moments of temporary transcendence of racial and national divides, Heinemann preserves gendered difference. Men and women in *Paco's Story* can occupy parallel positions of victimization, but the awkward positioning of the arm and the girl's incomprehensible speech argue that these parallel lines can never overlap. While proximity to women, especially women who are violently and sexually exploited, serves as a necessary vehicle in the construction of masculinity, the body of the male collective refuses to admit its gendered other.

These security measures emerge in the face of the perceived vulnerability of the uniform masculine body. The soldier and the veteran are drastically refitted by the military apparatus in wartime and then subject at home to the accommodations required by the newly disabled body. In the masculinist collective voice of the novel, Heinemann participates in the embrace of the social purported to shore up the material and conceptual costs of corporeal vulnerability. As the structural analogy to gang rape suggests, however, the reading positions allowed by the narrative address include only collusion with the masculine social body or resistance to its values. The novel performs the ideological force of collectivity—especially when the body politic looks like the U.S. Army or the nation itself—and demonstrates in its constant attempts to construct an obedient readership that the path of the resistant reader through the text requires constant struggle against the dominant mode. *Paco's Story* makes explicit, even hyperbolic, the ideological work necessary in nationalist and militarist interpellation. "James," as a form of address and as a constructed audience, imagines a secure position of acceptance in the social body, a safe port in the face of the imperiled physical body.

National Scars

Both Kovic's and Heinemann's texts locate the spectacle of physical disability as a multivalent signifier. The disabled veteran's body is at times the source of alienation and at others the site of masculine identification. As a symbolic force, the hybrid visuals of wheelchairs or scars with uniforms and medals embody the overlapping registers of military valor and political critique. Each form of spectacle, whether on the public stages of protests and parades or for the everyday audience of the small town, is constructed by the mediating discourses of technology, sexuality and military nationalism. The bulk of this chapter has explored how figurative structures make the body legible and how the body itself can stand as a symbol. In conclusion, I briefly turn to the metaphors of disability and the body that construct public understanding of the Vietnam War. How has the war itself become located in the body in the national imagination? And how do these metaphors of the body establish a model of reading the war?

Perhaps the most striking vision of Vietnam as a scar on the national body comes in David Levine's 1966 cartoon for the *New York Review of Books*. The cartoon plays on President Lyndon B. Johnson's press conference performance where he pulled up his shirt for reporters to reveal a scar from his recent gall bladder operation. In the cartoonist's revision, the scar is figured as the geographical outline of Vietnam. Johnson's sunken eyes and posture in the drawing embody the national fatigue of an undesirable and yet escalating war. Levine's cartoon traces Vietnam onto the representative national body, demonstrating the centrality of the body in imagining the Vietnam War. As an enduring icon of the Vietnam era, Levine's cartoon does more than brand Johnson with the scars of a failed war. The image plays on the president's form in a "king's two bodies" logic of the national body politic, encapsulating a pervasive sense of Vietnam as a barely healed wound on the national body.

Over and over in political rhetoric, the war becomes a scar or disease on the body of America. In 1991 President George Bush celebrated U.S. success in the Gulf War with the announcement, "And, by God, we've kicked the Vietnam syndrome once and for all" (qtd. in Tal, *Worlds of Hurt* 61). According to a similar formulation, James Gibson summarizes conservative perspectives on the war, which understand Vietnam as "just a normal part of growing up for a young nation, a childhood disease like chicken pox, which leaves behind some small scars, but builds character" (5). Metaphors of Vietnam as a scarring or lingering disease to be "kicked" relocate blame for U.S. failure to an external force. Much like pointing to wounded American soldiers as the exhortation to continued fighting, medical metaphors of the war excise an acknowledgment of Vietnamese success, or even involvement. Instead, struggles in the war are about America's growing pains or America's unwillingness to commit its full resources to the "problem." Figuring the war as a disease redraws the borders of the conflict within America. When George Bush described a "Vietnam syndrome," he referred more specifically to a faltering American confidence in the decades after the war than to the war itself. What was Bush's cure for America's self-imposed hesitation? Decisive success in a war two decades later: "The specter of Vietnam has been buried forever in the desert sands of the Arabian Peninsula" (qtd. in Tal, *Worlds of Hurt* 60). In this regard, disability and disease as metaphor for the war appears no less frequently in scholarly literature. In a collection titled *The Wounded Generation*, Richard Harwood opens in the prologue, "Beneath the healed surface of American life, painful scar tissue from the Vietnam War remains" (Horne ix). Harwood's claim gains rhetorical force from his turn to the body in its record of trauma as a slightly mysterious, permanent effect. The most common metaphor of Vietnam is as something contagious, a replicable virus that at any moment could produce Another Vietnam. In the years following 9/11, news articles resurrected the Vietnam syndrome that George Bush hoped to have buried with the Gulf War by asking of his son's war in Iraq, "Are we caught in another Vietnam?"

The potency of somatic metaphors in the decades following the war reflects a continuation of the heightened anxiety over bodily coherence during Vietnam and its immediate aftermath. That war serves as a flashpoint in the history of ideological approaches to the embodied citizen, enacting a period of intense scrutiny over the seemingly reliable spectacles of nation. Just as war prompts a very material challenge to bodily coherence in the form of wounding and death, the ideological coherence of the body as a representation of military might and national well-being is similarly disrupted. While the comparison of mortal injury and somatic symbolism may seem facile, or a mere play on the dual meanings of "coherence," the strategy of the U.S. commanders in a war of attrition demonstrates that the belief in the body's symbolic work had life and death consequences. The confluence of these spectacles of the body and their mortal stakes, in turn, draws attention to the extensive system of sense-making scripts and technologies that emerge to manage the increasingly threatened male body. Heinemann and Kovic both capture and participate in this endeavor, hoping to shore up a compelling account of a uniform body in the face of an encroaching sense of disintegration.

4 /   Conceiving the Freakish Body: Reimagining Reproduction in *Geek Love* and *My Year of Meats*

In the American political arena, the figure of the child carries special ideological weight. Candidates and special interest groups sell their positions as a promise to America's children of a better future. As denoted by pop songs and campaign ads, children are synonymous with the future, and as such, figures of reproduction and childhood take on heightened significance in the discourse of citizenship. In describing a similar political dependence on the alliance between the figure of the child and the appeal to the future, Lee Edelman argues, "We are no more able to conceive of a politics without the fantasy of the future than we are able to conceive of a future without the figure of the child" (11). But while political rhetoric makes heavy symbolic demands on the figure of the pregnant woman or the smiling grade-schooler, these figures are successful because they appeal to seemingly uncomplicated, unanimous values. Who doesn't want to make a better world for our children? Who doesn't believe that children should be protected and celebrated?[1] In employing the seemingly apolitical figure of the child, voices from the right and the left share an appeal to the notion of a universal citizen. Perhaps it is because the image of childhood has been so politically efficacious that the practicalities of conceiving and raising actual children have become so politically charged. The flip side of "children are our future" is an often violent and intensely divisive set of debates over abortion, reproductive technologies, fertility treatment, gay marriage, and adoption rights.

Each of these national debates takes place in and over the body in yet another valence of embodied citizenship. In her discussion of these issues as the ground of a newly "intimate public sphere," Lauren Berlant argues, "A nation made for adult citizens has been replaced by one imagined for fetuses and children" (1). In her account of how this move takes place, Berlant emphasizes vulnerability as the figural connection between the traumatized adult citizen and the imagined national child. She elaborates on the position of the "citizen-victim" with a series of terms: "pathological, poignant, heroic, and grotesque" (1). As much as any of these terms suggests the figure of the vulnerable child, they also evoke the image of disability as conceived in the popular imagination. Perhaps best captured in a literary figure like Tiny Tim, disabled people are often frozen in an infantilized role. The poster children and "Jerry's Kids" telethon subjects that dominate visions of disability in the popular imagination can arrest disability in a time of endless childhood, where the need for accommodations seems to equal childlike dependencies.

While typically less visible in the national conversation, the history of disability is similarly charged with struggles and debates over children and reproduction. In the sphere of reproductive rights, the documented history of forced sterilization and eugenics continues to impact the lives of disabled people. For women with disabilities like Down syndrome, the right to bear children has been fought in legal circles, and women who are infertile or have other reproductive problems face struggles with the medical and insurance industries. The question of who should or can have children becomes increasingly political as advances in reproductive technology require the articulation of new moral positions and social policy. As we move from the quest to have children to the desire to legally terminate or prevent pregnancy, the alignment of reproduction and disability can also change the terms of the debate. An ongoing conversation between feminists and disability theorists has demanded a reconsideration of, or at least a more nuanced take on, the pro-choice position that stands as a cornerstone of the contemporary women's rights movement.[2]

Approaching the question of reproduction and the ideological value of children through the lens of disability studies requires a reconsideration of orthodox political positions. These reconsiderations, however, can produce strange bedfellows as arguments from each point on the political spectrum articulate their position according to the perceived value of "life" and its preservation. In their arguments against aborting disabled fetuses or euthanasia, do disability activists have more in common with a right-wing "culture of life" than with the pro-choice, pro-euthanasia advocates on the left who couch their positions in terms of "quality of life"? While these debates are continuing daily in courtrooms, class-rooms, and LISTSERVs, this chapter steps back from the specific terms of these discussions to ask how the alignment of disability and reproduction in culture can produce revised conceptions of the embodied citizen. In looking at *My Year of Meats* (1998) and *Geek Love* (1983), two novels that explicitly thematize both disability and reproduction, I argue, first, that these novels conceive of America through the logic of embodiment, and furthermore that each work offers up a disability-inspired reconsideration of reproduction in imagining how to populate the national body.

Perhaps the easiest entrée into Katherine Dunn's sprawling and fantastic tale of the Binewski carnival family is to consider one of the lines most popularly quoted in criticism of *Geek Love*: "A true freak cannot be made. A true freak must be born" (20). *Geek Love's* narrator, Olympia Binewski, makes this claim while standing naked on the stage of an amateur strip contest, one targeting people with "specialities." As an albino, hunchback dwarf, Oly's physical difference immediately trumps the garden-variety faux-conjoined twins and obese performers behind her. While the neat parallelism and repetition of terms in her statement would seem to close down ambiguity, both the form and content of this declaration ultimately fold back on themselves. In a novel that self-consciously insists upon the binary between freak and norm only to both invert and then displace it, each of the terms in Oly's statement—"true freak," "made," and "born"—gestures toward a set of unfixed meanings.

Moving out from the level of the sentence to the scene as a whole, Oly's claim seems transparently true: her freakishness is strikingly authentic—the most of-the-body and obviously congenital—in the context of the imitators and amateurs on the burlesque stage. The episodic structure of the novel, however, offers the reader a reminder to locate truth situationally. Only a dozen pages earlier, Oly laments her "commonplace deformities" and her dim position in the constellation of her more extraordinary siblings (8). First there is her brother Arturo, whose flipper-like hands and feet extend directly from his torso to suggest his billing as "The Aqua Boy." Then, in comparison to her older sisters, beautiful piano-playing conjoined twins named Electra and Iphigenia, Oly's status as an albino dwarf offers less in the way of carnival marketability. This mutability in the definition of "true" freakishness places pressure on the negated term "made" in Oly's claim on page 20, suggesting that despite the unambiguous structure of her statement, embodied truths are constructed by and relative to their social contexts. Moreover, moving out another level from the novel itself to the sphere of intertextuality,

Oly's statement resonates as an inversion of Simone de Beauvoir's oft-cited claim that women are not born, but made. While *Geek Love* insists on the centrality of the body—often in explicitly essentialist terms—the novel also participates in de Beauvoir's feminist emphasis on the social construction of seemingly embodied categories.

Geek Love captures a Möbius strip of that which is made and that which is born. The central conceit of the novel—that Al and Lil Binewski have, through controlled experimentation with drugs, chemicals, and radioisotopes, bred freakish children to sustain the family carnival—offers a radical reconfiguration of the mode of reproduction such that the process more closely resembles the mode of production. The Binewski children are embodied commodities, as emphasized in the second most commonly quoted line of the novel: "What greater gift could you offer your children than an inherent ability to earn a living just by being themselves?" (7). I argue that in reimagining reproduction, *Geek Love* reconsiders the role of production and commodity in both the physical and the social body. Dunn's vision of America and its citizenry locates a shared logic in being made and being born.

In an exposé of the abuses of agribusiness and its toll on fertility, puberty, and secondary sex characteristics, Ruth Ozeki's *My Year of Meats* describes a tragic alliance between meat production and human reproduction. Published in 1998, Ozeki's novel follows narrator Jane Takagi-Little as she travels across the United States, producing a program for Japanese television sponsored by the American beef industry. Jane's Japanese and white American ethnic background suggests to her Japanese employers an ideal mix of familiarity with both representative American values and Japanese sensibilities. Jane speaks to these two masters in her hastily written proposal for the program:

> Meat is the message. Each weekly half-hour episode of *My American Wife!* must culminate in the celebration of a featured meat, climaxing in its glorious consumption. It's the meat (not the Mrs.) who's the star of our show! Of course, the "Wife of the Week" is important too. She must be attractive, appetizing, and all-American. She is the Meat Made Manifest: ample, robust, yet never tough or hard to digest. Through her, Japanese housewives will feel the hearty sense of warmth, of comfort, of hearth and home—the traditional family values symbolized by red meat in rural America. (8)

Jane's show is constructed around the exuberant slippage between the meat and its maker. Beef is the star of the show and communicates itself as message. The wife, by extension, is "appetizing," consumed by the television audience during her own act of consumption. In an interview with Ozeki reproduced for the paperback version of the novel, she refers to the above description as the kernel of the novel's genesis: "The meat was metaphorical, a gag if you will. . . . I was thinking of women as cows; wives as chattel (a word related to cattle); and the body as meat, fleshy, sexual, the irreducible element of human identity. I was thinking, too, of television as a meat market" (6). *My Year of Meats* operates under a similar principle of correspondence: through the course of the novel, Ozeki dramatizes the connections—sometimes metaphorical, but often very material—among corporate agriculture practices, international trade agendas, global media, definitions of family, gender, and nation. Each of these categories, for Ozeki, is rooted in the sense of meat as flesh and body, as she returns to the physical costs and possibilities of participation in production, consumption, and reproduction. Throughout *My Year of Meats*, Ozeki turns to disabilities, including infertility, paralysis, precocious puberty, and feminization in men, in order to demonstrate the tragic effects of profit-seeking shortcuts in agribusiness. The plot of *My Year of Meats* unfolds in two directions: as Jane learns more about meat production, she travels from the dinner table, to the supermarket, to the slaughterhouse, and finally to the feedlot; this backward movement contrasts with the forward movement from conception through gestation to birth marked by the pregnancies of the two central female characters in the book, Jane and Akiko, a Japanese viewer of *My American Wife!* Ozeki, like Dunn, offers a freakish revision of reproduction according to a model that, despite its protest at the costs of production, also follows its logic and allows for its value.

The reconfigurations of production and reproduction in *Geek Love* and *My Year of Meats* do not obviate the negative valences of these terms—production will still signal corporate abuses and reproduction will carry with it heteronormativity—but this reconfiguration can still challenge the totality of conventional alliances. While the two authors deploy disability according to opposing notions of its value—Ozeki uses disability to mark the tragic costs of corporate farming whereas Dunn celebrates the freakish body as a gift—these disparate starting points lead to similar conclusions about the symbiotic nature of the corporate, the national, and the human. Although Ozeki is more apparently didactic than Dunn, both novels use disability as a manifest critique of prevailing norms. Like the public spectacle located in the parades and protests explored in chapter 3, Dunn and Ozeki use disabled bodies to express political dissent. The fact that these bodies *also* reflect a widespread conceptual incorporation of the very systems they are challenging does not reflect the failure of the novels or their lapse into a hand-wringing ambiguity. Instead, disability inspires a model in which apparent collusion can be reimagined as accommodation. Because the physical and social demands of disability insist on a theory that can account for pain, compromise, and difficulty, the anomalous bodies in these novels represent the possibility of simultaneous critique and reconfiguration of dominant norms.

Americana and the National Body

In an essay on *Geek Love* and the paradox of American individualism, Victoria Warren introduces a term into the critical conversation surrounding the novel that I find central to readings of both Dunn's and Ozeki's work: "Americana."[3] In "American Tall Tale/Tail," Warren offers a catalog of the Americana found in Dunn's novel. Her list is extensive and convincing, including the heartland settings of the carnival circuit; Dunn's cast of American types like the cowboy, the self-made man, Ivy League fraternity boys, and the Boston aristocrat;[4] and homey family scenes of storytelling and berry picking. Warren then extends the concept of Americana to diction and the saturation of the novel with specifically American phrases—"Thus the narrative incorporates the language of an older, rural America, the contemporary language of urban slang, romantic, sentimental language, and the tone of the barker, establishing an auditory image of interconnected Americanisms" (326). While Warren uses these examples of Americana to explore Dunn's critique of foundational American values, I want to pause over the term, as it evokes for me a curiosity about the role difference, specifically embodied difference, plays in the construction of that which is recognized as "characteristically American."

The term "Americana" and its constituent objects and practices entail an interesting tension between the representative and the extraordinary. This paradox lies at the heart of embodied citizenship, in which the very characteristics that exclude people marked by disability, gender, race, and sexuality from full participation in the foundational logics of citizenship are the same properties by which we understand their national participation. The artifacts that occupy the status of Americana similarly come to notice by virtue of their difference. Often marginal in some way, these objects represent a lost time, a regional locale, or a physical oddity.

Apple pie manifests nostalgia for a lost gendered and heteronormative imaginary. The carnival and its freak show represent America through their extraordinariness, both in their itinerant nature and in the unusual bodies on display. As captured in the metaphor of conjoined twins examined in chapter 1, the national fantasy of an interconnected America is often discovered at its temporal, spatial, and bodily margins.

"Americana" is first defined in the *OED* as a book or literary artifact, but this definition seems most appropriately extended to include a series of circulating oral stories, including folk tales, songs, and family tales of origin. *Geek Love* begins with exactly this kind of storytelling, describing Al's inspiration upon seeing a collection of hybrid roses to breed his own family of freaks.[5] The repetition of the word "would" in Oly's recollection of these family tales—"Papa would say" (7), "nights on the road this would be" (7)—illustrates the ritual nature of the act and suggests a portable quality important to its inclusion as Americana. These repeated family stories reflect the broader rhythms of life on the carnival circuit, which is composed of a series of routines: mounting and dismantling the midway, tents, and rides; performing shows, usually scheduled two or three times a day; and the circular call of the barker. Together these activities form a node on another circular series, the route of the traveling carnival across the United States. Throughout the novel, Oly and her family repeatedly express their disconnection from the specificities of location and time—"It was a bright warm morning in Arkansas, I think, or maybe Georgia" (120). In a longer elaboration of this experience, Oly explains, "It may seem odd that I have no idea what town we were in, but when the whole show was alive and functioning—especially at night—it felt like the whole world and it always looked the same no matter where we were. In the daylight we might notice that we were in Coeur d'Alene or Poughkeepsie, but at night all we knew was us" (218). These lines describe a series of substitutions by which intranational differences are obscured so that "the whole show" can become "the whole world." The seeming call to specificity in naming cities is deflated by the conjunction "or" which seems to establish equivalence between Coeur d'Alene and Poughkeepsie. These cities and their regional differences are collapsed into the "alive and functioning" body of the carnival and its connection to a national body uncomplicated by the local.

The carnival produces a similar relation to time in which the specifics of global and national history become secondary to the family narrative. As a backdrop to their romance, Lil tells her children of meeting their father, "It was during a war, darlings. . . . I forget which one precisely" (4).

In contrast to the hyperbolic rhetoric of the carnival world in which each act is "Miraculous" or the "Most Curious," Lil falls into understatement in losing track of the military events that so often script national narratives of history. The distinction among wars of the late twentieth century is not a question of recalling "precisely," according to nationalist rhetoric. The principle of equivalence suggested above in the naming of Coeur d'Alene and Poughkeepsie becomes more fully established in this line. Wars become indistinct and subordinate to the background of personal histories. The Binewskis' story is novel, however, because even as it falls under the "meet cute" rubric of the romantic origin tale—a love story in which the carnival boss "boy" falls for the new ethereal geek "girl"—the grotesque details of the story are strikingly unlike any other member of the genre (the girl, after all, is seducing both boy and audience by biting the heads off live chickens). This quality of being both like and unlike familiar categories is one of the central appeals of Americana. Among collectors, value is often located in the novelty of the item, unique among its kind because others have been lost to time; or because in a world of mass production, it bears the obvious marks of its maker; or because the subject of the item is itself extraordinary, as in photographs of freaks that circulated widely as *cartes de visite* in the late nineteenth century.[6] The difference that makes these items valuable, however, always points back to their identity with other objects of the same class and their popular legibility.

Despite the extraordinary setting of *Geek Love*, much of its narrative energy emerges from a repeated slippage into recognizable modes of the familial and the national. Dunn is careful not to rely on an uncritical universalism in her characterization; the emergence of the familiar, instead, points to the dialectical nature of identity and difference. Even elements that seem unique to the sphere of the carnival resonate with the concerns of a more common world. An early description of the financial woes of the business reads as an allegory for national problems: "The show was burdened with an aging lion that repeatedly broke expensive dentures by gnawing the bars of his cage; demands for cost-of-living increases from the fat lady, whose food supply was written into her contract; and the midnight defection of an entire family of animal eroticists, taking their donkey, goat, and Great Dane with them" (7). These concerns parallel national crises in the seemingly extra-national sphere of the carnival. The lion points to health care and an aging population; the fat lady speaks to inflation as both an embodied metaphor and a material concern; and the defection of the animal eroticists anticipates the loss of industry cemented by policies like NAFTA. This tendency to see the familiar in the strange is nothing new. In fact, as I argue in chapter 1, the domestication of difference into a legible quality is one of the most profound ways for a social body to manage marginal citizens. The process of domestication, however, will always leave a residue of the anomalous, and *Geek Love* emphasizes this residue. The more startling moments in the narrative force readers to look across the familiar/strange binary to see ostensibly known categories in new lights. Dunn exploits the family epic and its reliance on the familiar as a self-reflexive trope. Familial and national belonging take on charged meanings as Dunn points back toward the unusual processes that constitute membership in both family and nation.

In *Geek Love*, the carnival functions according to the synecdochical logic of Americana in which the characteristic part represents the national whole. Similarly, categories like "the American family" or "the American novel" gain cultural meaning because of their presumed ability to balance general relevance with specificity. Ruth Ozeki is similarly concerned with the stakes of symbols and figurative substitutions. Ozeki's fictional commercial/documentary series, *My American Wife!*, functions on a pretext of representation in which meat, wife, and nation stand for each other. Set in 1991, the novel engages in a more subtle play with the reigning political symbols of the day. In a comment on modern militarism and the impact of foreign wars on the population at home, President Bush's Desert Storm forms a haunting presence in *My Year of Meats*; reminders of this largely out-of-sight war emerge most often in liminal spaces like airports or in symbols like yellow ribbons and military uniforms.

Both *Geek Love* and *My Year of Meats* suggest that America is perhaps most easily apprehended at its margins. Dunn's carnival succeeds as Americana because of its ability to stage, over and over, in each new town on the circuit, a contained, but thrilling, reflection of national values and concerns. Ozeki argues that dominant American culture is most visible as a series of repetitive acts, serial moments that contain an element of difference, just as the sideshow establishes the border of the midway. Like the recurring segments of the television show at the novel's center, life in America is revealed through scenes that are no less scripted or episodic than these TV vignettes. Early in the novel, Jane is forced to reconsider the familiar vignette of the departing American soldier through the eyes of her Japanese crew:

A brass band was playing when I arrived, and the ticket counters were decorated with proud banners of sparkling stars and stalwart stripes. Yellow ribbons festooned the departure lounge, and Mylar balloons floated like flimsy planets over the cloudlike tresses of blonde girls in pastel who had come to say good-bye.

At the center of all this effusion were the callow recruits, with brand-new crew cuts and bright-red ears, dressed in the still-unfamiliar pale of desert camouflage. Babies were pressed to their clean-shaven cheeks. Mothers' breasts heaved like eager battleships, while the soldiers' fingers lingered over ramparts of stone-washed thigh. (10)

The airport setting of this scene is central to its themes of international conflict and embodied symbols of national values. Two forms of foreign conflict emerge in the departure lounge: Desert Storm and the Japanese crew's witness of "Gulf War Fever." As a borderland site, the airport both represents and literally serves as the stage for the permeable limits of the national body. As soldiers leave to serve as national representatives on foreign soil, travelers to the United States cast an examining look at the cultural differences expressed by local symbols of militarism and citizenship. In the metaphors of the passage's closing sentence, the military apparatuses more familiarly located in the Gulf become domesticated in the bodies of mothers and wives. This gendered translation places American militarism in the realm of the family.

In *My Year of Meats*, Jane Takagi-Little uses episodic television to capture and construct families in the mode of Americana, emphasizing portability, marginality, and legibility. *My American Wife!* illustrates two layers of portability, first in the packaging of personal lives into a palatable thirty-minute episode, and then in the transmission of these programs into the milieu of the Japanese housewife. Just as the wife is the "meat made manifest," she also embodies America for an international audience. The fantasy of America shared by the beef industry and the Japanese advertising agency that produces the show, however, turns out to be more elusive than expected. In order to successfully cast episodes, Jane must follow a national route much like the carnival circuit traveled by the Binewski family. She and her crew eschew metropolitan centers in favor of rural agricultural communities. In the earliest episodes of the series, the wives profiled conform to the fantasies of the American Heartland; the women are white, middle-class mothers who serve straightforward meat-and-potatoes fare to their husbands and children. According to the model of modern homogenization, these families are holdovers from a disappearing era. In the first episode of the show, which, in turn, serves as the opening chapter of the novel, Jane's zeal for Americana backfires when her enthusiasm for the antique quilt belonging to Suzie Flowers (the wife) inspires Suzie's self-conscious shame over a bedspread that feels old and shabby in the face of outside scrutiny. Jane expresses her dismay upon returning to the home to discover that Suzie has shipped the offending/admired quilt to her sister and replaced it with a synthetic model just purchased from the local Wal-Mart. The exchange of the handmade quilt for the mass-produced comforter encapsulates Jane's sense of urgency as a documentarian of American culture. In her quest for what she sees as an increasingly elusive authenticity, Jane looks toward figures and places marginalized by the national agenda. Difference, in these episodes, becomes the requirement for representation.

In subsequent episodes, Jane's belief in the extraordinary as the most effective representative leads her to profile families that seem to break from the heartland stereotypes portrayed in the Suzie Flowers episode. Much to the dismay of Jane's conservative Japanese boss, *My American Wife!* begins to showcase atypical families such as the Boudreaux, a couple in Louisiana who have adopted ten children from Asia and South America, and Lara and Dyann, lesbian vegetarians whose young children were conceived by artificial insemination. In her initial departure from white America, Jane profiles Alberto (Bert) Martinez, a Chicano farmer living in Texas: "He'd lost his left hand to a hay baler in Abilene seven years earlier, a few months after he and Catalina (Cathy) had emigrated from Mexico, just in time for Bobby to be born an American citizen. That had been Cathy's dream, to have an American son, and Bert had paid for her dream with his hand" (58). In this character summary, Ozeki highlights archetypes of national belonging—immigration, citizenship, and the American dream—and locates them explicitly in the body. Martinez's amputated hand serves as a symbol for the family's loss of ethnicity, paralleled typographically in the parenthetical translations from Alberto to (Bert) and Catalina to (Cathy). The profile of the Martinez family illustrates that despite the idyllic portrait of a frolicking child and his pet pig—charmingly, but grotesquely, called "Supper"—national belonging requires embodied sacrifice. Prefiguring the deeply significant role of reproduction in the novel, the American son acts as a kind of prosthetic for Bert's lost hand, in which the next generation serves as a supplement for the limits of their progenitors.

The embodied nature of American citizenship—a model in which it is unremarkable to claim that a lost hand can serve as payment toward the American dream—provides the terms through which individuals understand their membership in the social body. *My Year of Meats* tells the story of Jane's production of "documentaries about an exotic and vanishing America for consumption on the flip side of the planet" (15). In its parallel plotline, the novel traces the reverse movement of Akiko Ueno from the consuming audience of Jane's program to a participant in the heterogeneous makeup of America. Akiko's triumphant rejection of her abusive husband—also Jane's boss—finds dual expression in her successful pregnancy after months of infertility and her climactic migration to America. For Akiko, national connection is literally a process of incorporation. During a train ride through the American South—a mode of transportation that is itself a form of Americana—Akiko feels "as if she'd somehow been absorbed into a massive body that had taken over the functions of her own" (339). She thinks, "*This is America!*" (339). While Akiko expresses joy in giving herself over to the "massive body" that "is" America, the description allows for a more menacing reading in its requirement of corporeal surrender. The body is not simply fodder for the metaphorics of national belonging. Understanding citizenship according to a somatic model raises the stakes of identification and emphasizes its potential physical costs. For Ozeki, assimilation into the national body involves loss, sometimes literally, as in the case of Bert Martinez, or figuratively, in the dissolution of Akiko's sense of her bodily limits.

Akiko's absorption into the American national body emerges in the wake of her communal participation in a scene of racialized performance. As I'll discuss in more detail at the close of this chapter, both *Geek Love* and *My Year of Meats* construct a hybrid genre in which fantastic elements are most often expressed in a realist mode. The train car in which Akiko experiences her American epiphany becomes a troubling site in which the realist expression of the novel collides with its fantasies of harmonious racial difference. According to the Amtrak attendant, a "kind, . . . wiry black man" named Maurice (335), the train from New Orleans to New York City is called the "Chicken Bone Special." Named for the homemade, fried chicken box lunches the working-class black passengers have brought along, the Chicken Bone Special becomes a mobile stage in the tradition of minstrel shows, exaggerating the multicultural themes of the novel in a form of grotesque parody. The routine begins with gentle banter singling out a single participant, but performed for the assembled passengers. After joking that perhaps Akiko has taken the train all the way from Japan, Maurice uses her as the straight man in explaining the history of the train's name and its working-class roots.

To this point, the scene seems to offer a model of vernacular, working-class histories and a celebration of down-home values in contrast to "the frozen cardboard sandwiches" served up by corporate America. The next act of the routine, however, veers toward the perverse, as Maurice encourages the passengers in a chorus of "*chicken bone chicken bone chicken bone*" and, "clapping his hands and slapping his knees," begins to sing, "Let me tell you a story 'bout train one-nine" (339). It is this performance, and Akiko's breathless "This would never happen on a train in Hokkaido!," that leads to her shivering realization, "*This is America!*" (339). In the world of the novel, this scene really happens, and it serves as the culminating expression of the multicultural fantasy that Jane has been documenting in *My American Wife!* Away from the mediating influence of the editing room and conservative pressure from both American sponsors and Japanese advisors, Akiko—the consuming audience of Jane's show—has her own experience of racial celebration, an "authentic" experience that she believes is identical to America and its radical incorporation of her own body. The danger of this celebration of difference, as both critics and supporters of the late-twentieth-century movement in multiculturalism have outlined, is that difference will become reified and unmoored from the power relations that have made this heterogeneity socially meaningful. A generous reader of this scene can find in its explicit use of minstrel traditions a foundation for the suggestion that Akiko's epiphany springs from an ironic performance of racial difference. The position of the scene as the climax of Akiko's plotline, however—and the sense that, like a train, the events of the novel have been inexorably leading her toward this sense of community with America's communities of color—suggests that, like the other fantastic experiences of the novel, the Chicken Bone Special is meant to be taken seriously.

As an expression of Ozeki's hopeful integration of the fantastic and the realist, Maurice and the Chicken Bone Special demonstrate the generative power and the danger of Americana. The minstrel tradition—with the blackface makeup and collectible dolls that are its legacy in the realm of Americana—is an example of a larger symbolic system in which objects and practices come to represent the nation. The body, especially the body marked as different, is constantly pressed into service as a symbol of America, both as a key metaphor for national belonging and as a model for cultural artifacts. On the one hand, Akiko's absorption into the social body is presented as a triumph in the novel. On the other, the hyperbolic performance of racial difference that sparked this national incorporation requires the flattening of heterogeneity into an easily legible and portable property. This translation of the body from subject to objectified symbol resonates with what I am describing as a central theme in both novels: the critical evaluation of production as a model for the reproduction of family and nation. In the next section of this chapter, I'll take up Ozeki's interest in agribusiness and in consumerist centers like Wal-Mart as a central mode in developing that which we understand as representative of America and consider how these corporate practices emerge and change in the face of her dual interest in mass production and reproduction.

My Year of Meats and the Business of Making Babies

Americana serves as a key touchstone in the discussion of embodied citizenship, calling attention to questions of symbolism and the alignment between the marginal and the representative. As a category emphatically populated by objects, Americana also foregrounds the role of the material in the social apprehension of concepts like patriotism and citizenship. Just as abstract elements of the nation attach to objects, so that an apple pie can convey a sense of country, these objects circulate differently in the national imagination and can become part of the figurative approach to understanding identity. For Akiko Ueno, in *My Year of Meats*, American cultural artifacts shape her vision of the world and her place in it. Akiko contrasts her own infertility with the apparent successes of *My American Wife!* star Suzie Flowers, manifested in Suzie's recipe for Coca-Cola rump roast and her brood of healthy children: "[Suzie's] children pushed between her sturdy, mottled legs and hung off her hem. They must have just poured out, Akiko thought, one after the other, in frothy bursts of fertility" (20). Like the descriptions of the roast itself, these passages equate health with fertility and locate both in the flesh, in the "sturdy" stock of the "rump," legs, and hips that lie above the hem. In Akiko's mind, the dish and the children are inextricably linked to American abundance. Coca-Cola, the giant among transnational commodities, moves from the main ingredient in the roast to Akiko's metaphor for fertility's "frothy bursts." Ozeki develops a figural system in which the body—made emphatically material in descriptors like "sturdy" and "mottled"—and commodities—represented by both Coca-Cola and the cut of meat—are woven into one another.

Fertility, as a sign of physical health, is especially significant in this scheme as production increasingly serves as a model for reproduction. *My Year of Meats* troubles the conceptual divisions between person, animal, and object, challenging, like Katherine Dunn, the difference between that which is made and that which is born. For Ozeki, conception and gestation are sites of great interest. The dangerous practices of corporate farming can imperil sexual health, but these same practices offer potential reproductive hope to single, queer, or infertile women. Hormonal intervention, artificial insemination, and genetic selection in breeding exact a high price when used on the feedlot, but have also radically changed human approaches to conception, for good and ill. Despite her explicit protest of the human and environmental costs of agribusiness and big-box retailers, Ozeki does not argue for a complete retreat from the corporate model. She demonstrates, instead, how production can suggest a freakish alternative to restrictive notions of procreation. These changes in human reproduction are as much conceptual as they are practical. Both Jane and Akiko come to understand their sexuality and fertility in terms increasingly analogous to corporate farming, hoping to breed for specific genetic or racial traits and wondering about the effects of technological intervention. Throughout the novel, Ozeki deploys disabled figures most visibly as a sign of corporate shortcuts and their tragic effect in America's food supply. In her exploration of the vulnerable body, however, Ozeki also develops a model of embodiment that accounts for conceptual and literal permeability. This corporeal openness serves as a warning against the potential harm of experimentation, especially when "progress" is driven by profit. But somatic permeability, even when it reflects the strategies of the transnational economy, can also suggest a more holistic understanding of the connections between humans and their environment and new possibilities for remaking that world.

Given the activist goals enacted in both the plot and the novel itself, this notion of corporate economy as a progressive model seems at odds with Ozeki's critical intentions. Certainly, Ozeki dedicates much of the novel to arguments against the negative effects of capitalist excess. Jane's circuit through Middle America brings her in constant contact with Wal-Mart, and as a documentarian, she both laments the homogenizing influence of the retail giant and exploits it as a visual symbol of American culture, ready for export to her Japanese audience:[7]

> *This* was the heart and soul of *My American Wife*: recreating for Japanese housewives this spectacle of raw American abundance. So we put Suzuki in a shopping cart, Betacam on his shoulder, and wheeled him up and down the endless aisles of superstores, filming

goods to induce in our Japanese wives a state of *want* (as in both senses, "lack" and "desire"), because *want* is *good*. We panned the shelves, stacked floor to ceiling, tracked women as they filled their carts with Styrofoam trays of freezer steaks, each of which, from a Japanese housewife's perspective, would feed her entire family for several days. "Stocking up" is what our robust Americans called it, laughing nervously, because profligate abundance automatically evokes its opposite, the unspoken specter of death. (35)

While the conceit of a documentary program selling meat to Japanese housewives lends novelty to Ozeki's description, her critique of "raw American abundance" is familiar. Given the strength of this critique, it is perhaps surprising when Ozeki's protagonist confesses, some twenty pages later, "Don't get me wrong. I love Wal-Mart. There's nothing I like more than to consign a mindless afternoon in those aisles, suspending thought, judgment. It's like television" (56–57). In a novel that advocates greater public scrutiny of the practices that bring food to our tables and goods to our pantries, phrases like "mindless" and "suspending thought, judgment" in this line might signal its insincerity. Part of my interest in this chapter, however, is to take seriously cultural elements, such as freak shows or Wal-Mart, that seem outlandish and even exploitative in giving pleasure. Shopping can feel like a private source of pleasure, as in Jane's afternoons given over to solitary browsing, but consumerism also serves as an essential node connecting individuals with the transnational economy. So typically denigrated as a woman's practice, shopping traces a circle uniting women, production, goods, and citizenship.

In the symbolic logic of the novel, Wal-Mart embodies America and locates a central place for women in that culture. Just as their confrontation with Gulf War Fever in the airport holds a mirror up to American militarism, Jane's Japanese film crew registers intercultural astonishment at the excesses of Wal-Mart. To Suzuki and Oh, the superstore is a manifestation of "the sheer amplitude of America, . . . the capitalist equivalent of the wide-open spaces and endless horizons of the American geographical frontier" (35). As a filmmaker, Jane preys upon a similar belief among Americans in the equivalence between nation and consumerism. In order to find wives for the show, she convinces women of their "civic duty to promote American meat abroad and thereby help rectify the trade imbalance with Japan" (35). In *My Year of Meats*, Ozeki insists that the most complex and distant-seeming concepts of agricultural production and international trade are, in fact, domestic in the most immediate sense.

Ozeki focuses on wives and families in order to bring home the harmful impact of corporate practices that often seem obscure and insurmountable. In leveling her critique, Ozeki constantly turns to the body as the site of revelation for corporate abuses. Disability, then, figures prominently in the novel as a way to make questions of economic policy and the mode of production tangible. Nearly all the characters in the novel, including Jane, Akiko, and most of the subjects Jane considers for *My American Wife!*—Bert Martinez, the Boudreau children, Christina Bukowsky, Rose Dunn, and Purcell Dawes—are in some way disabled, and each serves as a politicized sign of the human costs of corporate America. Disability calls attention to the body's vulnerability in the instability of health and seemingly fixed processes like dexterity, mobility, sexual maturation, and fertility. This vulnerability motivates a cautionary impulse that Ozeki hopes will urge the citizenry to reconsider its largely permissive attitude toward profit-driven enterprises. Vulnerability can also, however, suggest the need for new ways to approach the body and a more flexible attitude toward its maintenance. These newly "flexible bodies," to borrow a term from Emily Martin,[8] may offer a site through which to critique transnational corporations, but they also take a page directly from the capitalist playbook. A dominant tactic of the contemporary economy is, in fact, flexibility.[9] While their effects are often toxic, Ozeki's treatment of disabled people argues that corporate tactics can offer a surprising model for conceiving of embodiment.

Ozeki's characterization of Christina Bukowsky, a young woman paralyzed after being hit by a Wal-Mart delivery truck, illustrates the novel's complex relationship to corporate models. Most immediately, Christina serves as the embodiment of the devastating effects of Wal-Mart on local communities. Left paraplegic and comatose after her collision with the delivery truck, Christina has been literally "crushed" by the superstore, like the small businesses crushed by the chain's low prices and wholesale purchasing power. Her mother, working as a Wal-Mart associate, is denied both time off and access to unemployment by her employer and quits her job in order to provide full-time care for her daughter. In her profile of the Bukowsky family, Ozeki makes the local impact of retail giants even more immediate. In a narrative strategy that resurfaces throughout the novel, Ozeki uses the power of the body and disability to illustrate economic and cultural problems. In contrast to the slow strangle-hold that Wal-Mart places on local businesses, significantly called "mom and pops" by Ozeki (56), Christina's accident dramatizes the superstore's crushing effect in a single moment of trauma. The body, even when subject to seemingly permanent conditions such as paralysis, always contains a sense of immediacy in its social demands. Disability makes the needs of the body especially pressing as cultural and environmental norms fail to accommodate physical heterogeneity. For the Bukowskys and the town of Quarry, Indiana, Christina's unanticipated physical and spiritual requirements in the aftermath of her corporate injury prompt a radical restructuring of the social body. Ozeki exploits this disjunct between social expectations and physical practicalities in order to highlight the more abstract injury and its cause. Where the slowly mounting landscape of "out of business" signs or growing unemployment lines may fail to communicate the urgency of the problem, Ozeki turns to disability to focus a seemingly diffuse and overwhelming issue.

Although Christina serves as an embodied symbol of the negative effects of Wal-Mart on local communities, the chapter's critique does not extend to a condemnation of large-scale corporate economies as such. After the accident, the Bukowskys call on the townspeople to help treat their daughter. They ask the community to contribute food to their increasingly impoverished household and to share with Christina their hopes and pleasures. Although initially immobile and silent, over the course of seven months Christina begins increasingly to respond to her visitors with slight eye and finger movements and finally with a triumphant request for "lampchops." At first, the Bukowskys' model for treatment seems emphatically democratic: the underemployed townspeople talk to Christina and, in turn, these speeches have a therapeutic effect on the speakers as well. Mrs. Bukowsky describes the process in homespun terms with ingenuous plays on language: "Here she is, in the living room. You know. The Room for Living" (133) and "It was all about compassion. . . . Compassion: 'com' (with, together, in conjunction with) plus 'passion'" (134). The climax of this folksy, inexpert wisdom emerges when Christina regains speech and limited mobility. The family's success, however, also signals a turn toward the economic models that resulted in the initial injury. The Bukowskys open a 200-bed, long-term care facility; Mr. Bukowsky is elected mayor of the newly renamed town of Hope; and the majority of the townspeople work at the Hope Renewal Center or one of the supporting businesses surrounding it. In the language of the novel, "The town of Quarry had found a new natural resource—compassion—and they were mining it and marketing it to America" (135–136). The transition from quiet bedside visits to national commodity is complete with the making of a promotional videotape, *Welcome to Our Living Room: The Bukowsky Method of Compassion and*

Renewal, and an eponymous best-selling book (136). This section of the novel offers all the emotional satisfaction of a happy ending. Christina is cured, the town emerges in prosperity, and the little guy topples the corporate giant. What Ozeki's self-consciously economic language in these descriptions signals, however, is that while the little guy has won, it is because he has beaten the giant *at his own game*. Fantasy and the narrative pleasures of a happy ending recur to form the capstones for each of the plotlines in the novel. In this chapter, pleasure at the joyful resolution obfuscates the ambiguity of transforming compassion into a highly profitable "natural resource" to be "mined" and "marketed to America." The novel, in fact, celebrates this revisionist approach to the market economy and dramatizes the potential located in a flexible model.

Where Ozeki turns broadly to the disabled body as an effective device for demonstrating the personal effects of economic practices, she uses fertility and secondary sex characteristics more specifically as a sign for the body's vulnerability. Returning briefly to Ozeki's claim that the genesis of the novel was, for her, largely metaphorical—resting in her ability to make rich figurative and cultural ties between women, meat, wives, chattel, and cattle—it should be no surprise that the connections in her work between production and reproduction are more than merely linguistic. It is certainly a reflection of medical realities that the costs of hormonal intervention in feedlots will manifest themselves predominantly in the systems of the human body themselves controlled by hormones. But Ozeki narrows her focus to these abuses of the agricultural industry in part because she understands the cultural resonance attached to human gender and sexuality. Among the host of environmental and health dangers mentioned in the novel, the scenes with the most narrative impact dwell on sexual pathologies. In the American popular imagination, masculinity is identical to unchanging sex organs, girls reach puberty according to a preordained timeline, and fertility is an assured reward of heterosexual marriage. *My Year of Meats* dramatizes personal stories of deviation from each of these norms, aiming at a set of bedrock assumptions in the American mind as a way to challenge the similarly protected notion that "cheap meat is an inalienable right" (126). Ozeki's novel offers a catalog of injuries and then traces a common line among the causes of damage, connecting them both directly and through analogy.[10] In this agenda, disability performs as symbol, an embodied warning against corporate shortcuts and a reminder of the body's vulnerability.

As she develops her portrait of the vulnerable body, Ozeki consistently turns to individuals already closest to harm: the young and those already marginalized by the cooperating systems of racism and classism. She develops a seemingly unlikely alliance between Purcell Dawes, an older, working-class, black resident of Mississippi, and Rose Dunn, the five-year-old, white heiress to a ranching fortune in Colorado. Hoping to cut corners in the household budget, Purcell and the rest of his small Southern community eat mostly cheap cuts of meat, especially undesirable chicken or pork parts that can be purchased inexpensively from processing plants directly. As the couple discovers, however, the American palate's demand for white meat has been addressed by producers in the form of hormones like DES,[11] hormones that are stored in the cheap chicken parts that are then sold to poor consumers. Purcell explains in his newly high voice, "It was some medicines they was usin' in the chickens that got into the necks that we was eatin.' . . . An' that medicine, well, if it didn't start to make me sound just like a woman!" His wife, Helen, adds, "And look just like one too, with them teeny little titties and everything!" (117). The image of Purcell with an unnaturally high voice and swollen breasts is more disturbing ideologically than it is medically. While DES poisoning represents real dangers to the body (as illustrated by Rose Dunn and Jane Takagi-Little), the unsettling effect of the scene, especially as the tension is diffused by the couple's laughter, depends more on Purcell's physical deviation from gendered norms than serious concern for his health. Ozeki's use of dialect in the quotations and her reliance on the familiar figure of the smiling Southern Black serve as a reminder that this oppression is another in a line of racial and economic exploitations. Purcell's physical vulnerability serves to condemn two systems: profit-seeking shortcuts in meat production and the oppression that has made him economically subject to the dangers of those practices.

Purcell Dawes's experience sparks a narrative strand through which the novel interrogates the transnational impact of DES poisoning. Jane credits her own infertility to the common practice of prescribing DES to women considered poor candidates for gestation, a quality she believes was likely attributed to her small, Japanese mother in predominantly white Minnesota. Despite regulation in the United States, hormonal intervention continues to be used illicitly by farmers looking to increase milk production, control breeding cycles, and decrease the growth time before slaughter. On their visit to the Dunn ranch in Colorado, the distancing screen of the camera reveals for the documentary crew what makes Rose seem so odd: she has fully developed breasts as a five-year-old. Ozeki places Rose's affliction in the context of a transnational market: "She's 'precocious.' . . . It's premature thelarche. . . . I read about cases in Puerto Rico. Precocious puberty. These little girls with estrogen poisoning. They thought it was some kind of growth stimulants in meat or milk or poultry. I think they suspected DES. . . . Some of the girls were just babies, like a year old, with almost fully developed breasts. Some of them were even boys" (270). For feminist readers, this phenomenon recalls the international protests against the forced sterilization of Puerto Rican women. By emphasizing the alliances between Rose's experience in Colorado and the exploitation of women and children in Puerto Rico, Ozeki extends her critique from the local context of the family to a systemic practice. Ozeki understands, however, that the local is often the most impactful, so she plays up the family drama of the scene to increase its sense of immediacy. Watching Rose play with her decades-older half brother, the crew learns not only that Rose is physically "precocious," but that her brother is stroking her full breast. When Jane brings Rose's mother, Bunny, evidence of both the hormone poisoning and the molestation, Bunny consents to an interview detailing Rose's symptoms: "'Oh, what the hell. It's not like it's her fault. And with a body like that, who's going to be looking at her face, right?' . . . Her tone, part defeat and part bravado, was filled with the echoes of strip joints and neon, of tinsel and tassels and the hooting of men. All the pain of her own freaky career seemed to hang in the gaps between her words" (276). In these lines Bunny's tone reveals that her previous inability to recognize the severity of Rose's condition or to intercede on her daughter's behalf stems from her internalization of the culturally ubiquitous hypersexualized female body. Bunny assimilates Rose's poisoning symptoms to a familiar narrative of sexual scrutiny. Ozeki's word choice, "freaky," in the last line calls out the tragically familiarized figure of the stripper, locating her among other somatic deviants like the bearded lady. Rose's precocious puberty demands an intersectional analysis as her visibly enlarged breasts prompt inquiry into environmental racism in Puerto Rico, her half brother's molestation, her mother's sexual exploitation, and the illegal use of hormones in agribusiness. In these scenes Ozeki relies on the capacious quality of the body as a vessel able to contain complex and loosely interrelated personal, familial, national, and international phenomena.

Rose and Purcell's changing bodies serve as an alarm for us to look backward at the dangerous practices of the feedlot and, perhaps, an even broader cultural ambivalence toward exploited people of color and sexualized young girls. While disability in these cases calls for stricter regulation of hormonal intervention in meat production, physical difference is not merely a warning against the processes that exploit somatic vulnerability. Certainly, the major narrative force in *My Year of Meats* lies in its critical examination of agribusiness and its human costs. The more latent impact of this corporate focus, however, is to demonstrate the ways in which the model of production has enacted a change in the approach to the body. Just as disability in this novel calls for a revolution in corporate practices, it also reflects a revised notion of embodiment and reproduction that takes its shape from the very economic model it looks to unseat.[12]

Ozeki's novel demonstrates the extent to which corporate animal slaughter has assumed the role of the abject in American culture, cast away from notice as bloody, violent, and distasteful. *My Year of Meats* also illustrates the ways in which the abject will return, either thrust to our attention through the novel's documentary impulses or in a more subtle cultural creep. The action of the novel is explicitly focused on the former, bringing the reader and the documentary crew ever closer to the corporate systems that are responsible for bringing food to the American table. More implicit, however, is the extent to which the logic and practices that govern the transnational food market have crept back into popular notions about embodiment. The most outspoken activists in the novel often express their position in terms that resonate more strongly with a commodity economy. Grace Boudreau, for example, expands her family through both biological children and international adoption, arguing on the question of overpopulation, "I've always thought folks should just replace themselves in the world" (69). With the language of "replacement," Grace deflates romantic or fundamentalist notions of procreation, instead articulating her relationship to her family and environment in the vocabulary of inventory. Some progressive philosophies have entered the corporate vocabulary as well, with similarly unorthodox results. Gale Dunn, manager of the Colorado feedlot, expresses the bitter pride and defensiveness of one who works and lives behind the veil of taste and decency erected by the culture at large. He brags to Jane and her crew, "You East Coast environmental types are always going on about recycling. . . . Well, that's just what we're doing here with our exotic feed program and we're real proud of it. We got recycled cardboard and newspaper. We got by-products from potato chips, breweries, liquor distilleries, sawdust, wood chips. We even got by-products from the slaughterhouse—recycling cattle right back into cattle. Instant protein. Pretty good, huh?" (258). To Jane's aghast, "But that's cannibalism,"

Gale responds disdainfully, "They ain't humans" (258). This exchange between Jane and Gale illustrates the tendency to draw largely arbitrary lines between self and other and the extent to which these lines govern one's sense of propriety. Where Jane insists on the preservation of a split between the cow and its self, calling cattle eating cattle cannibalism, Gale draws the line between human and animal, inscribing the taboo as the sole domain of the human. As Jane admits later, while some of these developments in feed technology are dangerous (for example, cattle consuming the by-products from slaughter can cause "mad cow" disease), some forms of exotic feed make economic and environmental sense. Our distaste for such "recycling" stems as much from a belief in the firm divisions between object, animal, and human as from health concerns. American culture has turned its collective attention so far away from meat production that when the practice is forced into our awareness, we reinitiate the same cycle of abjection, denying any resemblance between the cast-out process and ourselves. As *My Year of Meats* documents, however, the lines between object, animal, and human are often faint and arbitrary, especially in the charged sphere of reproduction and sexuality.

In the same way that Gale sees his responsibility for the cattle's growth in terms of technology, Jane expresses her sexuality in ways only made possible by a late-twentieth-century economy. In a job that requires constant travel, Jane develops a relationship with another individual in transit, Sloan, a touring musician. Much of their relationship develops through "libidinous conversations" over the phone and in the exchange of erotic faxes to motels across Middle America. Sloan and Jane have sex by phone and fax before they meet physically, and much of their talk involves shaping their bodies for the other through often surprising sensual language. For Jane, much of her description reflects a fluid understanding of the borders between plant and human, masculine and feminine, or human and machine: "Exotic? Well, botanically speaking, yes, but not what you'd expect. I'm more of a hybrid or a mutant. . . . I'm tall. Very tall, pole thin. . . . Brown hair. . . . No, like really short. Like boy short" (51). Jane responds to Sloan's implied fantasy of "exotic" Eurasian difference by revising exoticism as a botanical or technical trait. Later in the exchange, however, she returns to the figure of the multiracial "exotic" and its sexual and commercial potential: "You know what [the motel room is] like? A 1960s porn set: exotic Eurasian of ambiguous gender, dressed in men's underwear and combat boots, lying on her back having phone sex on the damp polyester bedspread—sort of a post-Vietnam nostalgia-porn thing. A quick little R and R fantasy in Tokyo or Seoul. I should call the boys in to film it. There must be a market for this" (52). Phone sex for Jane and Sloan transpires according to a series of cultural figures and fantasies constructed through commodities like the porn film she imagines. Jane's multiracial body calls upon an already existing sexual network between American soldiers and Asian women. While her father's role as a botanist in the army and her parents' long marriage complicates the image of a "quick little R and R fantasy in Tokyo or Seoul," Jane's mixed-race background communicates a transnational racial fantasy and this fantasy, in turn, influences her relationships. In these passages Ozeki demonstrates the extent to which sexual expression is culturally embedded. Jane understands her body in terms that reflect an American preoccupation with race, nation, gender, and technology. Finding sexual tension in the meeting place between ostensible binaries, the phone sex scenes in *My Year of Meats* both transcribe and enact a model of physicality capable of drawing in seemingly disparate categories.

For Ozeki, reproduction is no less dependent on technology than on sexuality. Both Jane and Akiko embrace a freakish approach to procreation, imagining conception outside of the heteronormative. In Jane's case, reproduction and infertility are inextricably bound up in the promises and costs of both technology and miscegenation. During her teens and twenties, Jane fantasizes about the possibilities of giving birth to a multiracial baby, a child she thinks of as "an embodied United Nations" (149). According to the white supremacist logic of the American mainstream, Jane's imagined child is freakish in its manifestation of many races in one body. She is drawn to her first husband, Emil, an African living in Japan, as the ideal mate in her "breeding project" (151). Emil, in turn, participates in the miscegenation fantasy, offering to be "the genetic engineer of [their] love" (152). The couple's vocabulary shuttles among the language of romance, agriculture, and engineering as each sphere cooperates in directing their approach to reproduction. Sex between the couple is increasingly mediated by the technology of predicting ovulation: monitoring temperatures, timing menstrual cycles, and testing secretions (153). With each month of infertility, however, and the failure of her "experiment in biotech" (152), Jane comes to see her mixed-race heritage as the source of her reproductive struggles: "I have thought of myself as mulatto (half horse, half donkey, i.e. a 'young mule'), but my mulishness went further than just stubbornness or racial metaphor. Like many hybrids, it seemed, I was destined to be nonreproductive" (152). In this context, Ozeki's turn to the linguistic roots between "mulatto" and "mule" reflects the way that breeding, as an agricultural technology, is already embedded in popular notions of race. Jane's connection between race and reproduction, a connection that is facilitated through technology, is only a heightened expression of existing models.

Throughout *My Year of Meats*, Ozeki offers paired terms with shared linguistic roots and presses the significance of these ties to their limit. The connections between "chattel" and "cattle" that inspired the novel recur in Jane's concern over her infertility, a condition she locates in the ties between "mule" and "mulatto." Despite the energy and humor of Ozeki's work, this exploration of shared linguistic roots is not simply punning or word play; language, for Ozeki, both illustrates and reinforces a cultural network of meanings that have material and often tragic consequences. "Conception" as both a mental and reproductive process takes on a similarly heightened role in the novel. Akiko and Jane both experience infertility caused, according to the logic of the novel, by patriarchal abuse. In Jane's case, she suspects DES poisoning while she was herself in utero. Akiko, on the other hand, experiences irregular cycles and infertility when she develops an eating disorder in an abusive marriage. Ozeki uses shared symptoms—the failure of conception—to illustrate the connections between patriarchal norms enacted at very different levels. Akiko's body rebels against heterosexist norms in the face of her husband's surveillance and his collusion with the androcentric medical system: "But suddenly her periods became his business, and as soon as they did, she stopped having them entirely" (47). Ozeki's characteristic optimism emerges, however, when Akiko becomes pregnant upon leaving her abusive husband. When Akiko is hospitalized after being raped by her husband, she becomes convinced that she is pregnant and that she has created the embryo independently through her imagination: "But she could feel it and knew it was a miracle of sorts, watery, lunar, and profound. She looked down the length of her body, skeletal beneath the thin hospital sheet, and that's when she saw. Not saw, as with her eyes, but conceived in her mind" (305). Rejecting the violent abuse of her husband, Akiko insists on a new model of conception, one that emphasizes the term's dual meaning as thought. While Ozeki uses the language of "miracle" to describe this fantastic climax in Akiko's storyline, the possibility of this freakish, magical conception depends on Akiko's ability to imagine an embryo distinct from its parents, a process made possible by developments in the anti-miraculous realm of biotechnology. In a poem that immediately follows Akiko's realization of her pregnancy,

Ozeki enacts the process of conception according to strikingly medical language:

> a whip-tailed armada!
> zona pellucida, penetrated, now
> a small round egg made lively, and
> propelled downstream on ciliary currents through the darkness
> cleavages and shiftings,
> thickenings,
> zygote into morula into hollowed blastula, still suspended,
> free-floating, until . . .
> *now . . .*
> it brushes up against the soft and spongy wall. Parasitic
> it sticks tight, begins to burrow.
> ruptures,
> engorgement,
> hemorrhage,
> secretion,
> until finally the pugnacious morsel of life bores into the wall's
> warm embrace. (305–306)

In these lines Akiko's pregnancy transpires both physically and poetically. The striking turn to poetry at this moment, especially after Akiko's self-described failures at writing throughout the novel, undergirds Ozeki's case for the material effects of language and culture. Ozeki develops a scene that attempts to hold together the multiple meanings of conception, pointing to both the reproduction of the physical and the emergence of ideas. Akiko's ability to conceive this embryo, in both senses of the word, depends on medical imaging technology that tracks the progress of sperm and egg as personified actors in a process independent of the will or desire of the male "donor" and female "host."[13] While Akiko attempts to reassert herself as the agent of fertilization, the internal process she imagines requires a partner not in Joichi "John" Ueno, her abusive husband, but in the biotech industry that has captured and sold these images of conception. Akiko is familiar with this *Life* magazine–style vision because of her work writing freelance articles on pregnancy for a popular Japanese women's magazine, a role that aligns Akiko more fully with the medical authorities than with her lay readers. Both the articles and Akiko's conception rely on principles drawn from medicine and production: an emphasis on a reliable process, on naming and knowledge acquisition as control, and on a predictable route between beginning and outcome. In Akiko's poem, the tripping movement between often-enjambed lines and the strikingly active language construct a model of fertilization in which active agents are propelled toward a sure outcome. The proliferation of increasingly specialized terms for each element in the process reflects the power of medical authority to quantify a previously obscured, internal event. This expertise then projects a sense of control, a sense that is borne out by Akiko's successful conception.

Although medical technology fails Jane in her attempts to conceive and sustain a pregnancy, she operates according to a similar logic that is no less dependent on the reassuring connection between cause and effect. Both the critique staged by the novel and the hope for redress that underlies its activist goals reflect a principle in which consequences are knowable and able to be controlled or reversed. While, on the one hand, *My Year of Meats* suggests a global network of competing forces that seems too complex to manage or trace, on the other, the novel returns constantly to the possibility of drawing a line between cause and injurious effect or a link between two seemingly disparate events. Ozeki writes according to a metaphorical principle that seeks to draw elements constantly together. Although the novel acknowledges the obvious distinction between women and cows, for example, much of its force emerges in the ability to find connections between cattle and wives as chattel. In the sphere of injury and disability, the novel's exposition of corporate abuse relies on the activist potential in the principle of cause and effect. Hormone intervention causes vocal changes or precocious puberty. Wal-Mart's calculated exploitation of small-town markets and their introduction of massive delivery trucks cause Christina Bukowsky's paralysis. Jane Takagi-Little is particularly caught up in a dogmatic adherence to cause and effect. Although she has little evidence that her mother, in fact, was given DES during her pregnancy, she credits the practice with causing her own infertility, an assumption that becomes more and more secure in her mind as the novel progresses. Of her father's death, Jane describes herself as "always wondering if there was some connection" between his work in post-1945 Hiroshima and his cancer (235). When she miscarries during a visit to a Colorado slaughterhouse, Jane insists that the loss is her fault, caused by exposing the fetus to medicines and hormones days before at the feedlot. When Bunny Dunn explains that the fetus was dead a full week earlier and that the miscarriage could not have been caused by her contact with the feedlot, Jane insists, "It *is* my fault!" (294), finally crediting her failed maternal instinct for the fetal demise. Jane's belief in reasons, in a predictable world with clear links between behavior and consequence, reflects both activist fantasies of redress and the rationalist premises of corporate production.

Jane's faith in a world organized according to cause and effect mirrors the linear thinking sparked by both corporate production and human reproduction. In agribusiness, the cow's body bends to the constructive forces of technology and economy. Food, health, and growth all tend toward a bottom line that looks to a future outcome, either in dairy production or in readiness for slaughter. The cow is not so much subject to technology as it is itself a technology, part of a vast farming system where the lines between production, extraction, and commodity are blurred. Human reproduction requires a similar orientation to the future, an orientation that is shared by national politics. As described in the opening of this chapter, political life in the United States is constantly shaped by a turn to the figure of the fetus and the child (Berlant, Edelman). Jane participates in the national equation of reproduction with futurity, claiming, "That's the thing about involuntary infertility—it kills your sense of a future, so you hide out in the here and now" (159). The stakes of conception, then, rise high above the context of the individual or the family, circumscribing the temporal world of the imagination and collapsing the promise of the political agenda. After her miscarriage, Jane laments, "My thwarted progeny. My poor hope" (293). In a reference to *Frankenstein* and its "hideous progeny," Ozeki articulates Jane's sadness following a technological model of freakish reproduction. *My Year of Meats* outlines a series of conceptual alliances for Jane and Akiko's pregnancies, connecting their procreation to technology, corporate production, political rhetoric, and breeding practices. The multiple valences of these symbols claim a central place for reproduction in the exploration of the social body.

Pointing out the ways in which Ozeki's literary bodies are indebted to the corporate models they also critique should not be understood as a condemnatory reading, one which charges the novel with capitalist collusion. Instead, the reemergence of the corporate in Ozeki's work confirms her emphasis on an interconnected world. Ozeki turns to disability as a flashpoint embodying the costs of corporate economy because she understands that corporeal vulnerability can communicate dangerous practices that seem diffuse and distant. This final, most central pun in Ozeki's work—between the corporate and the corporeal—argues that to discover extensive ties between the body and the economy should not be a surprise or a mark of the novel's failure. Ozeki's use of disability as a warning sign reminds readers of the human costs of an economy that seems beyond the scope of the individual. But the links between capital and the body are not merely tragic; the inextricable nature of these ties argues that conceptual and practical approaches to both the body and the economy will influence one another.

Ozeki's insistence on locating and teasing out the shared linguistic roots among terms is a manifestation of her belief in the interconnected nature of seemingly disparate elements. While the novel preserves material differences among national cultures or between animals and humans, for example, much of its energy rests in locating underlying similarities and overlapping forces. Ozeki's model, then, places more emphasis on the holistic than the hegemonic. A holistic methodology, especially when it emerges through a discussion of disability, can offer an interesting alternative to politics seeking an oppositional relationship to power. The physical and social demands of the disabled body can include pain, discomfort, inconvenience, and exploitation. Complete eradication of these elements is a largely impossible goal in treatment of the body and theories of disability typically reflect an incorporation of this difficulty. "Incorporation," however, does not have to mean celebration or acquiescence. As in homeopathic medicine, creative strategies emerge in concert with the injurious element, reintroducing it to the body on different terms. Ozeki's writing performs this holistic approach, insisting on obscure connections and allowing for the simultaneous critique and incorporation of the corporate economy she protests.

Freakish Inheritance in *Geek Love*

First released in 1932, Tod Browning's film *Freaks* offers a lasting contribution to the national fascination with physical difference.[14] Much like Katherine Dunn, Browning turns his narrative eye to the daily life behind the sideshow curtain, dramatizing the domestic space of the carnival community. The climactic scene of the film centers on a problem that similarly preoccupies *Geek Love*, namely, how does the social body of the carnival cohere around the diversity of forms among its constituency? In *Freaks*, a proposed marriage between Cleopatra, the circus's able-bodied trapeze artist, and Hans, a midget, requires the lines between normal and abnormal to be redrawn among the social body.[15] In the ensuing wedding initiation ceremony, the freak community welcomes Cleopatra as one of their own. Their memorable chant, "Gobble, Gobble / Gobble, Gobble / We accept her / We accept her / One of us / One of us," offers a performative moment of induction. While the infectious nature of its

repetition seems to imply an easy passage from norm to freak, the opening babble in the chant preserves a sense of anti-rational inscrutability.
The ceremonial trappings of the scene preserve the authority of the freak
community, announcing that any permeability of its borders must come
from within. *Geek Love* explores similar questions of authority in the
construction of the body politic, asking where freakishness is located
and how it can be reproduced as a social and physical property. Each of
the narrative strands in the novel articulates a form of freakish reproduction, outlining a competing set of methods for becoming "one of us."

Even in a novel infused with a series of hyperbolic bodies and scenes,
perhaps the most difficult-to-swallow action is the form of reproduction
that opens the book. Inspired by the agricultural process of breeding
unusual hybrid roses, Al approaches the expansion of his family with the
zeal of a mad scientist, hoping to breed his own anomalous children. The
language describing Al's "experiments" makes self-conscious reference
to the American values of innovation and scientific progress: "The re-
sourceful pair began experimenting with illicit and prescription drugs,
insecticides, and eventually radioisotopes. My mother developed a complex dependency on various drugs during this process, but she didn't
mind. Relying on Papa's ingenuity to keep her supplied, Lily seemed to
view her addiction as a minor by-product of their creative collaboration"
(7). For the Binewskis, human reproduction becomes subject to the principles of scientific experimentation. Dunn offers a parodic allegory of
technological development, dismissing the human injuries of such intervention as the cost of doing business. Like Ruth Ozeki, Katherine Dunn
makes much of the double meaning of conception, as when Olympia
says, "I was born in a trailer. No idea where it was parked at the time.
But I was conceived here" (345). This linguistic link between thought
and reproduction speaks to the overlapping registers of creative work,
including production, parenting, and authorship. Dunn yokes each of
these spheres to conventional American values, turning Al Binewski
into a freakish Ben Franklin of reproductive technology.

In contrast to Ruth Ozeki's work, in which disability serves predominantly to mark the tragic effects of agribusiness, *Geek Love* assigns
radical value to disability, celebrating the children's difference from the
denigrated world of the "norms." Lily and Al use exactly the strategies
that *My Year of Meats* protests so they can breed children who embody
the kinds of deformities that Jane Takagi-Little hopes to prevent. Despite this split in their explicit approach to disability—as either tragedy
or gift—both Ozeki and Dunn develop a model of embodiment in which

the corporeal evidence that is so effective in critiquing the dominant system also serves to illustrate the ways in which these prevailing practices and values nevertheless shape that which seems to offer an alternative. Again, as in Ozeki's work, Dunn's attempt to simultaneously critique and incorporate national values results not in a novel bogged down in ambiguity, but in a disability-inspired methodology that acknowledges creative accommodation. Dunn uses anomalous bodies to test a series of foundational American principles, demonstrating the hyperbolic and contradictory results that emerge when these ideals are embodied.

Dunn's carnival setting dramatizes the notion of "property in one's person" that lies at the heart of American individualism. Lil Binewski's claim—"What greater gift could you offer your children than an inherent ability to earn a living just by being themselves?"—emblematizes Dunn's attempts to press the logic of the body as property and citizenship as its ownership to their limits. The novel consistently approaches bodies through the language and principles of economics in an examination of the cultural and human consequences of defining citizenship in these terms. *Geek Love* recognizes that social or aesthetic value in America exists in concert with economic value. In looking at the rose garden, Al sees that "oddity was contrived to give [the hybrids] value" (9). While the worth Al observes lies undeniably in the beauty of the rose, he also understands that the notion of value itself relies on the social and, in this context, the market. Facing the possible closure of the family carnival due to economic crisis, Al Binewski initiates a plan that calls for a radical conflation of the notions of inheritance as genetic process and transferable real property. "Inheritance," as a multivalent term, provides an underlying schema that directs the characters' approach to questions of business management, reproduction, individual identity, and family relations.

Al's "innovation" in the rose garden becomes the foundation for the family's reproductive program, now figured as a masculine endeavor. Dunn presents a hyperbolic vision of masculine authority, extending Al's power to the domain of the uterus. Upon giving birth to her apparently normal youngest son, Chick, Lil laments, "I did everything, Al. . . . I did what you said, Al. . . . What happened, Al? How could this happen?" (64, ellipsis in original). The repetition of "Al" in Lil's lines reinforces his authority over conception and birth. Lil's search for reassurance and her incredulous "How could this happen?" emerge from the couple's adherence to a mechanistic model of reproduction. Much like Jane Takagi-Little's belief in a logic of cause and effect, the Binewskis' lay scientific approach to procreation promises *some* kind of effect, even if the congenital abnormalities that emerge are not exactly predictable. When Chick is born without visible birth defects, this apparent return to the physical norm gets chalked up to another minor failure in a largely successful scientific experiment. The later emergence of Chick's telekinesis ultimately reassures the family of Al's position as paterfamilias.

This masculine authority finds its seat in each of the creative spheres at the carnival, both procreative and in Al's authorlike role as the spinner of family tales and master of ceremonies. In developing this analogy between creative practices, Dunn places the novel itself in conversation with the reproductive plotlines she develops. In their reading of *Geek Love*, David Mitchell and Sharon Snyder emphasize the literary resonance of inheritance, placing Dunn in conversation with the conventions of the modernist grotesque. They argue that Dunn is aware of the literary tradition of exploiting physical difference and that the novel caricatures the long-standing metaphorical connection between disability and perversity (146). Of the freakish breeding program that serves as the novel's central conceit, Mitchell and Snyder argue, "The stated need to reproduce with an eye toward the 'freakish' and 'bizarre' locates an allegory for literature's dependency upon idiosyncratic, scandalous subject matter" (148). Dunn, then, grapples with a literary inheritance of prurient curiosity, a motive she both skewers in the novel and exploits as cultural capital in the "cult" status of her own work (Mitchell and Snyder 146–147).

Dunn's exploration of the popular interest in freaks speaks to the social body that emerges through the sideshow. One of the carnival exhibits in particular demonstrates the ideological force that binds the audience. Advertised as a "Mutant Mystery, A Museum of Nature's Innovative Art," this display collects in jars the embalmed remains of "Al's failures," Binewski children whose deformities were so severe that they died shortly after birth (52). The exhibit's advertising scheme masks Al's work in intentionally freakish breeding. The call to "mystery" and "nature's innovation" articulates biological inheritance as a social threat, connecting the audience through the anxiety of the public's susceptibility to "natural" rather than technological mutation. The exhibit also expresses a menacing ambiguity in that "mutant" denotes both sameness and deviation. A sign in the display asserts that the jarred remains are, in fact, "HUMAN . . . BORN OF NORMAL PARENTS" (54). Here, the reference to natural and naturalized reproduction reminds us that while we imagine inheritance as a predictable process, the fact that it requires the transfer of qualities and property opens up the possibility of radical deviation.[16] The carnival display challenges the cultural fantasy of security that the concept of inheritance hopes to address. Oly's name for the exhibit of her dead siblings, "The Chute," denotes the display of throwaways as a performance of abjection. The simultaneous reference to garbage and a narrow passageway in Oly's term suggests an inevitable return of the usually repressed, cast-out other. Forcing the visitors through the opening maze of the exhibit car, the Binewskis stage the unruly nature of physical difference as that which enacts a constant confrontation. According to the trope of inheritance, both physical traits and material property are often difficult to negotiate and manage; *Geek Love* emphasizes this difficulty by conceiving the anomalous body in terms of commodity. One of the family's conventional speeches exhorts, "Step up, friends. . . . A vision of the miraculous extravagance of Nature for the same simple price as an overcooked hotdog" (46). The perverse parallels between the Binewski child on exhibition and the "overcooked hotdog" begin with their shared, cheap price, but extend to the unorthodox practices of production Al enacted during Lil's pregnancy.

While Al's desire to breed freakish children would seem to suggest a break with familial continuity in favor of absolute uniqueness, the terms of his reproductive program are, in fact, thoroughly caught up in the logic of inheritance. Like the hybrid roses that serve as his model, Al sees his children as a combination of his ingenuity, his and Lil's biology, and the result of a collection of external agents that become radically enfolded into the process of reproduction. Although Al's exploitation of environmental agents is startling, his plan reflects the popular notion that children are not merely the product of parental DNA, but also embody the effects of their surroundings. *Geek Love* does not so much express an ambivalent tension between nature and nurture as it violently shuttles from one to the other, insisting at some moments on the absolute determinism of the body and at others on the freakish body as the ultimate expression of the American ideal of the "self-made man." The opposing attitudes toward biological and individual determinism in the novel reflect a series of competing national fictions, each powerfully compelling in constructing narratives of the self and the nation.[17] Al Binewski himself embodies contradictory turns toward multiple national stories; while his success emerges from his celebrated individual ingenuity, he directs his efforts toward the preservation of family and the expansion of the carnival that he has, literally, inherited. In American culture, the discursive bond formed by the collection of names inscribed on the family Bible competes with the romantic tale of striking out alone for the wilderness.

As the novel's standard-bearer for biological determinism, Oly represents her father's insistence on the ties of the family. Oly serves as the narrator for the novel's two temporal registers, split between her recollections of growing up in the carnival and the sections entitled "Notes for Now." Both of these periods reveal Oly's efforts to preserve a coherent vision of the family, either placating her egocentric siblings in the past or secretly supporting her now-senile mother in a Portland boardinghouse. The Portland narrative also centers on family as it follows Oly's quest to connect with her own daughter Miranda. Following from Al's revision of reproduction, Miranda's conception was similarly freakish. Oly asks her telekinetic brother Chick to transfer sperm from her older brother Arty to her own uterus. Forced by Arty to place the infant in a convent school, Oly nevertheless insists that the nuns preserve the visible sign of Miranda's freak heritage: a small, curled tail at the base of her spine. Writing against the influence of Miranda's "normative" upbringing, Oly relentlessly expresses her connection to her daughter in the terms of biological essentialism. She imagines that "[Miranda] might harbor some decayed hormonal recognition of my own rhythms" (12) or that "there may be some hooked structure in her cells that twists toward all that the world calls freakish" (15). She later expresses a similar sentiment as "some twist in her genetic coil" (25), mirroring Miranda's visible difference—the "twisted" tail—as the product of a similarly twisted structure in her genes. For Oly, locating connection in the sphere of biology soothes her guilt at abandoning her child. In the symbolic context of the novel, the narrator's essentialism reflects a contradictory sense of the body as both source of power and indenture. Of Oly's defining statement, "A true freak cannot be made, a true freak must be born," David Mitchell and Sharon Snyder argue,

> The sentiment establishes one of the crucial paradoxes of physical disability in the novel: while the body hosts an array of parasitic social mythologies regarding abnormality and difference, it is also bound to a notion of biology as *inborn essence*. The Binewski children prove capable of adeptly manipulating fantasies of bodily difference in order to carve out a niche in a fetishistic commodity capitalism yet such a manipulation leaves them ambivalently tethered to a physical fate. Faced with the dictates of a culture that confuses biology with destiny, Olympia embraces a dubious ideal that she

and her sibling possess the "originality" of a "true difference," one that cannot be reproduced by pretenders to the throne of uniqueness and absolute individuality. (150)

The novel originates and turns on these scenes of freakish conception in order to dramatize the stakes of an unsettled debate over the role of the body in identity formation—whether national or personal. The reproduction that occurs in the novel is relentlessly intentional, conceived in both mind and body. This reference to the role of imagination in procreation speaks to the "social mythologies" Mitchell and Snyder cite above, as the fetus and infant that emerge from these moments of conception carry more than the gift of "twisted genes"; they also carry the ideological burdens attached to physical difference. It is this cultural baggage, however, which allows for the freak's social and monetary value. In this way Dunn simultaneously critiques and incorporates the dominant narrative; despite the Binewskis' disparaging attitude toward "norms," the family also takes its success from the norm population's fantasies of anomalous bodies as sexy, scary, and exciting.

In one elaboration of Oly's essentialism, she allows a sense of irony to infect her mostly stubborn adherence to physical determinism: "What's bred in the bones, when you have bones, comes through" (17). This line shakes up the axiomatic phrase "what's bred in the bones" by making the presumed fact of having bones radically contingent. The destabilizing irony in this statement balances Oly on a conceptual tightrope as her constant emphasis on embodied identity seeks to both challenge and accept conventional narratives of biological determinism. The freak show takes the premise that an individual is identical to her body and explodes any security attached to it. Instead of a safe retreat into the anonymity of a docile, normate body (or the hope of passing as an approximation of that ideal), freaks similarly equate the body with the self, but insist on making that equation shockingly visible: born without arms or legs, but with fins, in the language of the carnival, Arturo *is* The Aqua Boy.

Where Oly articulates the novel's interest in biological essentialism, her brother Arturo extends the American tradition of the self-made man in a freakish hyperbole. Arty serves as the antihero of the novel's carnival sections, which trace his rise from performing as The Aqua Boy to becoming the leader of a nationally recognized cult called Arturism. Much of Arty's success exploits the American ideal of personal reinvention. In contrast to Olympia, who constantly explains herself as the product of her father's reproductive experiments and his extensive vocal lessons, Arty insists on a personal history of self-creation: "Do you ever think that I *deserve* what I get? . . . You know what they do to people like me? Brick walls, six-bed wards, two diapers a day and a visit from a mothball Santa at Christmas! I've got nothing. The twins are true freaks. Chick is a miracle. Me? I'm just an industrial accident! But I made it into something—me! I have to work and think to do it. And don't forget, I was the first keeper. I'm the oldest, the son, the *Binewski*" (103). Arty's bootstrap narrative takes the form of insistence because he understands and feels the pull of essentialist accounts. He locates his sisters and Chick as "true freaks" and a "miracle," then denigrates his body as an industrial accident in order to demonstrate the depths from which he has risen.

In addition to the novel's interrogation of the split between freak and norm, Dunn emphasizes the heterogeneity within difference, outlining a series of positions within the category "abnormal." As in the above quotation, where Arty distinguishes among "true freak," "miracle," and "industrial accident," these positions are not socially equivalent and carry with them differential access to power both within the freak community and without. In a later scene, Arty sneers at McGurk, an amputee, "You've got yourself a little old disability there" (169). Particularly offensive for Arty is McGurk's willingness to use prostheses in order to pass among the norms. He challenges, "You're just going along with what *they* want you to do. *They* want those things hidden away, disguised, forgotten, because they know how much power those stumps could have" (170). Again, Arty emphasizes the transformative potential of inversion, locating power in disability. While the terms of the discussion are characteristically exaggerated, Dunn reminds us that the term "disabled people" can only mark a coherent group by obscuring difference within it. The political work located in the opposition to a world constructed for the able-bodied similarly turns away from struggles within the disabled community.

In Arty's constructed ladder of disability, he begins with himself at the bottom, only to flip this hierarchy; Arty now resides at the top as one who needed to combine will and embodiment in contrast to his siblings who are simply identical to their abnormalities. Arty's speech performs the reinvention he describes. In the line "Me? I'm just an industrial accident! But I made it into something—me!" Katherine Dunn captures the mutability of identity as "me" becomes transformed over the course of two sentences from its unstable, accidental status at the beginning, to the emphatic product of intentional remaking at the end. The closing lines in this passage evoke the pull of birthright and patriarchal lineage, but Arty insists on his triumph in the context of these demands. Identifying himself as "the first keeper," Arty displaces his father's labor in producing the children and instead reinvents him as a passive fisherman, pulling the fully formed Arty from the depths of Lily's womb.

Like most elements in the novel, Dunn presses this philosophy of reinvention to its absolute limits, carrying a foundational American ideal into the realm of freakery. Dunn's vision of Arty's cult offers another answer to the question from *Freaks* that opened this section, namely, how does a norm become "one of us," or, in Arty's megalomaniacal formulation, "one of me"? The cult of Arturism takes up the novel's interest in reproducing the freakish body; the centerpiece of cult membership is a gradual remaking in Arty's image through a series of amputations beginning with individual toes and ending in lobotomies. As Katherine Hayles argues, these scenes mark the novel's serious play with the positions of subject and object: "The inert desexualized, near-mindless torsos are as close to objects as human subjects could get. . . . They also serve as marks of difference distinguishing [Arty] as the true freak, the others as inferior imitations. . . . The genetic manipulation that had initially constituted Arty in the object position is thus re-marked to bestow originary status upon him, while making those who have surgical interventions mere copies of his form, objects he has created and can control" ("Postmodern Parataxis" 415–416). As Hayles demonstrates, and as the mutating repetitions of the term "true freak" throughout the novel confirm, "originary status" is always a relative position. The cult members embrace a radical form of imitation, but the novel suggests that the forces that have driven them to membership lie in their failure to approximate the assimilative standards of the norm world. As Oly replies derisively when asked if she would make her family normal if she could, "Why would I want to change us into assembly-line items?" (282). Accordingly, Dunn captures another phenomenon in which the very standards that become the object of greatest critique—imitation, homogeneity—also serve as the form by which that critique is expressed. While Arty's amputations lack the triumphant quality of the Bukowsky family's best-selling series, *Welcome to Our Living Room*, the practice demonstrates a similar principle. As in *My Year of Meats*, where the Bukowsky family's approach to their daughter's disability remakes the entire community, Arturism reflects the ways in which changing the physical body can construct a new social body. Eventually, the cult's caravan "would string out for a hundred miles" behind the traveling carnival (185), forming a massive community cohering around the freakish body.

Dunn constructs an allegory of assimilation, lampooning the imitative tendencies that characterize the norm population, but conceding that, nevertheless, this trend toward homogeneity is central to the creation of the social body.

* * *

Perhaps the foregoing readings will be understood as yet another frustrating example of critical fence-sitting, of crying "ambiguity!" in the search for literary complexity. After all, if there is one novel that seems straightforward in its message, it is *My Year of Meats*, where the good girls get rewarded with babies and film distribution deals and the bad guys get punished. Ozeki's desire to tie up her plotlines with a reader-friendly bow reflects her political optimism and the motivating force that encourages her audience to enact the corporate whistle-blowing the novel dramatizes. The central place of disability in both of these novels, however, suggests a new resonance to ambiguity, as the notion of a happy ending for characters with chronic infertility, congenital deformity, paralysis, or exposure to carcinogens must be rewritten against conventional models. The discovery of ambiguity in these novels does not signal the failure of their critique, but instead, a nuanced reading of the world that accounts for the incorporation of both difficulty and possibility, a methodology inspired by the novels' attention to disability. While Ruth Ozeki centers her novel on disability as a tragic effect of agribusiness, physical difference in Katherine Dunn's imagination is highly valued, both as a commodity and as a way of being. Both authors demonstrate the ways in which the objects of their critique have, in fact, reemerged in the very figures that serve as the most effective evidence in their arguments against those norms.

In *My Year of Meats*, despite a compelling case outlining various forms of disability as the effect of corporate exploitation and environmental intervention, the novel also reveals the ways in which disability and its necessary accommodations use the practices and values of global capital as a model. Rather than condemning the anomalous body as complicit in the corporate economy, the diversity of approaches demanded by the vulnerable body makes visible a more holistic account of life in which the divisions between animal, object, human, and land are routinely crossed and redrawn. Much of *My Year of Meats* seems to focus solely on the dangers of intervening in corporeal boundaries and the problems that emerge when humans manipulate animal hormones or doctors attempt to change the course of pregnancy. There is a latent strand in the novel, however, that acknowledges how incoherent these bodies are already and how sometimes objectionable interventionist and corporate strategies have reshaped the nation's approach to embodied questions like infertility and reproduction. While Ozeki's work can certainly be read as alarmist, protest fiction, these elements in her writing do not entirely obscure the pleasures that emerge from practices like big-box commerce or sex by fax machine. According to the holistic logic that I find in Ozeki's work, the fact that her characters find pleasure in the objects of their critique is not a failure of their will to resist the dominant order, but, in fact, suggests the possibilities of a homeopathic approach. The transnational economic and cultural structures Ozeki critiques are both immediately embodied and diffuse; in a worldview where we must take seriously the claim that corporate agricultural practices in Colorado will affect fertility in Japan, then we must also allow that these same practices and values will emerge in unexpected ways to change even deep-rooted concepts like reproduction or national belonging. In incorporating criticized elements, Ozeki reflects a homeopathic methodology, one which, like disability theory more broadly, acknowledges the impossibility of removing injurious forces at work upon the body and suggests that an attentive reconfiguration of these elements may produce new possibilities.

In a much rounder portrait of disability, Katherine Dunn injects an often-missing sense of realism and psychological depth into the carnivalesque. Despite its wild and fantastic elements, *Geek Love* takes the body seriously, especially as a site for exploring the most foundational ideals of American citizenship. The novel highlights a series of competing national myths and presses these narratives to their embodied and conceptual limits. In the case of Arturism, for example, the cult exposes the alienating fiction of normalcy but then proposes a radical form of embodied imitation as the antidote. As an analog for the nation, Dunn's carnival dramatizes an American courtship with physical difference, suggesting embodiment as the force that literally and conceptually makes the body politic coherent. Both Dunn and Ozeki ultimately offer an inclusive gesture, inviting readers behind the sideshow curtain or alongside Akiko and Jane on their national circuits. As the horrific ending to Tod Browning's *Freaks* suggests, however, the process of incorporation into the social body that will open the possibility of becoming "one of us" involves not only celebration but also violence, a process that Dunn and Ozeki model as disability-inspired creative accommodation.

5 / Some Assembly Required: The Disability Politics of *Infinite Jest*

Weighing in at over two pounds, David Foster Wallace's *Infinite Jest* cautions by its sheer heft that reading the novel will be an embodied experience. In finding a place to balance its weight or endlessly flipping back to the endnotes, reading the book becomes a curiously physical task. These excessive qualities call attention to the reader's body consuming the text, but the novel also announces the extraordinary bodies between its covers. At a distended 1,079 pages, the most obvious anomalous body is perhaps the text itself. Wallace constructs this unconventional textual body from a series of nonlinear episodes, shifting points of view, and nearly one hundred pages of explanatory endnotes. His experimentation with freakish textual forms finds expression in the bodies of the characters as well. Wallace populates his novel with wheelchair assassins, gargantuan infants, the "Union of the Hideously and Improbably Deformed," and a host of characters with congenital malformations. Rather than read these extraordinary elements as merely the offshoot of creative innovation, I argue that unusual physical bodies provide a model for reading the textual body and vice versa.

This homology of physical and textual forms finds its crystallizing expression in Wallace's image of the characteristic asymmetry of athletic bodies. Slipping into the boys' locker room at the Enfield Tennis Academy, Wallace describes how these teens have "the classic look of bodies hastily assembled from other bodies' parts, especially when you throw in the heavily muscled legs and usually shallow chests and the two arms of different sizes" (100). In imagining the body as a lopsided collection of parts, this scene offers the physical analog to Wallace's irregular, episodic narrative. The phrase "hastily assembled" evokes the sense of construction, representing both writing and embodiment as processes. In contrast to dominant conceptions of the body as natural and ahistorical, this image of corporeal assembly insists upon heterogeneity and social formation. Bodily assemblage runs counter to the cultural fantasy of the "able-bodied" as uniform and whole. In the proliferation of discourse that seeks to make sense of the in-coherent body, even exceptional athletes, who seem antithetical to traditional notions of disability, can fall under the more capacious reaches of disability as freakish anomaly.

The students at the Tennis Academy testify to embodiment as a matter of process and training. Although they are super-abled in athletic ability, the players' relentless conditioning results in hypertrophy, joint disorders, exaggerated appetites, and exhaustion. They blur the line between abled, disabled, and super-abled, reminding us that these divisions are flexible and not naturally determined. When the lines between these categories are socially meaningful, however, disability, as an analytical model, occupies the publicly marked position among the three. The typical collapse among these terms lies in the transformation of physical excellence into the invisible position of norm. Disability, by contrast, carries the ideological burden of the extraordinary to stand constantly in opposition to, literally, unremarkable models. As an embodied challenge to idealized norms, like health, beauty, and a natural body, disability both calls for a revision of conventional narratives and finds a new conceptual model in its own form. Even as "assembly" refers to the literal figure of disability and its visual suggestion of collected parts, it also contains a theoretical intervention as the rejection of unified ideals.

Wallace's description of the athletic body as an assemblage of visually discrete parts recalls centuries-old visions of the state as a somatic collection of citizens: the literal form of the body politic.[1] The second sense of the term "assembly" as a gathering or meeting draws the social body into necessary conversation with physical and textual bodies. Appropriately, the social bodies in Infinite Jest are no less extraordinary than the characters or the form of the novel itself. The Enfield Tennis Academy, the Boston chapter of Alcoholics Anonymous, and the hemispheric interactions of Canada, Mexico, and the United States all demonstrate the effects of communities built explicitly on the principle of collectivity. In place of the reigning cult of American individualism, disability proposes a model of ethical assemblage, a set of practices that acknowledges the interdependent nature of the body politic. Where chapter 1 explores the logic of liberal individualism in its paradoxical split between the representative and the extraordinary, my reading of Wallace centers on a disability-inspired alternative to individualism in the multiple forms of corporeal, textual, and political assemblage. Assemblage, as a conceptual frame, highlights both construction and a sense of deferred whole, challenging portraits of the body as natural or political ideology as inevitable.

Finally, in its textual assembly, *Infinite Jest* subverts traditional approaches and demands new reading practices. In its ballooning cast of characters, sentences that can span a full page, and elevated, often highly specialized vocabulary, the novel tests its readers' expectations of standard prose. The source model for these newly required reading practices can be found once again in the example set by the novel's anomalous bodies. Disability calls out the impossibility of conventional and naturalized categories. In the face of a poor fit between disability and the built environment, the extraordinary body requires innovation and creative redefinitions. As a heuristic model, disability valorizes rethinking fixed norms and offers its own strategies as a new paradigm for political and textual engagement.

My notion of bodily assemblage as a heuristic category requires a perhaps discomforting unmooring of disability from its strictly material effects. Theorists of disability have initiated this work in moving from a medical model of disability—in which difference is pathologized according to scientific truths of normalcy—to a social model of disability, which acknowledges the role of ideology in the construction of embodied identities. The state itself, in its definition of disability for the purposes of the 1990 Americans with Disabilities Act, turns to the intersecting realms of the body, the text, and the social sphere to temper the conflicting legal need for fixed categories with the heterogeneous causes and experiences of disability. As I outline in detail in my introduction, this definition serves as a conceptual springboard for the model of reading these interdependent spheres that I have followed throughout this book. In this chapter I press the stakes of this homology through a close reading of a single text, finding in these interlocking spheres of embodiment a new way of understanding Wallace's sprawling narrative. As described above, the ADA offers three components to its definition, with membership in any part constituting legal disability: "The term 'disability' means, with respect to an individual: A) a physical or mental impairment that substantially limits one or more life activities of such individual; B) a record of such an impairment; or C) being regarding as having such an impairment." In this definition, "impairment" (the body), "record" (the text), and "regard" (the social) are held in tension as an attempt to proscribe the open nature of disability. As located in even the height of its juridical expression, I argue that disability operates simultaneously through these three realms and that by understanding Wallace's construction of embodiment through assemblage, his textual excesses and vision of the social body emerge in sharper focus.

Despite its productive aspects, however, assemblage is not a utopian solution. The danger and the virtue in amassing a collection of parts lie in the tendency toward jagged seams and unequal distribution. While these mismatched qualities pose important challenges to the smooth tyranny of conventional assumptions, disability also conveys literal and figurative costs. This chapter discovers assembly in the physical, social, and textual bodies of Wallace's novel, arguing for the perils and possibilities of this conceptual and material intervention.

The Billboard Who Walks

As Tom LeClair's article on the novel suggests, Wallace fills his text with prodigies in several senses of the word.[2] The young people demonstrate precocious talents in tennis, math, language, or punting. Their bodies, however, recall earlier uses of "prodigy" as something monstrous and extraordinary. For Orin Incandenza, a professional punter with the NFL, his excessively muscled kicking leg becomes deified as The Leg, simultaneously part of and distinct from his body. Like the tennis players' uneven arms, The Leg recalls another archaic definition of prodigy as portent or sign. These athletes offer a visual representation of the broader phenomenon of corporeal assemblage. Even as their extraordinary abilities seem to appeal to ideals of health and wholeness, their prodigious bodies signify the seams in that ideal. These mismatched limbs point to the conditioning required to build these bodies and the ever-present threat of injury or loss of muscle. The extraordinary athletic body is not a permanent form, but an evanescent state, perpetually subject to change and possible only through constant work. The ideological power of physical ideals, however, is that popular narratives obscure this fleeting quality. Wallace's choice of images in his description of another talented tennis player reveals the aura of eternity attached to physical ability and attractiveness:

> Stice is one of those athletes whose body you know is an unearned
> divine gift because its conjunction with his face is so incongruous.
> He resembles a poorly spliced photo, some superhuman cardboard
> persona with a hole for your human face. A beautiful sports body,
> lithe and tapered and sleekly muscled, smooth—like a Polycleitos
> body, or Hermes or Theseus before his trials—on whose graceful
> neck sits the face of a ravaged Winston Churchill, broad and slab-
> featured, swart, fleshy, large-pored, with a mottled forehead under
> the crew cut's V-shaped hairline, and eye-pouches, and jowls that
> hang and whenever he moves suddenly or lithely make a sort of
> meaty staccato sound like a wet dog shaking itself dry. (637)

The aural contrast between "smooth" and "swart" could sum up the
distinctions that Wallace creates in this paragraph. Stice is yet another
example of the assembled body, in this case pieced together as a "poorly
spliced photo." As in this figure of photographic engineering, the recurring images of art—the oft-photographed cardboard cutout or the reference to the sculptor Polycleitos—announce the mediating role of representation in reading the body. Even as the passage dwells on incongruity,
the metaphors capturing the athletic body reinscribe myths of corporeal
unity. From the neck down, Stice is neat, smooth, and homogenous. He
is either a divine gift or the image of a god. While somewhat deflating in
comparison to Hermes, the superhuman cardboard persona is perhaps
the most apt image as it captures a fixed, unchanging ideal. By contrast,
the language associated with unattractiveness is itself ugly and messy:
"ravaged," "swart," and "mottled." Where his sculpted body is silent and
perfect, Stice's jowls flap around and produce a meaty, doglike smack.
This passage offers a complex model of assemblage; even as it names the
incongruity and disconnect between physical elements, the appeals to
divinity and classical models attempt to reinstate a fixed somatic ideal.

Disability theorist Lennard Davis offers an important contribution to
this discussion of physical ideals. In his 1995 text *Enforcing Normalcy*,
Davis offers an account of the emergence of the term "normal" and its
rise to dominance in shaping how physical and social bodies are conceived and managed. In historicizing the concept of the norm, Davis
creates a lineage beginning with the "ideal" and argues that the striking difference between the two models is that the ideal body was never
supposed to be attainable by the human body. Instead, in another process of assemblage, "the human body as visualized in art or imagination
must be composed from the ideal parts of living models. These models

individually can never embody the ideal since an ideal, by definition, can never be found in the world" (25). By contrast, concepts like "norm" or "average" establish an imaginary body and insist that this body is not only attainable, but already widely attained. As the norm becomes an imperative, however, the concept turns back paradoxically to the terms of the ideal as exceptional health and beauty come to occupy the position of the norm. These qualities are still exceptional among the population, but they differ from historical concepts of the ideal in that the extraordinary is now represented as ordinary.

As Davis argues, the rise of statistics in the nineteenth century and its accompanying concept of the bell curve or "normal curve" helped to entrench the hegemony of normalcy. No longer an unattainable product of the mind, these idealized bodies found their justification in scientific authority. Davis notes that many of the early statisticians were also eugenicists, a telling coincidence that suggests the political and human consequences of the drive to institutionalize norms.[3] Sir Francis Galton, often called the father of both fingerprinting and eugenics, devised a contraption to demonstrate the irrefutable law of averages; as balls dropped at random through a series of pegs and accumulated according to a bell curve distribution, Galton argued that normality was, in fact, a law of nature.[4] Much of the disciplinary strength of the concept of the norm stems from its formation as a natural, ahistorical property. Rosemarie Garland-Thomson joins Davis in querying the neutrality of social ideals, offering the neologism "normate" to designate the prototypical body that is pandemic in discourse, but so rarely occurs among individuals.

The normal body is no less imaginary than the model of the ideal that preceded it, but its ideological authority stems from the obfuscation of its constructed nature. Like the image of Stice's body as a "superhero cardboard persona," the power of the norm depends on its static nature and the easy dream of inhabitability represented by the cutout for the face. The national fantasy of the physical ideal takes the form of the carnival mainstay, imagining a narrow series of cutouts for a heterogeneous population to occupy. As the prodigies of the Enfield Tennis Academy demonstrate, however, living in these idealized forms is harder than advertised. The chronic pain and joint disorders that result from constant physical training expose the costs and extensive support apparatus that supplement an athlete's "raw talent." Disability's lagging institutional recognition in civil rights and academic struggles has a complex history, but one of the major reasons for its location in the *après-garde* is because the discourse of normalcy is so entrenched that distinctions like disabled or able-bodied seem simple, another fact of nature. Corporeal assembly challenges the myth of the discrete, asocial body, insisting on its formation as a complex process that impacts a heterogeneous spectrum of shapes and abilities.

Wallace signals the multiple meanings at the heart of corporeal assemblage in describing Mario Incandenza, the most strikingly disabled figure in the novel, as living with a collection of "character-building physical challenges" (313). As a textual practice, assembly discovers a pun in the suggestive phrase "character-building." The expression most directly refers to a telethon-inspired tradition of imagining integrity as the positive effect of overcoming obstacles. At another level, "character building" describes an author's turn to disability as the raw material from which to construct a character. In their 2000 volume of the same name, David Mitchell and Sharon Snyder name this dependence on physical anomaly as a mark of character "narrative prosthesis." Citing classic examples including Richard III and Captain Ahab, Snyder and Mitchell argue, "This defining corporeal unruliness consistently produces characters who are indentured to their biological programming in the most essentializing manner" (50). *Narrative Prosthesis* describes characterization as a form of textual biological determinism. In his description of Mario Incandenza's body, Wallace seems tongue-in-cheek in his reference to "character-building physical challenges," but this phrase also resonates with the deployment of disability as the constitutive force of literary character. Wallace literally builds Mario in the novel through highly technical descriptions of arachnid birth, bradypedestrianism, mucronate and nonprehensile fingers, and homodontism. And yet, despite the proliferation of medicalized terms, we are left with the sense that Mario as a subject exists in excess of this language that yearns for facts and specificity. This characterization emphasizes the break in Snyder and Mitchell's strict determinism, and fulfills their model of disability as narrative supplement in its most productive sense: while disability clearly directs Mario's fictional life, as a prosthetic function, it marks its own incompleteness as a full account of his character. Given the complexity of Mario's artistry and interpersonal relationships, the descriptive assemblage of congenital defects may pretend to build Mario fully as a character, but the attempt fails.

The fantasy of constructing a character through an elaborate naming of symptoms and conditions reflects the dominant position of the medical model as the most common means of approach to disabled people. At times, *Infinite Jest* reads like a lengthy medical chart, as though a collection of increasingly specific diagnoses will be able to account for a character completely. In a striking example of this proliferation of medical language, listeners to Joelle van Dyne's radio program would require a specialized dictionary to understand the terms of a pamphlet for the Union of the Hideously and Improbably Deformed: "Come one, come all. . . . The hydrocephalic. The tabescent and chachetic and anorexic. . . . The dermally wine-stained or carbuncular or steatocryptotic or God forbid all three. Marin-Amat syndrome, you say? Come on down" (187). In this short excerpt we can hear how Wallace juxtaposes the exhortations of a carnival barker with a list of physical conditions to merge the two most profound systems for the discipline of anomalous bodies: the sideshow and the medical. These methods of managing difference lead us back to the constructed nature of bodily identity. Following the model of assemblage, the discourses of medicine, entertainment, religion, race, gender, and sexuality operate in a network to construct how we understand bodies. *Infinite Jest* reflects a mid-twentieth-century shift away from the ethnographic and visually exploitive venue of the freak show toward a program of diagnosis and cure. Medicine works both materially and ideologically, acting as the central agent in the physical management of disability as well as reinforcing the logic of abnormality through which disabled people are made socially legible. Like the mismatched parts of the tennis prodigies, however, these disciplinary regimes always move toward a deferred whole, inscribing the failure of these systems in the management of heterogeneous populations.

Perhaps the most profound effect of the medical model of disability lies in the exaggerated value of "fixing." Once again appealing to an inflexible and imaginary norm, contemporary medicine locates individuals along a spectrum of health and illness centered on a theoretical average.[5] In contrast to this perfect norm, the promise of medicine lies in making the lived body perfect*able*. This principle serves as the foundation for the mutually reliant disciplinary regimes of medicine and consumption. Just as developments in anatomy, germ theory, and genetics have remade the modern body, so have the expanding spheres of consumption brought an entirely new kind of attention to the hygienic and aesthetic needs of that body. In *Infinite Jest*, perhaps the most striking example of this new vision of the body comes in the phenomenal rise in sales for NoCoat tongue scrapers. Television advertisements showing the "exaggerated hideousness of the near-geologic layer of gray-white material coating the tongue" produce a "nation obsessed with the state of its" mouth (413–414). According to Wallace's pithy formulation, "It did what all ads are supposed to do:

create an anxiety relievable by purchase" (414). As Wallace suggests, the best products are the ones that construct their own problem, forcing buyers to reconceive of their bodies. Much of the drive toward the normal body is wrapped up in these false corporate promises, in both senses of the term. The myth of wholeness becomes the animating goal for both medical and consumerist models of fixing. While the concept of corporeal assemblage insists on the impossibility of achieving a unified, ideal norm, it also dovetails dangerously with the logic of fixing. Commercial enterprise and its reliance on the notion of lack also depend on the accompanying understanding of the lived body as potentially changeable. This acknowledgment of variety, however, does not topple idealized norms from their privileged position, but instead suggests that with a tongue scraper or liposuction or the right aspirin, that ideal can be reached.

In addition to the visual piecemeal of limb size and shape, corporate sponsorship interrupts any possible corporeal autonomy for the most talented Enfield Tennis Academy students. Racquets, which act as a necessary prosthesis in tennis playing, advertise a second master of the body: the equipment supplier. The second mark of success for a player is to turn over her feet or torso as advertising space through a commercial endorsement deal. Wallace's narration of this phenomenon is telling: "Most of the higher-ranked ETA students are free to sign on with different companies for no fees but free gear. Coyle is Prince and Reebok, as is Trevor Axford. John Wayne is Dunlop and Adidas" (266). This simple, declarative phrasing enacts the move from the students' individual identities to their sponsors'—Coyle *is* Reebok. The players' clothing brands their limbs as sponsored by Dunlop or Wilson, but the ideal is a return to somatic wholeness with outfits that demonstrate total corporate sponsorship: Nike from sweatband to socks. This promise of corporate completion shares with medicine and consumerism a turn to the logic of somatic assembly. While the lived body will never quite reach completion, the promise of "fixing" sustains the supremacy of a unified physical ideal. Even as these discourses construct the body as a complex of mutable parts, they undo the progressive work found in the notion of assemblage, paradoxically reifying the imaginary body as an idealized norm, seductive in its apparent attainability.

Individualism and Interdependence

The surprising link between a tennis player's mismatched, corporate-sponsored limbs and Mario Incandenza's striking physical difference is that each body announces the regulatory system that manages it. The disciplinary regimes of sports entertainment, consumerism, and medicine structure the relationship between these bodies and the world around them. As such, the physical body is an emphatically political body, working within the ideological categories that seem to both construct and limit subjectivity. In the United States, the tradition of liberal individualism serves as one of the most enduring of these categories. The properly individual body is first independent, governed by the mind, just as the social body is governed by its heads of state. The paradox of individualism emerges, however, when considered alongside democracy's foundational principle of equality. This equality is centered on the notion of a standardized body among citizens, a concept encapsulated by the Declaration of Independence's proclamation that "all men are created equal."[6] The contradiction in the promise of simultaneous equality and individuality reaches its height with disability. As Rosemarie Garland-Thomson argues, "The disabled figure speaks to this tension between uniqueness and uniformity. On the one hand, the disabled figure is a sign for the body that refuses to be governed and cannot carry out the will to self-determination. On the other hand, the extraordinary body is nonconformity incarnate" (*Extraordinary Bodies* 43–44). By marking heterogeneity where democracy wants a level playing field and taking the desire for uniqueness into the realm of freakery, disabled bodies call for a new ideal of citizenship. Instead of valorizing individualism, disability offers a model of interdependence. Accommodation and support, which are so visible and contentious in the political context of disability, are only signs of failure according to an individualist doctrine. Interdependence, by contrast, acknowledges that accommodations, even when not conceived as such—like lights for the sighted and chairs for the ambulatory—are always necessary. A democratic ideal of mutual reliance may not serve as the utopian foundation for a new society, but it can counter the paradoxical and exclusive tenets of liberal individualism.

As a model for political participation, interdependence overlaps with a disability-inspired rejection of discrete and autonomous bodies. The ethical model of interdependence offers a political analog to the conceptual model of corporeal assemblage. Exemplified by the incongruous image of two mismatched arms on a single athlete, dominant cultural categories—including beauty, health, and strength—work together in a piecemeal fashion to construct bodies that cannot reach naturalized norms. While I argue that it is conceptually productive to consider these bodies as an assembled collection of parts never achieving an imaginary whole, I must also acknowledge that the term carries with it a perhaps inevitable simplification. At one level, assemblage seems to imply that these social categories and their discursive foundations operate along distinct, but intersecting, lines.[7] If, however, the disabled body serves as a theoretical reminder of anything, it offers a figure of complexity and contingency; democratic assembly is no less difficult or complex. Any attempt to account for the dense correspondences among disciplinary regimes and their material subjects begins to look like Borges's unforgettable image of the map of an Empire that is itself the size of the Empire.[8] As the political implications of this representational endeavor reflect, the work of description is itself bound up in the limits of knowledge and the regulatory effects of language. Assemblage, then, does not offer a clear diagram for building bodies and nations, but instead exposes and reorients traditional approaches. Rather than emphasizing the apparent divisions between parts—and in the process paradoxically reinstating concepts of individualism and corporeal unity—I focus on assembly as it highlights the process of bringing together these seemingly independent elements, allowing for new and productive readings of mutual reliance. Assembly, and the construction it denotes, challenges staid concepts of corporeal and political norms even if it cannot offer an accurate map of the process by which physical and social bodies are constituted.

In addition to these conceptual limitations, interdependence loses some of its utopian luster in the international context of *Infinite Jest*. By issuing a temporary split between Wallace's geopolitical and local spheres, and then placing them side-by-side for comparison, the perils and possibilities of interdependence begin to emerge. In Wallace's hyperbolic vision of future international relations, Interdependence is the euphemism for American policies exploiting the rest of the continent. As a radical solution to rising levels of pollution in the United States, President Johnny Gentle forces Canada to annex pieces of New England, now the location of a massive, uninhabitable toxic waste dump. Gentle literally commits these crimes in the name of Interdependence, perverting the concept of an international community. At the local level, however, the Enfield Tennis Academy and Alcoholics Anonymous discover positive effects in the practices of mutual reliance and support. In the tennis world, Enfield's champion doubles team embodies the ideal of successful interdependence: "E.T.A.'s infamous Vaught twins, Caryn and Sharyn Vaught, seventeen, O.N.A.N.'s top-ranked junior women's doubles team, unbeaten in three years, an unbeatable duo, uncanny in their cooperation on the court, moving as One at all times, playing not just as if but in fact because they shared a brain, or at least the psychomotor lobes of one, the twins Siamese, fused at the left and right temple, . . . using her/their four legs to cover chilling amounts of the court" (217–218). The figure of conjoined twins so deeply undermines norms that even linguistic conventions like pronoun assignments—"her/their"—seem insufficient to account for their existence. On the court the women move "as One," but the simile in this case reasserts an important distance between the twins and their assignation as a single individual. In fact, the women are banned from singles play and achieve success only to the extent that they cooperate as a team. The Vaught twins may represent an unattainable height in interdependence, but their striking form evokes the success that can emerge from inverting dominant norms.

For Wallace's tennis prodigies and addicts living in Boston, individualism's celebration of personal freedom and self-determination contains their downfall. Wallace most strikingly undermines the concept of will through his portrayal of the addict's mind and cravings. For members of Alcoholics Anonymous such as Gene M. and Don Gately, addiction is a corruption of the will called the Spider, whose web is so entangled with desire and rational thought that the only escape is to admit powerlessness and, in taking the third step, "turn our will and our lives over" to a higher power. As a model of ethical assembly, AA can be described as a network of empathic listeners and storytellers that defeats the ensnaring web of the Spider.

In the parallel tennis community, ETA's pedagogy rests largely on subordinating the individualism implied by the singles game. The academy's coaches describe this process as "self-transcendence through pain" (660) or revising the game so that the opponent becomes "the partner in the dance . . . [,] the occasion for meeting the self" (84). Even where training allows for inward direction, this turn to the self must proceed through the interdependent practices of the academy and its students. In order for the players to approach success, they must rely on a thoroughly constructed set of maxims, exercises, support staff, and even a sweat-licking guru. Rejecting the notion of super-ability as natural, the students and teachers participate in a vast system of accommodations. Prorector Aubrey deLint describes the stakes of this training: "If they can get inculcated right they'll never be slaves to the statue, they'll never blow their brains out after winning an event when they win, or dive out of a third-story window when they start to stop getting poked at or profiled" (661). This "inculcation" requires movement toward the self in which the lines of the court, the opponent, and the memory of the strokes must be contained in the player's body. The tragedies deLint describes happen to unaffiliated players like Eric Clipperton, whose ego-driven playing can be predicted by the IND for "Independent" next to his name. Wallace includes the Clipperton legend and the similar Nestle Quik suicide-homicide incident to demonstrate the fatal ends of an independent star.

Even at the communal level, however, interdependence can be read as a risky form of proto-fascism. Although distinct from the paradoxical and exclusionary tenets of U.S. liberal individualism, Gerhardt Schtitt's doctrine of athletic development references the sinister state ends of self-subordination. In his program, "jr. athletics [is] basically just training for citizenship . . . learning to sacrifice the hot narrow imperatives of the Self—the needs, the desires, the fears, and the multiform cravings of the individual appetitive will—to the larger imperatives of a team (OK, the State) and a set of delimiting rules (OK, the law)" (81). In the context of Alcoholics Anonymous, a similar wariness of individual appetites and rational thinking opens the program to accusations of being a cult. Wallace includes its members' skepticism toward its clichés, capital letter Slogans, and loose monotheism, but the shocking fact of the text is that it all works. As the most successful technology of anti-addiction in the novel, AA is an imperfect and anti-rational but ultimately salvific program of interdependence.

While these proto-fascist and cultish elements suggest a slippage between the communal and the geopolitical, Wallace's ethics of interdependence rely on a wedge between these two spheres. In Wallace's North America, Interdependence-with-a-capital-I is the obvious lie of American exploitation. As the acronym ONAN suggests, any mutually beneficial union between nations is selfishly interrupted by the American partner. This masculinist form of international relations is led by Johnny Gentle, former Las Vegas lounge singer turned president. He is perhaps the embodied conflation of the terms of Mary Esther Thode's ETA course: The Personal Is the Political Is the Psychopathological (307). Gentle broadcasts his personal fear of germs and uncleanliness on his body by wearing surgical microfiltration masks and rubber gloves and showing raw skin from multiple daily showers. He then translates these phobias to the political sphere in promising citizens an America "you'll be able to eat right off" (398). At this level Interdependence is in fact the inversion of self-transcendence, because one man's will has been made grotesquely manifest. In his political vision Wallace remains interested in the corruption of the self by neuroses and addictions but here demonstrates the potential failures of an ethics of interdependence when mixed with global capitalism, commercialism, and national interests. The geopolitical context of *Infinite Jest* is the specter lurking above the possible solutions offered by the mutually dependent programs of the tennis academy or Alcoholics Anonymous.

Diagnosis and Cure

The disabled body prompts a nearly constant inquiry into the cause of impairment and its possible cure. Onlookers wonder, how did it happen? What's the extent of the injury? Is there any treatment? In provoking this curiosity, disability seems to point simultaneously backward and forward: back to the original site of injury, congenital condition, or illness and toward the possibility of cure or fixing. As the embodiment of this turn to past and future, disability offers an analog for the historicist logic that so often structures citizenship in the United States. The origin tale and the campaign promise surface again and again as the most familiar narratives of political elections. Icons like George Washington's cherry tree or Benjamin Franklin's kite decorate elementary school classrooms, locating the mythology of the nation in the personal experiences of its "founding fathers." The 2008 election cycle found Democrats staging a game of one-upmanship in finding the most humble origin story. From John Edwards the son of a mill worker to Barack Obama's goat-herding father, these narratives conform to the logic of progress epitomized by the American dream. The structural similarities between diagnosis and origin tale, prognosis and campaign promise are no coincidence, but demonstrate the shared logic of cause and effect that shapes our relation to both disability and politics.

In the world of *Infinite Jest*, teleological narratives are bound up inextricably in political agendas. The complex political landscape of the novel unfolds through Mario Incandenza's puppet show, a film shown at the tennis academy during its annual Interdependence Day celebration. Given the impulse to diagnosis sparked by his deformed body, it is perhaps not surprising that Mario Incandenza offers the most traditionally historical narrative of the novel. His film follows a linear path, describes events in a chain of causality, and deals with influential political figures. The mediating layer of Mario's work allows Wallace to create an artifact of the narrative convention of cause and effect that he deconstructs throughout the rest of the novel. Mario's film answers the question the novel's extraordinary setting raises, namely, how do we end up here?

The answer to that question begins and ends with President Johnny

Gentle, the germaphobic architect of Interdependence. Appropriately, Mario's film starts with a quotation from Gentle's second inaugural and a "full-facial still photo of a truly unmistakable personage" (381). This opening image confirms the slip between the body politic and the physical body, as it locates the nation in the form of its leader.[9] The quotation, in turn, heralds the temporal preoccupation that structures Gentle's rhetoric: "Let the call go forth . . . that the past has been torched by a new and millennial generation of Americans" (381). This call for a new era in national life rehearses familiar progressive narratives and campaign promises. While Gentle's answers—including ceding portions of New England to Canada as a massive waste dump—are shocking, his appeal to a halcyon past and hopeful future conforms to the teleological preoccupation of American citizenship. Staging his speech before a smiling Lincoln Memorial, Gentle promises to "rid the American psychosphere of the unpleasant debris of a throw-away past, to restore the majestic ambers and purple fruits of [American] culture" (382–383). Gentle uses historical conventions to invoke two static images of the past: first, a mythic origin to be restored and, second, a recent America in decline. He exploits the catchwords of patriotic songs and the benevolent image of Abraham Lincoln—the embodiment of liberation—to trade on past glories. For the portrait of decline, he constructs a reified version of history to be cast away as trash. Gentle makes his case to the public by imagining the nation as an embodied individual, a retired World policeman getting his uniform deep-cleaned and relaxing into "quality domestic time raking its lawn and cleaning behind its refrigerator" (383). Again, these personal metaphors ground the abstract political realm in the reassuring world of tangible familiarity. These calls to the familiar also find their place in Gentle's figure, as vestiges of his celebrity lounge-singer days emerge in his political persona—surely he must be the first U.S. president to swing his microphone around by its cord at an inauguration (382). Mario's opening photo of Gentle serves as a palimpsest, holding together each phase of the exceptional character: "This is the projected face of Johnny Gentle, Famous Crooner. This is Johnny Gentle, né Joyner, lounge singer turned teenybopper throb turned B-movie mainstay" turned fringe third-party candidate turned president turned radical architect of a reconfigured North America (381). Each new professional iteration contains the ones before it, offering a relentlessly linear catalog of Gentle's progress into the Oval Office.

Although intended for "woefully historically underinformed children" (380), Mario's film is most popular with the adults and adolescents who gather together to view it each year. This ritualized celebration of a founding political myth shores up the boundaries of the imagined ONAN community.[10] As the film dramatizes the history of continental reformation, its annual screening constructs a national identity among the viewers. At the tennis academy, the celebration takes on an air of irreverence as the cafeteria fills with students, coaches, and teachers wearing wacky hats and gorging themselves on the sugar and complex carbohydrates prohibited the rest of the year. These exceptional elements further distinguish the event, seeming to construct a democratic space of shared identity with hats and sweets. Wallace characterizes the scene with the benign elements of multiculturalism—costume and food—in an ironic nod to the violence such celebrations can mask. Irony, in fact, becomes the dominant mode of participation among the viewers as they cheer sarcastically and mimic Gentle's delivery. In this scene, mockery and parody do not unmake citizenship, but instead become its performance. Despite their staged distance from political events, the viewers' shared ironic response nevertheless achieves the purpose of Interdependence Day by illustrating a collective relation to the state. This very desire to demonstrate their detachment from the nation becomes the characteristic that is most classically American in the eyes of their Canadian colleagues. In the face of raucous cheering and yelling, "a handful of . . . Canadian students sit unhatted, chewing stolidly, faces blurred and distant. This American penchant for absolution via irony is foreign to them" (385). The Canadian students, exiles from their exploited homeland, perform their disidentification with American citizenship, rejecting the traditional celebratory hat and refusing to focus on the unfolding historical narrative. The terms "distant" and "foreign" manifestly apply to the students' faces and to American practices, but the words resonate at another level as the Canadians present are literally made foreign by the ritualized celebration of American history. As the film dramatizes President Gentle's search for a foreign scapegoat, the screening itself enacts these international divisions.

This parallel between the film's plot and its effect on the viewing community mirrors the tie between Mario's artistic strategies and teleological state principles. Even as Mario applies a critical stamp to the events he represents, his formal choices confirm nationalist narratives by relying on linearity. In one scene, a turn in national relations "is foreshadowed as ominous by a wavered D-minor on the soundtrack's organ" (384). This musical foreshadowing relies on a fixed narrative of cause and effect, the same logic that Gentle uses to usher in these dangerous changes. In a later segment, Mario weaves real and fabricated news headlines into a montage that narrates increasing U.S. pressure on its neighbor to the north (385). Like the students' ironic celebration of Interdependence, Mario's bogus headlines cannot dismantle the authority of news sources or constructed political narratives. The film seems no less accurate for its artistic license and, in fact, appeals to standards of coherence and progress in its historicist account. Mario's creative techniques make no radical departure from national political tactics. In an era of media campaigns only slightly exaggerated from our own, President Gentle's success stems from the power of focus groups and advertising principles. Mario's critical approach follows the same formal strategies discussed by Gentle and his advisors.[11]

Mario's film and its exhibition offer a surprisingly emblematic demonstration of the constitutive tie between linear narratives and national belonging. Once we locate the ultimate investment in historicism on the part of a sinister, "experialist" government, Wallace's episodic narrative seems to take on a more openly political agenda. In contrast to the driving teleological structures of nationalist rhetoric, Wallace's chronological experimentation produces a narrative principle of events without causes. Like destabilized notions of the body produced by (literally) corporate sponsorship, *Infinite Jest* radically disorients the security of linear progression with the advent of subsidized time. Instead of 1997, 1998, we move from the Year of the Whopper to the Year of the Tucks Medicated Pad. When years are designated by the name of their corporate sponsor, time lacks the numerical sequence that serves as a touchstone for order. The text repeats this temporal disarray in making jumps forward and back among days and weeks. As time becomes unmoored from its reassuring linearity, it loses much of its power to structure and make sense of events. This temporal instability requires a similarly shaky representation of action, such that the notion of plot*line* in the novel can only be approached by way of loops, breaks, and branches. Wallace places his characters in crisis—Where are the missing drugs? Will Pemulis be expelled? What is the prognosis of Don Gately's condition?—and then turns back in time to postpone or, in some cases, never deliver these answers. Wallace denies conventional structures of crisis and denouement. Instead, his characters are all poised at the brink of personal and national disasters, the climactic action is never realized, and to turn to the beginning of the novel—the latest time in the book—initiates a second cycle of reading without offering resolution.

This search for answers at the beginning of the text casts the opening page of *Infinite Jest* in a dual role, in which it serves as both the introduction and, strangely, the epilogue. The framing chronology of the novel opens with an effect: Hal's profound failure to communicate. We then read the novel with the disability-inspired impulse for diagnosis, for cause. While the novel never fulfills this desire for medical solutions, the influence of a progressive model of time lends extra weight to the most recent moment, even when it falls as the first scene in the book. The nature of Hal's disorder—his inability to manage his face, body, and language—takes on added significance in this doubly important position in the novel. The scene announces its strangeness with a series of phrases in which Hal voices excessive attention toward his body—"I have committed to crossing my legs I hope carefully"—or concern over a possible lapse between an intention and its physical manifestation—"I believe I appear neutral, maybe even pleasant, though I've been coached to err on the side of neutrality and not attempt what would feel to me like a pleasant expression or smile" (3). Hal's aphasia embodies the disruption of cause and effect staged in the novel's aesthetic strategies. This break between desired meaning and its expression in speech or body language unseats the body as a reliable signifier. Wallace represents Hal's disability from his first-person point of view, placing the reader alongside Hal in the shared inability to know what his language and body are representing. The horrified responses of Hal's companions—"What in God's name are those *sounds*?" (12)—offer the only clue to the disjunct between the intended and expressed speech. Hal's unruly body challenges models in which the mind acts as the secure captain of the body. Rather than serve at the pleasure of the mind, disabled bodies reject narratives of this personal hierarchy as easy or natural. As an analytical category, aphasia highlights difficulty as a property of language. Both Wallace's experimentation with narrative strategies and the reader's search for meaning are marked as labor, excluded from the creative and interpretive ease offered by foreshadowing and climactic action.

Just as the disabled body sparks the desire to know, reading is no less driven by the search for answers and resolution. While Wallace's refusal to diagnose Hal's expressive disorder is the most extreme example of symptoms without diagnosis, he also subordinates the cause of injury to Les Assassins des Fauteuils Rollents (The Wheelchair Assassins) to the notes. As most critics of the novel have described, Wallace typically locates crucial information in the subsidiary position of the footnotes. These notes are actually the essential prosthesis to the body of the novel. By challenging hierarchies of knowledge, the novel exposes the reader's desire for complete information and origins. We eventually learn about the Canadian tradition of working-class teens playing chicken with trains, but the answer is buried in a lengthy footnote and further mediated by layers of third-person narration, plagiarism, and the Quaalude-inspired academese of a scholarly article. *Infinite Jest* reconfigures the epistemological drive of conventional narratives, locating clear origins, linear history, and causality in a dysfunctional marriage with disciplinary regimes such as medicine, mass entertainment, and government. The novel does not deny meaning entirely, but subverts traditional approaches to demand new reading practices. These practices are found in the example set by the novel's anomalous bodies. Disability similarly dramatizes the impossibility of such conventional and naturalized categories. In practice, the extraordinary body requires innovation and creative redefinitions; as a conceptual model, disability valorizes rethinking fixed norms and offers its own strategies as a new paradigm for political and textual engagement.

Case Studies in Assemblage

Near the close of the novel, the newly sober Joelle van Dyne offers a striking metaphor in which she captures the deeply untenable nature of a recovering addict's investment in origins or ends. She begins by describing that familiar early sense of hope and commitment to sobriety, shaking her fist at the sky, declaring "never again" and "I quit for all time" (859). While counting each day and looking ahead to the next, these sober days become cars that must be jumped over in an Evel Knievel–style act. Even if two cars or ten cars seem possible, a lone daredevil will never clear the three hundred cars representing an entire year. Instead of this impossible stretch of days, AA's foundational aphorism, "One Day at a Time," places each day in a series of isolated juxtapositions. Wallace's aesthetic principles of nonlinearity, resistance to closure, and masking cause find their ethical counterpart in AA's temporal model. Interdependence and focusing on the present offer an alternative to the metaphor of an isolated motorcyclist contemplating a leap into infinity. In turn, this practice of placing days in a series, not a continuum, offers a hermeneutic key for finding meaning within Wallace's episodic narrative. From page 370 to page 379, *Infinite Jest* inextricably weaves together form and content in order to aesthetically and thematically enact a rejection of both etiology and teleology. These nine pages move back and forth between two memorable evenings. In the longer narrative strand, Don

Gately attends a speaker's meeting that dramatically clarifies the AA ban against causal attribution. In the second, a drunken James Incandenza conceives "anticonfluential cinema"—an artistic movement in film that refuses to resolve multiple narrative lines. Separated by years in the novel's timeline and following distinct communities among the book's cast, these events are connected only by their proximity on the page. When read together, however, Incandenza's filmic rejection of resolution offers a clear aesthetic analog to the recovery principle "One Day at a Time." I argue that Wallace's thematic interests on these pages offer a model for reading the text, a way of finding meaning that enacts the principles of assembly that construct physical, textual, and social bodies in the novel. In contrast to political campaigns which construct heroic origin tales and make promises for the future, assemblage offers an alternative model of ethical and literary conduct.

Despite Alcoholics Anonymous's explicit cautions against looking for past causes or future sobriety, the personal histories at the center of the program commonly take the form of progress narratives. At a speaker's meeting, each individual story of recovery follows a predictable, linear structure in order to facilitate identification—the familiar self-effacing jokes, the stories of loss followed by greater loss until the speaker hits bottom and turns to recovery. Just as founding myths, performative rituals, and linear histories shore up national belonging, narratives of addiction and sobriety conform to similarly rigid conventions. Both political and personal histories pull from the raw, diffuse material of daily life to construct legible plots of decline, climax, and success. For Alcoholics Anonymous, the central value of identification requires this legibility, but unlike most political propaganda, the program's doctrines and their relational methods of enforcement deconstruct the progressive and seemingly individualist narrative structure. Boston AA is a self-policing community where aphorisms and cringing distress force newcomers to deny the search for the source of their addiction. Gately describes the coercive force of group disapproval: "If you start trying to blame your Disease on some cause or other . . . everybody with any kind of sober time will pale and writhe in their chair" (370). The central contradiction of speaker's meetings is that while first-person point of view and deeply personal revelations reinforce the speaker's difference from those present, the conventional plotting serves to establish a basic identity among the group. The interdependent nature of these performances means that listeners can also deny identification, breaking eye contact and squirming in their chairs to undermine a speaker's reliance on the origins and ends enabled by a linear history. Gately describes the ideology behind this rejection of causes:

> The self-pity itself is less offensive . . . than the subcurrent of explanation, an appeal to exterior *Cause* that can slide, in the addictive mind, so insidiously into *Excuse* that any causal attribution is in Boston AA feared, shunned, punished by empathic distress. The *Why* of the disease is a labyrinth it is strongly suggested all AAs boycott, inhabited as the maze is by the twin minotaurs of *Why Me?* and *Why Not?*, a.k.a. Self-Pity and Denial, two of the smiley-faced Sergeant at Arms' more fearsome aides de camp. . . . Though it can't be conventionally enforced, this, Boston AA's real root axiom, is almost classically authoritarian, maybe even proto-Fascist. (374)

Again, the impermissibility of "whys and wherefores" returns to the risks of a communal ethics of subordinated will. The key difference, however, between a proto-fascist program of recovery and an exploitative national political agenda is the dependence on others necessary for any return to personal responsibility and agency. AA strays from "conventional enforcement" to embrace a model of "empathic distress," a relational structure that withholds identification and interpersonal connection. While speaker's meetings rely on historicist narrative structures to promote identification, the group simultaneously rejects the turn to possible cause or secure future. Like Joelle's daredevil metaphor of the line of sober days she cannot possibly jump over, AA's success relies on the radical denial of both origins and future orientation.

Don Gately's musings on the AA rejection of etiological narratives stem from the striking juxtaposition of two newly sober speakers. The specter of physical difference resides at the heart of each story, establishing a common thread to connect the two women. In these recovery narratives, disability functions as a mark of total incapacity to self-determination. Both women locate their own failures of will in another body, either as the cause of their struggles or as the revelatory sign of their addiction.

In the first speaker's autobiographical tale, she is forced to run away, strip, and use drugs *because* of her adoptive family's dysfunctional behavior toward her congenitally paralyzed and catatonic sister. The foster mother pushes the concept of inclusion to its absolute limits by insisting that her catatonic daughter accompany the speaker in every extracurricular activity. The stereotypical norms of adolescence—slumber parties, softball practice, and double dating—become perverse in the face of such striking physical and mental difference. While the relational principles of assemblage provide the key to finding meaning in the text as a whole, the disturbing combination of unlikely forms in this section places it more firmly in the mode of the grotesque. At its core, the grotesque suggests the simultaneously ridiculous and unsettling effect of mixing dissimilar forms or the eruption of one category into another.[12] In this story, the mother adheres so dogmatically to the normalizing promise of universal categories that she fails to recognize her disabled daughter's total inability to participate. Consumerist guarantees break down as expensive clothing and makeup become "lurid" in the absence of muscle tone and animating facial expressions. While the foster mother struggles against the daughter's failure to conform to social norms, the father finds in his daughter a completely pliable object of sexual fantasies. Again, a grotesque fusion of elements structures the speaker's domestic history. During his nighttime sexual assaults, the father calls his daughter "Raquel Welch" and eventually goes so far as to procure a full-head rubber mask for the daughter to wear. The story concludes in a horrifying conflation of the sacred and profane when the speaker sees the sister's postcoital expression of ghastly bliss mirrored in a Catholic statue's ecstatic face (373). For both the father and the speaker, the disabled sister serves as an outlet for the expression of their own desires, whether sexual or escapist. If the mother's behavior toward the daughter demonstrates the breakdown of universal norms, the father and the speaker use disability as an embodied permission to transgress those same norms. The speaker forfeits her life of Campfire Girls and slumber parties when those rituals of suburban happiness fail to blend with the realities of her daily life. Instead of taking personal responsibility for her addiction, the speaker fixates on her sister, telling a roomful of writhing listeners, "That's what caused it" (374).

The disabled sister, conceived of as the ultimate mark of denied humanity, will, and self-determination, exaggerates the sister's own failure to acknowledge agency. The speaker walks a tricky line of subjective identification/disidentification whereby she denies responsibility for her actions, but must remain unlike the abject and helpless sister. With each repetition of an italicized "*because*"—she was a dope fiend *because* she'd become a stripper at sixteen *because* she'd been forced to run away from her foster home *because* . . .—the speaker further alienates herself from personal responsibility and locates herself alongside her pliable, disabled sister. She flees her house, however, out of the deep desire for distance from the sister, even in memory, and to avoid the sister's fate. In another example of interdependence, the speaker cannot describe her position except through relation to her sister. This section of the novel extends disability's influence to the subjectivity of the able-bodied as well. This brand of interdependence offers not a utopian expression of mutual care, but a portrait of the inevitable shuttle between identity and difference in subject formation.

In the second story, offered just a page later, the congenitally malformed body is no longer the "not-me" figure, but instead becomes grotesquely assimilated into the speaker. After months of free-basing cocaine while pregnant, this twenty-year-old delivers a stillborn baby. Caught in intense withdrawal and denial, the young mother wanders for days, clutching the dead infant to her chest. Despite its graphic horror, the woman's story is a success, silently celebrated by the empathic audience, because her narrative turns responsibility inward. Wallace demonstrates the difference between cause and responsibility by magnifying the necessary acceptance of personal agency through the figure of the dead baby. At a moment of "facing the business-end of the arrow of responsibility," the mother enters a state of absolute Denial (377). She takes up the morbid effect of her addiction, and the hot, underdeveloped flesh attaches to her breast. This horrifying image is actually a metaphor for personal accountability. By drawing the impact of her addiction toward her, instead of citing it as just another reason to get high, the mother enacts a grotesque stage of recovery. In offering a model of pulling a terrible experience inward—an act repeated in her metaphor of "trying to tell a truth she hopes someday to swallow, inside" (378)—the speaker demonstrates the interdependence at the root of AA. Wallace peppers this story with a series of directional images—a pointing arrow, swallowing, drawing an infant to the mother's breast—to describe the power of identification to change the self. In this case, the recollection of attaching another body to her own creates an avenue through which the speaker can approach recognition of her role in addiction without seeking an external cause. More broadly, sharing this story with others and participating in the ritual of public speech enact the mutually dependent practices of Alcoholics Anonymous.

Tucked neatly between the pages of these AA stories, we find a description of the creative community of James Incandenza, Lyle the sweat-licking guru, and Mario in his role as production assistant. James turns to Lyle in a drunken depression, concerned that even writers from avant-garde journals discuss his failure to construct an appealing plot. Much like a politician or an AA speaker, James finds that plot forms a kind of aesthetic hegemony, serving as the first requirement for involving the viewer. Incandenza acknowledges that his "efforts had no sort of engaging plot, no movement that sucked you in and drew you along" (375). The turn to second-person pronouns in this line enacts the very involvement it describes. Just as recovery narratives and political rhetoric depend on conventional plot arcs to construct national or interpersonal connections among listeners, film conforms to a similar logic of engagement. To counter the demands of a legible plotline, Incandenza conceives of "anticonfluential cinema," described in an endnote as "an après-garde digital movement a.k.a. 'Digital Parallelism' and 'Cinemas of Chaotic Stasis,' characterized by a stubborn and possibly intentionally irritating refusal of different narrative lines to merge into any kind of meaningful confluence" (996). This celebration of parallel stories and characters with no satisfying outcome is the hyperbolic extension of the episodic and unresolved form of *Infinite Jest*. The paradox of anticonfluence as an aesthetic practice is that the text's failure to provide "meaningful confluence" constructs its own interpretive model. Meaning emerges in the writerly text by locating subtle connections among narrative elements laid side by side. The fragmented nature of the text itself mirrors the AA doctrine "One Day at a Time," which in turn mirrors an ethical model of interdependence. In textual assemblage, the seemingly unrelated elements come together to construct another layer of meaning and to offer a model of reading the novel. The AA tradition of speaker's meetings addresses the narrative impulse attached to disease, but radically displaces the dependent assumptions of origin and cure. In its circular and episodic form, Wallace's novel offers the aesthetic counterpart to these principles.

The Burden of Realism

For James Incandenza and his search for realism in art, even anticonfluential cinema involves the excessively mediating hand of the artist. As the next step toward realism, Incandenza offers Found Drama, in which a dart thrown at a page torn at random from the Boston phone book determines the protagonist. No footage is ever filmed, no cartridge is ever released, and the subjects go about their business, oblivious to their role in the Drama, because in reality there are no cameras, no scripts, and no directors. The only medium that is produced in Found Drama comes in the form of the scholarly manifesto, pumped out by critics and tenure seekers who rush to hail the project as the ultimate in avant-garde neorealism. In the end, however, these scholars are the butt of the joke; Incandenza conceives of Found Drama as a way to confound the critics, recognizing the absurdity of a film that has never been recorded. Wallace plants a trap, lurking in an endnote of his novel, for the ambitious critic. In analyzing *Infinite Jest*, we can never be sure that the joke is not, in fact, on us. I'll take the risk, however, of taking Found Drama seriously, and offer it as an emblem of the mutual desirability and impossibility of realism. Despite the hopelessness of ever reaching a truly realist text, Wallace sees small-"r" realism as a project with both formal and ethical goals. The most striking aesthetic elements of *Infinite Jest*—breathless sentences, tenuously braided strands of events and characters, and the pervasive influence of television and advertising—mimic the mediation and isolation of contemporary life. The ethics of fiction, as he describes them in a 1993 interview with Larry McCaffery, are grounded in the possibility of keeping loneliness at bay. Wallace argues, "We all suffer alone in the real world; true empathy's impossible. But if a piece of fiction can allow us imaginatively to identify with characters' pain, we might then also more easily conceive of others identifying with our own. This is nourishing, redemptive; we become less alone inside" (127). Wallace offers a vision of fiction that, like the model of assemblage, acknowledges inescapable boundaries even as it draws together. Imagination and written expression are not the failure of realism, but its possibility: we can only approach empathy through the mediating structure of imagination. Ethical interdependence, then, both mirrors and requires textual interdependence as the most effective strategy for representing what seems real.

Wallace's description of the redemptive potential of fiction sends up a red flag, however, in dwelling on the language of pain and suffering. While disability offers an exemplary model for the practice of interdependence, disabled people are too often pressed into service as the object of sympathy and the mark of reality. As the forlorn gaze of a March of Dimes poster child can testify, disabled people have been the enduring sign of a public discourse on pity.[13] Although Wallace's language of "true empathy" and identification look to ameliorate the hierarchical nature of pity, his focus on pain and suffering nevertheless names disability as the largely static vehicle through which these "nourishing" connections can be made. If pain and its communication stand as the goal of realism, then disabled characters become objectified as the embodiment of the real.

In the context of *Infinite Jest*, Wallace loads this added burden of the real onto Mario Incandenza's shoulders. Throughout the novel, Wallace locates Mario's delayed physical and mental development as the source for his laudably underdeveloped sense of irony and cynicism. Wallace naturalizes Mario's interpersonal skill, citing it as the result of his congenital malformation:

> Mario is basically a born listener. One of the positives to being physically damaged is that people can sometimes forget you're there, even when they're interfacing with you. You almost get to eavesdrop. It's almost like they're like: If nobody's really in there, there's nothing to be shy about. That's why bullshit tends to drop away among damaged listeners, deep beliefs revealed, diary-type private reveries indulged out loud; and, listening, the beaming and bradykinetic boy gets to forge an interpersonal connection he knows only he can truly feel, here. (80)

Instead of elevating Mario's position, Wallace's slip into second-person point of view pitches the disabled body as a flexible and inhabitable vessel. The passage enacts the very forgetting it describes, pushing Mario aside so the reader can take his place. By the end Mario has been reduced to "the boy." This turn to the second person undermines the specificity of person and place suggested by the closing phrase, "only he can truly feel, here." While Mario's disability allows him greater access to commonly protected truths and a higher form of "interpersonal connection," this moment of textual interdependence suggests that Mario can serve as a conduit to reality, valued primarily for his ability to bring the reader closer to truth. The disabled body is no more real than the able body, but this passage demonstrates that disabled bodies carry an ideological burden of being *conceived* as more real. Although Wallace is quick to call this characteristic a positive for Mario, this perceived access to reality often serves as the conceptual limit for figures of disability. If experiences located in the body are viewed as the most real, then identities seeming to stem from the body—like disability, age, race, or gender—will be read as inescapable. Physical difference becomes both constitutive and exhaustive of disabled people's social interaction. Despite Wallace's optimism, the mantle of reality carries with it a sense of being apolitical and ahistorical, of being more object than subject.[14]

Mario's movement from exceptional listener, to a universal "you," to an objectified "the boy" demonstrates how disability can serve in the object position in the process of identification. Disability serves not just as object, however, but also as the cast-off abject. In the AA speaker's story described above, the molested and catatonic sister offers an emblematic case of the disabled as the abject. The speaker turns to drugs and prostitution to forget the debased image of her sister, an image that persistently recurs to "show [her] what [she] permanently thrust aside in order to live."[15] In able-bodied subject formation, disability often serves as an essential, but cast-out, element. This form of abjection is no less descriptive of the constitution of the social body. The geopolitical perversion of Interdependence enacts a radical slide from democratic connection to hierarchical exploitation. As a member of Les Assassins des Fauteuils Rollents explains of the toxic dump that was once New England, "Fans do not begin to keep it all in the Great Convexity. It creeps back in. What goes around, it comes back around. This your nation refuses to learn. It will keep creeping back in. You cannot give away your filth and prevent all creepage, no? Filth by its very nature it is a thing that is creeping always back" (233). If Julia Kristeva describes the abject as that which "does not respect borders, positions, rules" (4), then "creepage" in this case demonstrates the inevitable permeability of constructed borders. As both a political and a psychic model, abjection demonstrates the instability of narratives that imagine the nation or the self as static and whole.[16] The giant fans that the United States has mounted to send airborne pollutants back into Canada are the technological manifestation of a vast system of strategies, both discursive and material, used to construct and preserve the image of secure borders. A related set of disciplinary regimes looks to regulate physical difference, but disabled subjects cannot be entirely contained, erupting back in the face of those narratives that look to cast them out.

Disability and experimental neorealist narrative strategies serve analogous functions in *Infinite Jest*: both act as facilitators, bringing readers closer to reality even while acknowledging the impossibility of ever getting there. The value of realism is expressed by all the artists in the text, from Incandenza's Found Drama to Mario's earnest commendation of Joelle van Dyne's radio show: "It is increasingly hard to find valid art that is about stuff that is real in this way" (592). Like the use of the second person in the passage describing Mario's embodied talent for listening, textual strategies become the vehicles through which individuals can access disabled persons and the proximity to real they manifest. Toward the end of the novel, Wallace stages another moment in which Mario embodies the possibility for redemptive interpersonal connection. In this scene, Barry Loach, the future trainer at Enfield Tennis Academy, has to restore his brother's faith in humanity. The two decide on a scheme where Barry must stand outside the train station and ask passersby to touch him. No one will. Days turn into months with Barry standing outside the station begging, "Touch me. Touch me, *please*." As Wallace describes it, the appeal for touch is "taken literally" by Mario and he "extends his own clawlike hand" to shake Loach's filthy one (971). The underlying meaning of "taken literally" in this scene suggests that interdependence emerges specifically through reading strategies. Mario's exacting sense of language elevates writing as the necessary instrument of interpersonal connection. His fidelity to the manifest level of meaning stems from his mental disability and his consequent proximity to reality. While the moral code developed in *Infinite Jest* certainly suggests that we should value Mario's act, this disabled hand reaching out for contact is a familiar trope. Balancing out a literary tradition of villainous Richard IIIs and Captain Ahabs, we find the disability-produced purity of Tiny Tim.[17] The danger in this kind of characterization is that the "clawlike hand" becomes metonymic for Mario himself. While this scene of handshaking dramatizes the kind of human connection Wallace wants his fiction to produce, it also demonstrates the dark side of interdependence. Loach's experience of abjection is temporary, relieved by a shower, a job, and perhaps some antibiotics. The most cynical reading argues that the movement enacted by the scene resides only in Loach's experience; Mario becomes the vessel through which others grow and change. This service as the instrument of others' transformation suggests that disability is more permanently abject. Although Wallace seems to envy Mario's facility with connection and posits it as one of the most successful models of anti-addiction and health in the novel, physical difference in the novel often slips into a dangerously static role.

Mario's position as the vehicle for change in others represents perhaps the most significant danger lurking in the model of assemblage. While at one level, disability resides at the necessary center of challenges to dominant norms, at another level, assemblage always contains the potential for unevenness among its parts. Sympathy and interdependence are inherently relational structures, similarly threatening to place disability in this object position. At the textual level, *Infinite Jest*'s preoccupation with extraordinary bodies at times slides into this exploitative practice, depending on disability for its exuberant reputation. We should not forget that in the tennis player's mismatched body, the swollen arm is the result of excessive use.

Conclusion: Inclusion, Fixing, and Legibility

As I hope to have shown throughout these chapters, embodiment is a mutable discursive and material category shaped by the reading practices of a no less dynamic social body. But the contours of these reading practices are themselves shaped by long-standing ideological categories that tempt with their promise to fix what is inherently fluid. I use the term "fix" here to call upon a productive double meaning of (1) fixing as correcting and curing, an approach most commonly associated with the medical model, and (2) "fix" as it describes attempts to make shifting phenomena static and capable of control. These related forms of fixing comprise one side of civic debates over how to address disability in the public sphere. Models of inclusion, I would argue, commonly constitute the other side. "Inclusion" serves as an umbrella term, capturing legal battles over public access, mainstreaming in schools, and increased awareness of disability in cultural expression, political agendas, and academic study. Both inclusion and fixing have stakes in the overlapping public stages on which battles over embodied citizenship are fought, including medicine, schools, courts, employment, public space, media, and the academy. The tension between these two approaches can perhaps best be captured in the question often asked regarding access: If medicine promises to eliminate disability through technology and cure, why should we undertake the expense and disorientation of reshaping public space to include disabled people? In placing fixing and inclusion at odds with one another, this question reveals the ways in which these competing models diagnose problems and offer solutions according to frameworks that are often mutually illegible. By way of conclusion, I hope to outline a few emblematic examples of this complex illegibility, to demonstrate how these frames find their roots in the foundational ideologies of American individualism, and to propose how disability itself can serve as a conceptual model for rethinking these problems of illegibility.

Having laid the foundation for my argument in an opening reading of "disability" as defined by the Americans with Disabilities Act, it seems only appropriate to close with the ADA as well. As Ruth Colker describes in her 2005 study *The Disability Pendulum*, the judicial history of ADA enforcement has tended to swing between narrow, pro-defendant inter-pretations of the law and pro-disabled decisions more in keeping with congressional intent and statutory history. The battle for greater inclusion in U.S. schools, jobs, restaurants, and transportation is typically fought in the courtroom. Without a national agency to enforce its aims, the suc-cesses and failures of the ADA depend upon legal redress. As such, the judicial sphere is essential to understanding the contemporary condition of embodied citizenship. While a vast apparatus of cultural texts and political theater supports this litigation from both sides,[1] the disciplin-ary effect of the law itself cannot be underestimated. This turn to the courtroom to uphold the promises of the ADA requires entering into the limiting narrative frame of the law. Barriers of access, both financial and physical, are the first hurdles to inclusion in the legislative domain. No less limiting, however, are the constraints imposed on the imagination of the courts and on the possibilities for restitution imposed by adher-ence to concepts like "reasonable accommodations" or defenses of cost and "undue hardship." More abstractly, legal redress constructs a limited narrative by characterizing the state as a disinterested judge rather than as an agent of oppression and, as Wendy Brown argues, fixing the com-plainant's identity upon the site of injury.[2] These constructions of the state as a neutral protector of individual rights, capable of resolving per-sonal injury, compose central narratives according to which citizenship can be legibly expressed. Litigation determines the possibilities of inclu-sion through its requirements of specialized legal language, costly expert advocates, reliance on case history, and a narrow list of available com-pensation. The limitations imposed by these elements, however, should not obscure the fact that the law has vast material and symbolic effects: constructing an influential definition of disability; structuring concepts of justice and rights; and regulating the form by which inclusion can be pursued.

The history of the ADA and its legal enforcement demonstrates the complex movement between the legislature's desire to address the needs of populations and the requirement of litigation to condense widespread forms of political inequality into isolated instances of injury to individuals. The rhetoric of individual rights allows for a comforting return to the foundational promises of American citizenship. This enduring emphasis on the individual serves as the governing trope for public narratives of disability advocacy and activism, typically understood as having their roots in personal experience. Accounts of the strikingly bipartisan nature of congressional support for the ADA often cite the leadership of individuals across both parties who count themselves or family members as disabled. In her history of the ADA, Ruth Colker describes how one of the bill's sponsors, Senator Tom Harkin (D-Iowa), opened his remarks on the day of its passage with a signed thank-you to his deaf brother. In his conclusion to *Disability Theory*, Tobin Siebers critiques this individualist emphasis in approaches to disability, arguing, "Disability is nearly always interpreted in our society as a personal tragedy, as inherently individual" (188). One cultural legacy of this fantasy can be found in the overuse of disability to signify personal tragedy in the sentimental novel. The material impact of this individualist logic has been to privilege making isolated accommodations to bring individuals into social space, rather than to change the organization of space itself. Inclusion, then, typically locates the problem in the individual, seeking to change the public space only as much as necessary to address the needs of a narrowly conceived deviation from a fantasized universal norm. In a familiar model of accessibility, a small wheelchair-accessible space might be added to a stadium theater, as though architects can only imagine one or two wheelchair users attending a movie at the same time.

Given this widespread understanding of disability as a painful, personal struggle, it is perhaps not surprising that the political fights with the most immediate—if unacknowledged—correspondences to disability are expressed according to emphatically individualist terms. Proceeding under banners reading "Pro-Choice," "Right to Life," or "Right to Die," these movements—whether progressive, conservative, or from the complicating interventions of disability—enact citizenship through the rubric of liberal individualism. Debates over abortion and euthanasia are only two of the many arenas in which leftist orthodoxies must be reconsidered in the face of challenges from a disability perspective. In their critique of "choice" as overdetermined by ableist ideologies concerning "quality of life," disability activists may find they have more in common with anti-abortion conservatives. As these nuanced conversations illustrate, including disability in contemporary politics requires the acknowledgment that the conventional notions of "choice" and "freedom" are necessarily constrained according to ableist ideology that similarly scripts the legible definitions of concepts like "health," "family," and "dependence."

Perhaps surprisingly, including the interests of disabled citizens on the agenda of political parties is no less difficult than reshaping public space according to a principle of universal access. Integrating the complicating perspective of disability rewrites familiar political rhetoric, and presupposed political lines are redrawn according to seemingly peculiar alliances. While these interventions into traditional leftist agendas have not found consensus among disability activists and scholars, the terms of such critique are now widely known within these circles. Such complexities have become commonplace in disability studies, but they are significantly less cited among feminists, progressives, and American studies scholars. Americanists' lack of attention to disability perspectives in these debates excludes a rich terrain of study, since the mobilizing rhetoric across multiple sides falls so commonly into the language of American citizenship. While the project of American studies since its inception has included defining and reconsidering foundational concepts like liberal individualism, few scholars outside of disability studies have accounted for the difference disability makes. In taking up familiar terms and canonical texts that resonate with an American studies readership, the preceding chapters seek to make the case that, as in the examples of entrenched debates around abortion or euthanasia, an analysis of disability can shake up conventionally held notions of U.S. citizenship.

The inclusion of disability as a central term in the academy or in civic debates, however, cannot simply be an additive category in the familiar multicultural list. The complexity at the heart of inclusion more broadly demonstrates the impossibility of simply tacking disability onto the already-established agendas of political parties or civil rights campaigns. Disability antidiscrimination measures, for example, cannot adhere to the template established during the civil rights movement, because disability-centered concepts such as "reasonable accommodation and accessibility" lack clear counterparts in laws addressing race discrimination (Colker 11). A universal agenda within disability communities is no easier, as illustrated by intense internal debates over mainstreaming in public schools or cochlear implants. Even these brief examples capture the necessity to reckon with the difficulty inherent in models of inclusion. This difficulty, however, emerges in part from the heterogeneity, pain, and compromise at the heart of disability itself.

From the outset, disability's status as an inclusive identity category must allow for acknowledgement of its marked heterogeneity. The term addresses a stunningly wide collection of impairments and experiences and, according to the 2000 U.S. Census, includes nearly fifty million Americans. Disability can be temporary, chronic, congenital, onset with age, visible, or (seemingly) invisible. If disability can be in any way meaningful as an inclusive category, its usage must be understood to contain these internal differences. The immediately striking variability of disability can provide instruction to contemporary debates over internal difference that have emerged among pan-ethnic communities in the wake of strong periods of cultural nationalism. Any history of pan-identarian movements should include accounts of internal struggles and competing agendas among, for example, recent and established immigrant communities; white women and women of color; Latino/a women and men; gay men and gender queers. Rather than see internal struggles as the failures of these movements, disability's unavoidable internal differences can demonstrate the value of temporary coalitions and a diversity of tactics. In this sense, disability serves not just to query terms like "individualism" at the heart of American studies, but can also offer an avenue out from the consuming debates over multiculturalism of the past few decades. As I suggest in my introduction, however, as disability studies and disability rights become increasingly secure in the academy and political sphere, it is essential to remember the costs and benefits of institutionalization through the valence of disability history. Taking the lead from the heterogeneous constituents and diverse physical and social requirements of disability, it is possible to make these competing interests legible to one another by starting from the understanding of difference as constitutive of identity itself.[3] Such competing aims, then, are not the failures of a unified social body, but the condition for its existence.

These remarks on the possibilities and limits of inclusion return to my opening question regarding the cost of adapting public space as contrary to the promise of fixing disability through medical and technological intervention. For example, an increase in prenatal diagnostic testing and access to abortion appeals to national fantasies of eliminating some forms of congenital disability. As Tobin Siebers reminds us, however, "A society with a universally accessible built environment and laws designed to offer equal protection to all people would produce far fewer disabled citizens in the future" (190). At first glance this statement seems impossible; how can changing space alter physical bodies? Upon further reading, it is clear that this statement relies on an understanding of the social model of disability, a model that flies in the face of the medical investment in the clear split between "normal" and "pathological." For readers unfamiliar with the major tenets of disability studies, a universally accessible public sphere would not in any way reduce physical impairment among individuals. From this perspective, universal access cannot be read as a way to "eliminate disability"; such a premise flies in the face of the promise of the medical model. Universal access would, however, decrease the number of disabled citizens by changing social perception and removing some of the barriers that limit daily activities. This conceptual privileging of interdependence and the social sphere in our understanding of bodies exists in sharp contrast to more conventional approaches to embodiment as natural, needing cure, and adhering to strict standards of either normal or abnormal. In concert with the medical model, liberal individualism's celebration of independent agents with the power to shape the material world obscures the extent to which the world, in fact, shapes individuals. Accordingly, political debates structured by the logics of liberal individualism would not just disagree with Siebers's statement on the embodied impact of universal access; it would be baffling and illegible.

Such conceptual illegibility occurs not just between opposing adherents to the medical and social models, but within these spheres themselves. I'll explore just one extended example here of such illegibilities within medicine, drawn appropriately from Annemarie Mol's work on complexities in knowledge production. In her essay "Cutting Surgeons, Walking Patients," Mol demonstrates the complexities of diagnosis, treatment, and clinical evaluation through a case study of two competing methods of treating arterial disease. Throughout *Reading Embodied Citizenship*, my analysis has centered on unpacking a series of textual strategies that seek to make sense of the unfamiliar by locating these anomalous bodies in the comforting terrain of familiar stories. The centrality of narrative framing throughout Mol's inquiry similarly demonstrates how thoroughly storytelling and reading practices are embedded in seemingly objective, ahistorical accounts of embodiment. Reading practices take on a special significance in Mol's work in the practical problem of assessing competing treatments. In addition to the typical complexities of measuring comparative success, these treatments for arterial disease in the legs—surgery and walking therapy—require such different approaches to problems of symptom, cause, and success as to make walking therapy nearly illegible to surgeons. The philosophy underlying surgery is that leg pain during walking—which typically brings the individual to the doctor in the first place, casting him or her as "patient"—is a sign or symptom of an underlying structural problem: clogged arteries. The solution to the problem is to address the underlying disease by surgically "fixing" the blocked artery. Walking therapy, on the other hand, cannot fix arteries; it does not change blood flow or reduce blockage. In fact, the success of the treatment maintains a vexing sense of mystery; patients experience clinical improvement in increased pain-free walking distance, but researchers are unsure why. Mol quotes an internist who uses an apt plumbing metaphor to describe the seemingly incommensurate natures of these competing approaches: "But if you look at their angiographies you see a pipe and it's clogged up. So the image itself suggests what should be done about it. Go ahead, unplug it. Or insert an extra pipe, if need be. It's plumber's work. . . . No one would ever invent walking therapy by staring at angiograph pictures" (227). The mechanistic approach contained in the "plumber's" fix literally cannot see a solution that falls outside the frame of the angiograph. This restriction in vision lies in the surgeon's reading of pain as the sign of an underlying problem; advocates of walking therapy, by contrast, treat pain as a problem itself without addressing possible structural causes. Neither my goal nor Mol's is to identify which of these treatments is more successful. My interest lies in demonstrating the ways in which the construction of the narrative frame can make certain solutions or explanations illegible. In the case of chronic conditions like those Mol describes and in disability as a fact of human variation more broadly, complete cure is impossible. Given a competing series of models for diagnosis and treatment as well as multiple parameters for assessing success, the tactics of close reading are essential for exposing the constructed nature of these frames.

The realities of chronic and permanent disabilities are not just failures of the promise to fix and cure, they call out the lie of the medical model as a universal solution. At a fundamental level, medicine cannot address the complexities of human physical variation and experience. Despite the pretense of facts and data, patient records are no less constructed than autobiographical narratives. Rather than simply reject the medical model for its failures, we should pause over its difficulties in order to understand how certain terms get privileged and which experiences fall out of view.[4] Analyzing complexity as an object of study itself can also offer a helpful caution against base postmodern and multicultural tendencies to uncritically value difference and difficulty. Disability's requirement of difficulty as the starting point for critical analysis can expose previously unseen contours in our constructed narrative frameworks. While the cultural and literary readings within this book may seem less practical than clinical assessments of treatment models or legislative rulings regulating public access, I have tried to show how coming into social legibility for anomalous bodies can often stage an uneasy moment of confirmation and challenge to the dominant ideological frame.

As I hope to have demonstrated through these examples, the competing promises of both inclusion and fixing are limited by a series of complex illegibilities. Not only are the demands of universal access often made outrageous by the dream of eliminating disabilities, but so do the ADA-mandated sphere of the courtroom, the orthodoxies of progressive politics, and competing forms of medical treatment all reveal the regulatory effect of both inclusion and fixing. As I have argued throughout this book, disability requires the reconsideration of long-held ideals and offers an alternative model to utopic political expectations caught up in the desire for fixing and cure. The social and embodied realities of disability require that any ideological approach centered on disability must include pain, difficulty, inconvenience, and temporary or inadequate solutions. Despite the seeming pessimism of these characteristics, the value of this inclusion of difficulty lies in providing a path out of stalemated political debates in which the participants can only envision change as oppositional resistance to power, uncompromised solution, or uniform consensus. As described in chapter 4, acknowledging the widespread influence and possible inclusion of injurious, critiqued elements in a holistic model can offer a productive alternative to the well-documented limits of a politics centered on resistance.[5]

In addition to moving away from universal narratives of the social body, a conceptual model grounded in disability understands the physical body as similarly diverse and socially contingent. In their own way, this book's chapters have all made this claim: in contrast to naturalized, totalizing models of the body, disability understands embodiment as a process of diverse incorporation, including prosthesis, social interdependence, medical treatment, litigation, and narrative positioning. Against the long-standing belief in a closed, individual body, anomalous forms remind us of the radically open and fluid nature of embodiment. This openness, however, can often signify vulnerability as well as possibility. The threat of injury, pollution, illness, or dismemberment in part produces the potential for reconsidering old ideas. This somatic diversity can lead to productive, if strange, alliances and possibilities for new readings of previously illegible narratives.

What I have tried to describe here is a disability-inspired model of creative incorporation. I find the study of disability so rich because it can offer both a practical and a conceptual methodology that acknowledges the impossibility of total political fixes and medical cures, instead taking its lead from the necessary incorporation of both difficulty and change. Because the material and symbolic demands of disability insist on a theory that can address pain and difficulty, such theories will inevitably reflect a simultaneous critique, incorporation, and reconfiguration of foundational ideals. This simultaneity makes the narrative complexity of the writers discussed herein all the more significant. These readings draw from disability to reveal a dense interdependence among physical, textual, and political bodies. Complexity in these textual readings demonstrates not only interdependence and ambiguity but also the desire to domesticate uncanny forms into familiar narratives. Rather than simply rehearse my part in a tired deconstructive chorus of "ambiguity," I argue for a complex interdependence as the conceptual and material root of disability itself. The value, then, of these literary readings is to open newly legible narrative forms not just among disability scholars, but for long-standing debates in American studies as well. This notion of incorporation as suggested by disability offers a new lens through which to read familiar narratives of American citizenship, a lens that exposes the textually contingent and embodied nature of liberal individualism.

NOTES

Introduction

1. The importance of this historical moment, however, should not obscure the decades of disability rights activism leading up to its passage, nor the similarly tireless work in the decades since to protect this promise of civil liberties from incursion by courts and lawmakers. For a history of this struggle, see Shapiro and Switzer.

2. In his essay "Disability and the Justification of Inequality in American History," Douglas Baynton demonstrates the centrality of rhetorics and categorizations of disability to three major citizenship debates of the nineteenth and twentieth centuries—women's suffrage, African American freedom, and immigration. Baynton argues that repressive notions of race, gender, and ethnicity were often couched in terms of disability, as in medical narratives of blacks' biological inferiority or women's inherent frailty. Baynton goes on to demonstrate the complexity of disability in struggles for civil rights by cataloging the ways in which groups made arguments against their own inequality by seeking to distance themselves from the label "disabled." Such distancing carries with it the notion that disability itself is a legitimate category for exclusion and repression. Baynton's essay offers a dual reminder of the often-overlooked centrality of disability in debates over citizenship as well as highlighting the complexity of simply adding disability to a list of multicultural historical and cultural categories. His brief history underscores the competing agendas and statements of bias among targeted groups.

3. Both quotes from Garland-Thomson, *Extraordinary Bodies* 41–42.

4. To similar ends, Emily Martin's "Body Narratives, Body Boundaries" and Barbara Duden's *Woman beneath the Skin* both work from medical texts to argue that narratives of the body which masquerade as "biological fact" are historically contingent and socially constructed.

5. This is the language of the 1976 statement from the British Union of the Physically Impaired against Segregation (UPIAS), quoted in Shelley Tremain's "On the

Subject of Impairment." Tremain draws from Michel Foucault to outline the complicity of the social model in the disciplinary constructs that present impairment as a "real," biological condition. I am interested in a similar troubling of splits that assume a pre-social body, but I also want to focus on the ideological effects of the continued persistence of the social model within disability studies.

6. Grosz uses the phrase "embodied subjectivity" to hold together the mutually constitutive forces of body and subject. While my own understanding of how bodies and subjects are constructed is heavily influenced by Grosz's usage, its proximity to "embodied citizenship" might evoke confusion. *Volatile Bodies* stages itself as an intervention into philosophical traditions that have failed to account for the primacy of the body in the development of the self. The reassertion of the body into these conversations is a positive move. My own argument about embodied citizenship suggests that while broader recognition of the role that bodies play in constructing all acts of citizenship is important, embodiment acts also as an unevenly distributed ideological burden. "Embodied citizenship" evokes a reminder that bodily difference acts as the compromising and conditioning force of national participation for people with anomalous bodies.

7. Mitchell and Snyder stake their claim for disability's "unique" position on the compelling observation that liberatory work within race, gender, and sexuality is often undertaken with the desire to escape association with physical and cognitive limitations (2–3). These challenges to biological justifications for racial or gendered inferiority or the assignment of homosexuality to the status of mental illness result in what Mitchell and Snyder call the "dual negation" of disability, in which physical deviance serves as the "master trope of human disqualification" (3). While Mitchell and Snyder offer an important reminder of the violence and repression that takes place within and between disempowered groups, their desire for disability's "difference" risks reinscribing physicality as a static property of identity formation.

8. In his chapter from *Crip Theory*, "Composing Queerness and Disability: The Corporate University and Alternative Corporealities," Robert McRuer challenges the institutionalized compulsion for orderly, disembodied final products in the college composition classroom. McRuer advocates a model of "de-composition" that reflects the "difficult, messy, disorienting" (146) process of writing in contrast to the "corporate model of efficiency" (148).

9. For more on the effects of these traditions on literature of the mid-twentieth century and a discussion of the ways in which their assumptions mingle to produce the prevailing approach to disability, see chapter 2.

10. For a more extended critique of Butler from a disability studies perspective, see Siebers's *Disability Theory*, particularly his argument in "Disability Studies and the Future of Identity Politics" that Butler's work privileges the psychic over the corporeal and that, for Butler, "materiality" is most often found in the "materiality of the signifier" (75–76).

11. This concept of the burden of materiality calls upon Jose Muñoz's theory of "the burden of liveness." He writes, "The story of 'otherness' is one tainted by a mandate to 'perform' for the amusement of a dominant power bloc. If there is any acceptable place for queers in the homophobic national imaginary, it certainly is onstage—being 'funny' for a straight audience. The minoritarian subject is always encouraged to perform, *especially* when human and civil rights disintegrate" (187). This burden stems, in

part, from the sense that queer performance is less mediated by an external apparatus of representation like film or text. This pressure of live performance emerges from the view that sees minoritarian subjects' staging as anti-aesthetic—camp and comedy or pain and tragedy are seen as the natural outgrowth of these identities. Muñoz argues that the live performance becomes a substitute for historical and political representation (188). The paradox of this substitution lies in the fact that the burden of liveness positions this performance as a more direct representation of minority experience so that the performance of racial tragedy, for example, is read as unmediated and real suffering, but does not translate to greater rights. I'm interested in expanding the scope of Muñoz's model to the unstaged, performative elements of everyday life as they stem not from the "fact of the body as real," but from its construction as such. For me, the burden of this constant perceived collapse into reality can be mitigated by demonstrating how the construction of identity in more local circumstances draws on the strategies and legacies of performance.

12. See Ong and Appadurai. In chapter 1, I also discuss briefly the transnational debt of American exceptionalism in a longer examination of the paradoxical alignment of the extraordinary and the representative.

13. Tobin Siebers levels a thorough critique against a zeal for heterogeneity that denies the material experience of the body in *Disability in Theory*; while allowing for this caution, I discuss the productive reaches of incorporating difficulty in theories of embodiment in chapters 2 and 5.

1 / Domesticating the Exceptional

1. See Rowe and Marcus, respectively.

2. For more details of Chang and Eng's history situated among arguments about the epistemological impact of ambiguous bodies (specifically hermaphrodites, intersex persons, and conjoined twins), see Grosz, "Intolerable Ambiguity."

3. Even the sentence structure of Twain's essay comes to mimic the conjoined form of his subject. Semicolons and compound sentences proliferate among Twain's descriptions of the twins' lives. A common construction reads, "When one is sick, the other is sick; when one feels pain, the other feels it; when one is angered, the other's temper takes fire" (252). In the closing section of this chapter, I discuss how these correspondences between textual form and physical form illustrate the discursive production of disability in the national imagination.

4. More than a century later, this enduring fascination with the twins' intimate lives served as the focus for much of Darin Strauss's 2000 novel, *Chang and Eng*.

5. In his genealogy of American studies, Gene Wise identifies Perry Miller's "jungle epiphany" as a "paradigm drama" in the formation of the intellectual movement. The legacy of Miller's work (along with Vernon Louis Parrington's) was to lay out a series of foundational assumptions for the study of America, including belief in an (essentially homogenous) exceptional American mind with an investment in a canon of great books and thinkers (306). Wise locates Miller within an emerging corporatism and cold war nationalism in American studies during which interdisciplinary programs and departments were well funded by major grant centers.

6. For a specifically political celebration of individualism as the central virtue of the U.S. character, see Herbert Hoover's *American Individualism*.

7. While Macpherson's *Political Theory of Possessive Individualism* focuses its

inquiry on English political thought in the seventeenth century, these thinkers have served as the foundation for liberal democracy in America. My understanding of individualism in the specific context of the United States, especially studied through the lens of its literature, stems from Yehoshua Arieli, Joseph Bertolini, Gillian Brown, Wai-Chee Dimock, Thomas C. Heller and Morton Sosna, and Myra Jehlen.

8. In the second chapter of *Extraordinary Bodies*, "Theorizing Disability," Garland-Thomson also explores these problems of self-government and liberal individualism. See 41–44.

9. See Gillman, Fredericks, and Sundquist.

10. If the fundamental split in critical work on sentimental literature has been the Douglas-Tompkins debate, a similar divide occurs in disability-centered analyses. Within disability studies, these disputes over the liberatory potential of the sentimental genre have been less entrenched and generally more conciliatory, but they share the concerns of the field-defining discussions of the mid-1980s. Aligned with Ann Douglas in their shared, critical view of the genre, Rosemarie Garland-Thomson argues that sentimental fiction exploits disabled figures to confirm the interests of individualist ideology and what she calls "benevolent maternalism" (see chapter 4 of *Extraordinary Bodies*, "Benevolent Maternalism and the Disabled Women in Stowe, Davis, and Phelps"). Mary Klages's work in *Woeful Affliction* intersects more closely with Jane Tompkins's, as both emphasize the importance of textuality as a means of extending political engagement to middle-class women or in presenting disabled people as writing, speaking selves. Klages concedes that nineteenth-century literature commonly positions disabled people as "posters" meant to evoke sympathy, but she also identifies the more powerful role of the "empathic actor."

11. T. M. Parrott, first published in *Booklover's Magazine* (Philadelphia) 3: 145–154, as reprinted in the Norton Critical Edition, 245.

12. Shirley Samuels's work describes another level of complication in the focus on embodiment for both abolitionist and proslavery literature; she argues for a dual impulse within sentimental discourse to locate identity within the body but also to make the body the sign of an identity that transcends it. These competing narratives both suggest, however, that American notions of subjectivity center on embodiment.

13. Michael Rogin and Sarah Chinn each discuss fingerprinting and palmistry in *Pudd'nhead Wilson* and elaborate their arguments by noting the influence of Francis Galton, the father of both fingerprinting and modern eugenics. In separate essays, both scholars describe Galton's deeply held, but unsuccessful, desire to blend the two disciplines as he searched for a way to correlate human performance to fingerprint characteristics. Shirley Samuels makes similar connections between phrenology, palmistry, and photography as nineteenth-century attempts to "fix identity at the surface of the skin" (169).

14. Leslie Fiedler's characterization of Twain's humor in *Pudd'nhead Wilson* is interesting in this context because he describes it as "the humor of the freak." He goes on to argue, "In the chamber of horrors of our recent fiction, the deformed and dwarfed and dumb have come to stand as symbols of our common plight, the failure of everyone to attain a purely fiction norm. Toward this insight, Twain was fumbling almost without awareness, believing all along that he was merely trying to take the curse off of a bitterness he could not utterly repress by being what he liked to think was 'funny'" (250). While Fiedler takes a critical approach to Twain's humor, calling

it "violent" and "appalling" and, perhaps most seriously, hinting that it is actually not funny, he does suggest the potential value of humor in dismantling normative codes. Fiedler's claims in this 1955 essay for the *New Republic* (reprinted in the Norton Critical Edition, 248–257), anticipate his publication in 1978 of *Freaks: Myths and Images of the Secret Self*. For a closer examination of Fiedler's work and his study of disabled figures as "symbols of our common plight," see my chapter 2.

15. For my understanding of the intellectual history of sympathy in the United States, I am especially indebted to Elizabeth Barnes and Kristin Boudreau. In my review of studies of sentimental literature, I was also influenced by Ann Douglas, Markman Ellis, Mary Klages, Shirley Samuels, Julia A. Stern, Karen Sánchez-Eppler, Rosemarie Garland-Thomson, and Jane Tompkins.

16. For more sustained attention to the history of Julia Pastana, billed as "The Ugliest Woman in the World," "Bear Woman," "Ape Woman," and "Hybrid Indian," see Garland-Thomson, *Extraordinary Bodies* 70–78.

17. In his chapter "Mark Twain and Homer Plessy," Eric Sundquist offers a reading of these lines that connects them to the minstrel tradition and its use in unpacking the performative nature of racial categories (228–229). In his turn to *Plessy v. Ferguson*, Sundquist offers an illuminating link between the novel and key moments in the racial crisis of the late nineteenth century. Homer Plessy is an especially interesting figure to note in this section because his protest against segregation laws was a staged act of racial performance. While riding in a whites-only Louisiana railroad car in 1892, Plessy announced his black identity according to the logic of the "one-drop rule." This challenge to segregation relied upon Plessy's ability to pass and the chance to dramatize his surprising move from whiteness to blackness.

18. In *Sideshow U.S.A.*, Rachel Adams makes a case for reducing the distance between audience and viewer implied by the term "spectacle" and extending analysis of the freak show to include the varying dynamics enacted by the participatory viewer.

19. In my second chapter, I offer a more thorough discussion of Siebers's theory of "bodily reality" and its relationship to representations of disability by placing his work in conversation with the literary traditions of realism and the grotesque.

20. For a more extensive analysis and history of the freak show tradition, see Garland-Thomson's *Freakery* and Adams's *Sideshow U.S.A.*

21. See Bill Brown's "Monstrosity" and Garland-Thomson's "The Cultural Work of American Freak Shows, 1835–1940," in *Extraordinary Bodies* (55–80).

22. Garland-Thomson makes a case for the ideological effect of physical restraints, arguing that containment assuages fears of diversity in the political sphere as well as the personal: "By exoticizing and trivializing bodies that were physically nonconformist, the freak show symbolically contained the potential threat that difference among the polity might erupt as anarchy" (*Extraordinary Bodies* 66).

23. See Parker for an extended discussion of the anomalies produced by the texts' composition history.

24. Quoted in Albert Bigelow Paine's *Mark Twain's Autobiography* from an 1872 letter in which Twain responds to Howells's favorable review of *Roughing It*. The quote commonly recurs in *Pudd'nhead Wilson* scholarship, including work by Eric Sundquist and Hershel Parker. Arthur G. Petit includes the quote and its original citation in "The Black and White Curse" (reprinted in the Norton Critical Edition, 331).

25. Freud quotes at length from a German dictionary to demonstrate that "*heimlich*

212 / NOTE TO PAGE 60

is a word the meaning of which develops in the direction of ambivalence, until it finally coincides with its opposite, *unheimlich*" (226). This movement from certainty, through ambivalence, to reversal offers a striking example of the multiple nature of signs.

2 / "Marvelous and Very Real"

1. There are two major schools in reading the grotesque as a symbolic commentary. In the first mode, physical anomaly is read as a metaphor for a chaotic world. This group sees physical and formal heterogeneity as an avenue to describe a larger destabilization of trusted categories, but the street is one-way; there's no reciprocal attention to the subject position of disabled people. Examples of this school include critics Wolfgang Keyser, G. Wilson Knight, and Francis K. Barasch. Philip Thomson offers a summary of this common approach in his contribution to the Critical Idiom series: "Where previous ages had seen in [the grotesque] merely the principle of disharmony run wild, or relegated it to the cruder species of the comic, the present tendency . . . is to view the grotesque as a fundamentally ambivalent thing, as a violent clash of opposites, and hence, in some forms at least, as an appropriate expression of the problematical nature of existence. It is no accident that the grotesque mode in art and literature tends to be prevalent in societies and eras marked by strife, radical change or disorientation" (11). While he shares the sense of ambiguity as a critique of the nature of existence, William van O'Connor argues that to see the grotesque emerging out of social upheaval or injustice is too narrow. Instead of reading the works of Stephen Crane and Nathaniel West as describing social problems that need to be solved, O'Connor claims that the most profound effect of the grotesque is a sense of cosmic pointlessness. Thomson wants to claim that civil struggles produce grotesque literature; O'Connor agrees but locates the necessary work of analysis as pointing forever out to a problem on a cosmic level.

The second mode of criticism of the grotesque is more explicitly grounded in the social sphere. Mikhail Bakhtin—at the influential center of this group—is less interested in the formation of anomalous bodies than he is in their transgressive potential. In his chapter "The Grotesque World of the Body," Bakhtin assimilates extraordinary bodies into his larger theory of carnival. The carnivalesque figure represents "the right to be 'other' in this world, the right not to make common cause with any single one of the existing categories that life makes available; none of these categories quite suits them, they see the underside and falseness of every situation" (159). In concert with the poststructuralist bent toward heterogeneity and deconstruction (see Harpham), the carnivalesque is a liminal figure with the transgressive power to challenge conventional unities. For these theorists, the characteristic blending of unlike forms and its unsettling effects makes the grotesque a form of counter-hegemonic discourse.

For a disability studies project, however, these methods of analysis fail to take seriously the material conditions of disability. Both modes require an aestheticization of bodily difference where the representation of abnormality can produce social or ontological critique, but neither discusses the subject positions available for disabled persons. While it can be helpful to remember Bakhtin's emphasis on transgressing norms and Keyser's willingness to move from the body to metaphor, studies of the grotesque and disability should also retain a sense of the price attached to their serving as a symbol.

2. The literary turn to freakery often serves as a catalyst among critics to locate a similar contagion where the freakish aspects of the work spread through speculation onto its author. In this mode, authors become scrutinized for their own disabilities and novels become marginalized as grotesque or minor regional works. Both Flannery O'Connor and Carson McCullers are striking examples of this phenomenon, in that the grotesque elements in their fiction have infected their critical histories. From their first publications, O'Connor and McCullers were called out for their strange heroes. For critical histories that include or describe early reviews of both authors, see Clark and Friedman. Rath and Shaw. and Robillard. Both O'Connor and McCullers have been aligned with a love for freaks in both their lives and their literature (Carr, Adams). After their deaths, biographical claims dominate the critical landscape of their works, with reviewers citing the authors' experiences with long illnesses as the motivating force in their writing. In addition to their novels acting as primary examples of the Southern grotesque, their experiences with disability carry the elements of anomalous bodies from the page to accounts of their lives.

3. Laura B. Kennelly similarly argues that, until the end of the novel, Hazel does not believe in Jesus Christ because he cannot see him. For Hazel, "what he sees is what *is*" (164), but O'Connor demonstrates the failure of this formulation in Hazel's frequent misprision.

4. Decades of criticism on *Wise Blood* have centered on the problem of redemption in the novel. Do sin and the Church of Christ Without Christ paradoxically offer a way to return to Jesus? Does Hazel's self-blinding and mortification lead to a Christian awakening? Is Enoch's rejection of the city a sign that he is on the same path to redemption as Hazel? Since numerous books and essays have already been written on O'Connor's alignment of the grotesque and the religious, including her own thoughts as compiled in *Mystery and Manners*, I will refer the question of Christian redemption to these sources. As it relates to my argument here, however, I'll suggest that O'Connor represents pain and disfigurement as one avenue toward the depths of the real; she does not see spiritual pursuits as a casual or unscathing endeavor. She writes, "I have found that violence is strangely capable of returning my characters to reality and preparing them to accept their moment of grace. . . . This idea, that reality is something to which we must be returned at considerable cost, is one which is seldom understood by the casual reader, but it is one which is implicit in the Christian view of the world" (112). In the absence of answering these questions more neatly, I'll offer my favorite quote from Bernard McElroy on the complexities of O'Connor's work and her tendency to undermine her own apparent solutions: "O'Connor always offers the reader an escape hatch while trying to persuade him not to use it" (139).

5. Flannery O'Connor's Christian commitments inform her understanding of the necessary ties between realism, regionalism, and the grotesque. From the moment *Wise Blood* came upon the literary scene in 1952 and for the remainder of her career, Flannery O'Connor's writing was branded with the related terms "regionalist" and "grotesque." In response, she often meditated in essays and lectures on the apparent symmetry between the grotesque and Southern literature. As documented in the posthumous collection of these occasional writings, *Mystery and Manners*, O'Connor would frequently tell audiences, "When we look at a good deal of serious modern fiction, and particularly Southern fiction, we find this quality about it that is generally described, in a pejorative sense, as grotesque. Of course, I have found that anything

that comes out of the South is going to be called grotesque by the Northern reader, unless it is grotesque, in which case it is going to be called realistic" (40). Although she approaches the question here with her characteristic dry humor, O'Connor, like Bakhtin, registers the connection between realism and the grotesque, especially when viewed through the lens of regional differences. O'Connor understands Southern culture especially as it is influenced by her Christian worldview. Accordingly, the primacy of the loss of the Civil War among Southerners takes on a spiritual cast as a second Fall. This lapsarian view of the world shapes O'Connor's understanding of realist fiction and the role of the grotesque in demonstrating the distance between the modern sociopolitical world and the depths of reality. Modernity becomes synonymous with artifice, and "realism," in its deepest sense, will reflect not the mundane details of life, but the often jarring and grotesque elements that unseat established norms. As O'Connor puts it, "The novelist with Christian concerns will find in modern life distortions which are repugnant to him, and his problems will be to make these appear as distortions to an audience which is used to seeing them as natural" (33-34). O'Connor's Christian commitments give these arguments an emphatically spiritual cast, but her belief in the disjunction between the modern world and reality is characteristic of a much wider school of modernist thinkers.

6. While Elaine Scarry's *The Body in Pain* remains the foundational work on this subject, Patricia Yaeger's article "Flannery O'Connor and the Aesthetics of Torture" offers a more focused look at the literature of this period. Yaeger argues that the use of the grotesque among Southern women writers forms a subversive attack against a conservative system that looks to suppress nonconformity. See also Louis D. Rubin Jr.'s "Carson McCullers and the Aesthetic of Pain."

7. Among the characters in these novels with chronic disabilities, including *The Heart Is a Lonely Hunter*'s John Singer (who is both deaf and nonverbal), it will become increasingly clear that their function in the novel is to serve as the embodiment of threat or fantasy, providing a temporarily fixed center for the psychic projections of the other characters.

8. For more on the relationship between the concept of flexibility and its connection to disability and embodiment, see McRuer's introduction to *Crip Theory*, "Compulsory Able-Bodiedness and Queer/Disabled Existence," and Martin's *Flexible Bodies*.

9. This formulation resonates with late-twentieth-century work by feminists of color on the tactical advantages and critical insights gained by women of color given their position at the interstices of multiple oppressions. Chela Sandoval argues for U.S. third-world feminism as a "differential consciousness" predicated on mobility and transformation. In place of a static approach, this form of resistance moves among oppositional ideologies to best confront shifting currents of power. In her essay "Notes from the (non) Field," Rachel Lee outlines the limitations in scope of a resistance predicated on these counterintuitively privileged positions of critique. Addressing similar trends in the work of Chela Sandoval, Gloria Anzaldúa, and Elaine Kim, Lee argues that the risk of this constantly mobile consciousness is the failure to gain the kind of territory that is required for theoretical attention toward themselves: "It is tempting, in short, to envision our exploitation, dispossession, unsafe spaces as our own strengths. But though we may be rich in 'psychic terrain'—in our ability to grasp dualities simultaneously, precisely because we are not allowed space in any singularity—we remain materially and practically impoverished, without a stable ground on which to stand" (102).

10. In his 1989 study *Fiction of the Modern Grotesque*, Bernard McElroy argues that grotesque figures always offer a comment on their environment, as the grotesque necessarily reflects the artist's vision of a context in which surprising and abhorrent combinations are possible: "To imagine a monstrosity is to imagine a world capable of producing that monstrosity" (11). While I agree with McElroy that the grotesque is typically a comment on its context, I also hope to show that the grotesque is just as often placed at odds with the modern world as it is aligned with its excesses.

11. Wolfgang Kayser—a founder, along with Bakhtin, of grotesque studies—would agree. His 1957 volume *The Grotesque in Art and Literature* (translated into English from German in 1963) offers a definitive study of the grotesque from the Romantic period to the twentieth century. He argues that the humor in the grotesque is cynical, scornful, and satanic, a sign of an alienating modern world. Bakhtin, by contrast, positions *Rabelais and His World* in part as an intervention into Kayser's pessimistic vision of the grotesque, arguing that the rejuvenating folk laughter of the medieval grotesque is the central characteristic of the form.

12. O'Connor at times chafed under her regionalist label, but she also took seriously the alignment between Southern writing and the literary grotesque: "Whenever I'm asked why Southern writers particularly have a penchant for writing about freaks, I say it is because we are still able to recognize one. To be able to recognize a freak, you have to have some conception of the whole man. . . . In any case, it is when the freak can be sensed as a figure for our essential displacement that he attains some depth in literature" (*Mystery and Manners* 44–45). The displacement O'Connor describes here lies between contemporary Americans and Christ's image, a perspective that reflects her Catholic background and convictions. For O'Connor, freaks, by virtue of their startling difference, disrupt the status quo and illuminate the extensive fictions that obscure the "whole man" or, what she calls elsewhere, the "ultimate reaches of reality" (41). In contrast to the mundane world of modernity, the grotesque body serves as an avenue toward the real. While O'Connor's writing treads in explicitly religious waters, her alignment between the anomalous body and an obscured material real resonates with the broader tradition of the literary grotesque.

13. To deal more thoroughly with Riesman's innovative work would inevitably derail the focus of this chapter. Setting aside the nuances of his description of social character, I draw Riesman's work and its popularity into my own analysis as a manifestation of the mid-century preoccupation with the crowd. Fortunately, much of the critical ground dealing with Riesman's work has been covered; see especially Lipset and Lowenthal. By way of very brief summary, *The Lonely Crowd*, which draws from methods in both sociology and psychoanalysis, charts three major overlapping stages in a history of social character in the West. The first type, centering in the Middle Ages, is "tradition-directed," during which the social order is largely unchanging and individuals are guided by their prescribed roles. The next type, emerging in the Renaissance and through the Industrial Revolution, is "inner-directed," in which mobility and expansion are grounded by individuals whose source of direction is implanted in childhood by the nuclear family. The final type, the "other-directed," emerged in the twentieth century among the professional/managerial middle class with the rise of the organization-man. These individuals are focused primarily on the peer group, whether immediate or as represented in the media. They are more uncertain, more approval-seeking, and they have more leisure time and money than in previous eras.

Riesman is careful to argue that each of these types will coexist in every era and that the application of these terms to individuals makes static what is intended as a more fluid diagnosis. Despite cocktail party conversations in which individuals tried to assess their social type, Riesman argues that no one is exclusively inner-directed or other-directed.

14. For more on the uncanny, see the concluding discussion of chapter 1.

15. In his chapter "The Eye and the Body," Marshall Bruce Gentry takes the opposite position, arguing that Hazel Motes's redemption in *Wise Blood* emerges as the triumph of the body and the community over individualism. Gentry draws from Bakhtin and Wolfgang Kayser, respectively, in outlining a positive model of communal grotesquerie and a negative, alienating vision of the individualist grotesque. Gentry, however, imports Bakhtin's value system too completely, finding in *Wise Blood* a far sunnier portrait of familial community than the novel or O'Connor's oeuvre would seem to support (*Religion of the Grotesque* 125–127).

16. Others have described McCullers's illnesses as rheumatic fever contracted in childhood followed by frequent strokes, alcoholism, and pleurisy until her final stroke and death at age fifty.

17. In her chapter on Carson McCullers in *Sideshow U.S.A.*, Rachel Adams's analysis similarly emphasizes visibility as a central category in approaches to physical difference. In "'A Mixture of Delicious and Freak': The Queer Fiction of Carson McCullers," Adams argues that the terms "freak" and "queer" take on a special position in McCullers's work as the opposition to normative behaviors and social distinctions. "Queer" suggests deviance that is at least partially hidden, where "freak" insists on visibility. In her readings of *Member of the Wedding* and *Clock without Hands*, Adams discovers liberatory alternatives found in characters' fantasies that are inevitably repressed by social norms, often in the death of a character or an apparent assimilation. For Adams, McCullers views race and sexually as mutually constitutive identities, but race often emerges as carrying an irresolvable social stigma, meaning that "some differences, unfortunately, would continue to matter more than others" (111).

18. Sarah Gleeson-White's 2003 study *Strange Bodies* opens with a chapter on "Freakish Adolescents." In her readings of Mick Kelly and Frankie Adams, Gleeson-White demonstrates their affiliation with freakishness as characters at odds with gendered norms. She goes on to argue, however, that where the freak represents a static role, the grotesque and its emphasis on Bakhtinian "becoming" and transformation is more appropriate for these adolescent narrators who, despite their seeming conformity at the novels' ends, point to the possibility for change beyond the close of the text. Gleeson-White's work stands as the most thorough treatment to date of gender and sexuality in McCullers's writing. As I've suggested in this brief summary of the first chapter, she draws heavily on Bakhtinian theories of the grotesque in her analysis.

3 / The Uniform Body

1. Gibson locates the practice of inferential counting as part of the larger emphasis on "productivity." U.S. officers faced increasingly tight competition for limited available promotions. In some cases, counts were openly falsified to satisfy ambition, in others, officers or soldiers felt tacit pressure to use inflated enemy body counts to compensate for American losses.

2. Kovic takes on the virtue of a laboring body as an activist through the performative

work of his disabled body. Part of the stigma attached to disabled veterans stems from public perceptions of them as "free-loaders." Kovic must redefine his relationship to the state, and especially his working-class family, when he returns as a "nonproductive" citizen.

3. For a longer look at the sexualized idiom of the war, see Jacqueline Lawson's "She's a Pretty Woman . . . for a Gook." Lawson includes a list of GI slang that figures the Vietnam War as a "protracted and brutal act of sexual intercourse" (24).

4. Lawson offers an instance of this gendering of the home nation, more explicitly in the guise of the loving mother than the girlfriend or wife. In Philip J. Caputo's memoir, *A Rumor of War*, he equates his own fear of failure with the desire to avoid his mother's placating words: "That's all right, son. You didn't belong in the marines, but here with us. It's good to have you back." Lawson argues, "For Caputo, failure is equated with home, home is defined as mother, and mother is the source of 'emasculating affection and understanding,' the soothing presence who will celebrate his failure as a marine, thereby confirming his failure as a man" (21).

5. For an example of this reading of the film and its connection to Vietnam narratives, see Bonn.

6. In their work on impotence and counseling, Fracher and Kimmel argue that the stakes of sexual potency and masculine identity are often the same. Any claim to adequate male identity takes place on the proving ground of sexuality (474).

7. Perhaps the most hopeful candidate for masculine redemption lies in the novel's emphasis on physical labor. Paco's job as a dishwasher is a spiritually cleansing expression of the already working-class values of military patriotism: discipline, pain, methodical order, and hard work.

8. Kovic and Heinemann rely on experimental narrative techniques in their texts, most strikingly in both locating the moment of injury to the early pages of the book. It has become almost a cliché of literary criticism of the Vietnam War to argue that the moral and strategic ambiguities of the conflict require new literary forms to properly represent the experience. For many at home and abroad, the rationale for fighting seemed unclear. Soldiers often struggled to identify guerilla fighters in the National Liberation Front. In a war where ground would be won, abandoned, and fought for again, there were few clear examples of conventional narrative climax. As Philip Caputo tells the *New York Times*, "It was an incoherent experience in many respects. With previous conflicts, the events themselves formed the broad structure for the narrative of the novel. A novelist seeking to portray the experience could take his characters on a literal level from A to B to C, and the reader could observe what changes everyone went through as they passed through these events toward some identifiable end. Trying to impose the sort of narrative thread you find in *The Naked and the Dead*, *The Thin Red Line*, or *For Whom the Bell Tolls* was literally impossible with Vietnam. It was a square peg in a round hole" (qtd. in Kakutani 39). In two major book-length studies analyzing the literature of the war, Philip D. Beidler insists upon the importance of fantasy, myth, and imagination, even for those texts that occupy the nonfictional status of memoir. For Beidler, the most successful work on the war demonstrates the mutually reliant forces of imaginative invention and memory as suggested in the proliferation of experimental narrative techniques. Other texts on the war that exemplify this open reflection on the role of fiction and imagination in the war include Tim O'Brien's *Going After Cacciato*, Norman Mailer's *Armies of the Night*, and Michael Herr's *Dispatches*.

9. The previous borrower of my library copy revealed his or her frustration with Kovic's voice, writing in the margin, "this is *so* self-indulgent" and "please not another shift!" At the same time, he or she demonstrated a critical reading of the war and the cultural manipulation that prompts Kovic to enlist by writing comments including fifteen identifications of "propaganda!" and the lament "but it [the war] was in vain before it ever happened." For this reader, a feeling of superiority to Kovic was matched by the ability to identify points in the text that are open to a more radical position than Kovic allows himself.

10. For a more detailed analysis of the possible referents of the name "James," see Grieff, who argues that naming in the story constructs a literary and historical brotherhood as part of Heinemann's desire for men of his generation to reconcile their experiences of the war.

11. All Jeffords citations refer to *The Remasculinization of America: Gender and the Vietnam War* unless otherwise noted as "Tattoos."

12. Qtd. in Scott 74.

13. While the primary focus of identification lies in military masculinity, *Paco's Story* adds a class dimension to the homosocial bond, insisting on community among working-class grunts. Nearly a cliché of Vietnam War characterization, Lieutenant Stennett embodies military command as ineffectual, cowardly, and dangerously narrow-sighted. The nursery rhyme cadence of his name and rank robs Stennett of any individuality beyond his position. Heinemann's refrain throughout the gang-rape scene, "Good morning to you, Lieutenant," makes a mockery of structures of authority in the face of unchecked sexual violence. During this episode, Lieutenant Stennett—"the English major from Dartmouth"—turns his back to the rape and murder and makes coffee. In *The Remasculinization of America*, Susan Jeffords observes that personal narratives of the war emphasize a separation between the soldier and government (here figured as a naïve commander), in part expressing a desire to reclaim masculine values for the individual even in the face of a potentially emasculating military loss. By locating failure in the structures of government, individual participants can recuperate their own claims to heroism. Characters as diverse as John Rambo and Richard Nixon have taken refuge in this heroic individualism, blaming defeat on military command and the U.S. Congress, respectively (Jeffords, *Remasculinization* 2).

4 / Conceiving the Freakish Body

1. Lee Edelman, in fact, would like to challenge the universal appeal of these seemingly rhetorical questions. He takes as his starting point the constant alignment of the political with the child/future on one hand and, on the other, the oppositional figure of the queer as, by definition, outside these heteronormative fantasies. In his self-described polemic, *No Future: Queer Theory and the Death Drive*, Edelman argues that instead of using liberal logic to refold queers into the "reproductive futurism" of the political—which would focus on the fact that, of course, queers have rich and healthy relationships with children as parents, relatives, and friends—there is value in taking the negative figuration of the queer seriously. Psychoanalysis, for Edelman, provides the theoretical framework to demonstrate the ways in which this oppositional structure can disrupt the political and social order.

2. For an account of disability's intervention in the abortion debate and the connections between disability studies and feminism more broadly, see Garland-Thomson's "Feminist Disability Studies." See also Fine and Asch.

3. The *OED* definition of "Americana" and selected examples of its usage offer a fascinating collection of items included under the term. Given the context of *My Year of Meats*, a 2001 quote from the *Atlanta Journal and Constitution* seems particularly germane: "In Japan, Americana is always in style whether it's golf courses, water parks, baseball—or bass fishing." Another press quote from 1994 calls Richard Nixon "a piece of Americana and a chunk of history." This alliance between the quotidian practices of American culture and a figure of national rise and fall points to the interesting ways in which "Americana" can hold together both the representative and the extraordinary. In another example, a 1962 reference describes an "Americana" column that collected "regional press absurdities of all kinds." Two of these terms—"regional" and "absurdities"—outline another interesting valence in our collectively held notions of that which is characteristically American. While Americana can include images of the ubiquitous, such as apple pie or diner jukeboxes, it also emphasizes that which is specific, local, and unusual.

4. The mother of the Binewski clan, Lillian Hinchcliff is described by her daughter as a "water-cool aristocrat from the fastidious side of Boston's Beacon Hill. . . . She has the long-faced, thin-nosed stamp of the Protestant aristocrat" (7, 13). In this portrait Dunn illustrates the ways in which the stock figures of Americana are commonly located in the body. In this case Lillian's face is imagined to bear the imprint of her race, class, and religion.

5. In their discussion of *Geek Love*, Mitchell and Snyder offer an extended reading of this scene, including an analysis of Al's moment of realization in the rose garden as a classic modernist epiphany (147–148). This "epiphany," in turn, supports their larger thesis that in citing her literary antecedents and their tendency to exploit physical difference, Dunn develops an allegory for narrative dependence on the bizarre and "investigates the site of metaphorical operations themselves" (146).

6. In the section of *On Longing* titled "The Collection: Paradise of Consumption" (151–169), Susan Stewart argues that in contrast to the souvenir, the collection is an ahistorical practice, focusing on example rather than sample, an aesthetic endeavor that replaces context and origin with classification (153). In its dissolution of traditional historical and local markers in favor of the itinerant social body of the carnival, *Geek Love* engages in a similar form of ahistorical collection in order to stand in for a national body that privileges the general over the specific.

7. Ozeki further locates Wal-Mart as a site of national homogenization, writing, "But as a documentarian of American culture, Wal-Mart is a nightmare. When it comes to towns, Hope, Alabama, becomes the same as Hope, Wyoming, or, for that matter, Hope, Alaska, and in the end, all that remains of our pioneering aspirations are the confused and self-conscious simulacra of relic culture: Ye Olde Curiosities 'n' Copie Shoppe, Deadeye Dick's Saloon and Karaoke Bar—ingenious hybrids and strange global grafts that are the local businessperson's only chance of survival in economies of scale" (57).

8. Martin's *Flexible Bodies*, articulates both the possibilities and the dangers of this notion of "flexibility." In charting changing conceptual approaches to the immune system, Martin finds that the controlling cultural metaphors of the body are radically democratic, emerging both from medical "experts" and from patients looking to account for their own conditions. The recurring trope of flexibility across many sources suggests possibilities for Martin, as in the corporate training courses that challenge

traditional hierarchies by suspending employees up on tightropes. She worries, however, about individuals for whom flexibility is not a choice or an exercise, but the mandate of their low-paying jobs. The ambivalence reflected in Martin's book emerges in Ozeki's work as well, allowing for a compromise position in accounts of the body.

9. Monica Chiu elaborates on the flexible arm of global corporations in this description of McDonald's creative expansion into new markets:

> The overwhelming success of McDonald's cheap, high-fat meals . . . stems neither from rigorous standardization—offering a uniform product to homogenous populations world wide—nor from mere good fortune. Rather, in a world of rapid corporate globalization, the restaurant chain has adapted to cultural preferences and demands much to its financial advantage: vegetable McNuggets and mutton burgers grace menus in India, while Japan, Hong Kong, and Taiwan offer the ever popular teriyaki burger. . . . In the Philippines, McSpaghetti is regularly dished up, and Ronald McDonald is regularly joined by Aunt McDonald at Beijing birthday parties as a nod to China's emphasis on family values. (99)

10. Shameem Black eloquently describes how Ozeki's ability to draw connections between abuses that occur on wildly different scales and on different continents lays the groundwork for a transnational feminist network: "[Ozeki] emphasizes the conceptual similarities among all the sources of harm in the book. . . . DES scars Jane as domestic violence and rape scar Akiko, and while the novel refuses to conflate these problems, it asks us to recognize these experiences as one basis for their eventually collaborative relationship. . . . This parallel format seeks to identify recurring agents of violence, such as patriarchal privilege, capitalist expansion, and dehumanizing forms of labor, while attending to the diverse ways that women experience and respond to such violence" (237–238).

11. Reflecting the didactic nature of the novel, Ozeki breaks from the action of the plot to allow her narrator to present a "Documentary Interlude" on the subject of DES (124–127). According to Ozeki, diethylstilbestrol, or DES, is a synthetic estrogen introduced in 1938. Its primary use was in poultry farming, where injected DES in male chickens caused chemical castration and the development of female characteristics that make the birds more marketable. The FDA banned the use of the hormone in 1959 because working-class Southern men (like Purcell Dawes in the novel) were themselves showing female traits after eating cheap parts. Despite the FDA ban in the poultry industry, DES use in cattle production only grew after 1954, when a nutritionist at Iowa State learned that cattle would fatten and could be brought to slaughter sooner with DES. Hormonal and antibiotic intervention in farming made assembly-line-style massive feedlots possible, driving many smaller farms out of business. In addition to the agricultural uses of DES, obstetricians used the hormone to prevent miscarriages and premature births. In 1971 researchers discovered that young women whose mothers were treated with DES were at risk for cervical cancer, irregular menstruation, and difficult pregnancies. In addition, researchers learned that not only was DES ineffective at preventing miscarriages, but it also could cause infant death. In 1979 the United States banned the use of DES in livestock production, but subsequent tests demonstrate that many farmers continue to use the hormone illegally despite its carcinogenic properties. Ozeki drives home this cautionary lesson by citing the statistic that "95% of feedlot cattle

in the United States still receive some form of growth-promoting hormone or pharmaceutical in feed supplements" (126).

12. Shameem Black, by contrast, argues for a more secure split between transgressive physical changes like gender-bending personal style and "unwanted" disabilities: "Differentiating these unwanted bodily changes from postmodern celebrations of transgressive gender identities and nontraditional constructions of the body, the novel refuses to romanticize these particular physical shifts as anything other than the effects of patriarchal and corporate violence" (232). Black continues in a footnote to the above sentence, "Ozeki explicitly contrasts liberating transgression of gender norms with corporate manipulations of the human body. As a tall, boyish, half-Japanese woman in Japan, Jane Takagi-Little soon abandons norms of Japanese femininity and accentuates her androgynous, nontraditional physical appearance. Her DES-related infertility, however, reminds us of the costs of unwanted physical changes" (251). While Black's distinction conforms to the dominant logic of Ozeki's novel, in which disability stands as the tragic effect of corporate and patriarchal abuse, I argue there is a latent understanding of disability in Ozeki's work that allows for injury as not just misfortune, but also as a more accurate reflection of embodiment as a complex relation between human and environment, including corporate practices.

13. Much of Emily Martin's work counters self-authorizing claims of "natural fact" among scientific authorities, instead outlining the ideological assumptions that underlie the medical model. In her essay "Body Narratives, Body Boundaries," Martin demonstrates the ways that accounts of fertilization in medicine, popular culture, and science education unfold according to gendered and heterosexist norms—for example, in familiar figures like the agile, conquering sperm and the docile, conquered egg. Ozeki references the former image in her description of the sperm as "a whip-tailed armada!"; both the figure of the battling armada and the exclamation point confirm standard accounts of the sperm's active role.

14. Browning's work was especially revolutionary in casting disabled people in the film as sideshow performers instead of relying on special makeup and costume effects. In an era when, over half a century later, Hollywood stars are rewarded for their "daring" choices in portraying disabled people, we might wish that Browning's legacy in this respect had been more far-reaching.

15. For audiences, the problem at the heart of this proposed marriage lies entirely in the simultaneously sexed and asexual freakish body. The film's producers understood this curiosity as a motivating interest in seeing the film and, for the 1949 re-release, created a series of accompanying posters tempting audiences to "See—what sex is the half man half woman? See—do Siamese twins make love?" As I argue in chapter 1, the sexual intricacies of disability lie at the heart of cultural approaches to the anomalous body. As in the bedroom scene where Twain piques the reader's interest in the undressing Cappello twins, Dunn's conjoined twins, Ely and Iphy, offer a succinct explanation of their audience's fascination: "You know what the norms really want to ask? . . . How do we fuck?" (207).

16. In his essay on the novel, Michael Hardin argues similarly, "The sign implies that instead of being something truly other or alien, the potential for being or bearing a freak exists within the 'norm' population. It suggests that we are not as far removed from the freak as we might like to think" (340).

17. Michael Hardin's essay on *Geek Love* draws from his background in

fundamentalist Christianity to elaborate on the competing national expectations for the body. On the one hand, he argues, we have inherited the Protestant tradition of denying the physical body, but on the other we face the constant cultural imperative to focus on the body and push it toward perfection (338). Such arguments are helpful in elaborating the always-plural nature of cultural constructions of America and its embodied citizens, even as each of these sometimes conflicting, sometimes cooperative traditions imagines itself as a singular force.

5 / Some Assembly Required

1. Most famously, see the frontispiece to Thomas Hobbes's *Leviathan* (1648).

2. While magazine and newspaper reviewers were quick to herald *Infinite Jest* as "the next step in fiction" (*Atlantic Monthly*, cited on the novel's back cover), academic critics have been predictably slower to take up Wallace's work. Of the handful of articles published on the novel in peer-reviewed journals, Tom LeClair's was the first. "The Prodigious Fiction of Richard Powers, William Vollmann, and David Foster Wallace" meditates on the multiple meanings of prodigy—as extraordinary, enormous, excessive—to class Powers, Vollmann, and Wallace as writers of a new form of fiction in which the novels themselves are conceived as information systems. Two recent book-length guides of Wallace's work offer readers an orientation to *Infinite Jest*; see Burn and Carlisle.

3. Davis, *Enforcing Normalcy* 29–35.

4. Davis describes this experiment and its consequences for both political organization and disabled people in a chapter of his 2002 collection of essays, *Bending over Backwards* (111).

5. Davis offers a helpful historical perspective on the medical emphasis on averages. He describes the century-long evolution from a Manichean model of illness, which staged a battle between health and disease, to the system that becomes dominant by 1850, in which health and disease are no longer opposed forces but exist along a continuum. In this system, illness becomes measured as either lack or excess and "disease becomes associated with prefixes like 'hyper' or 'hypo,' becoming in essence an extreme of normal health" (*Bending over Backwards* 112).

6. In his essay "The Rule of Normalcy ," Davis similarly notes the paradox of individualism in order to argue that democracy requires a notion of the "average citizen" (108). Included in his 2002 follow-up to *Enforcing Normalcy*, this essay demonstrates the implications of the reign of normalcy for both politics and disability. He closes the essay by cautioning that a civil rights paradigm for disability movements draws from the same ideology of equality that constructs limited and oppressive models of embodiment.

7. Wendy Brown explores the disciplinary and philosophical limits of discrete models of subject formation in her 1997 article for *Differences*. Brown describes the occasion of the article, provocatively titled "The Impossibility of Women's Studies," as the struggle within her department to establish core courses for a degree program in women's studies. She argues that as the object of study within women's studies, theoretical challenges to the coherence of "woman" require a discussion about the viability of the discipline. She takes up the call from feminists of color for a greater multiplicity of analysis, but critiques this scholarship as failing to account for the ways in which subjects are produced as well as regulated by discourse. Instead of an intersectional

or overlapping framework which suggests that different mechanisms of power operate independently, Brown outlines the challenge to scholarship represented by a model of power that sees marked subjects as created through multiple kinds of discourses in varying ways, but for which linear and discrete accounts will fail to describe subject production.

8. Jorge Luis Borges, "Of Exactitude in Science," *A Universal History of Infamy*, trans. Norman Thomas di Giovanni (New York: Dutton, 1972), 141.

9. In "The King's Two Bodies: Lincoln, Wilson, Nixon, and Presidential Self-Sacrifice" (in *"Ronald Reagan," the Movie* 1–43), Michael Rogin works out the contemporary political legacy of the Elizabethan doctrine that aligned the natural body with the body politic. His chapter studies key moments in which American presidents represent themselves as the physical embodiment of the nation.

10. My discussion of ritual and shared cultural texts as constitutive of national identity draws from Benedict Anderson's *Imagined Communities*.

11. David Foster Wallace describes a similar correspondence between critics' formal strategies and their objects of critique in his essay "E Unibus Pluram." He argues that the postmodern strategies of cultural critique have lost their bite as television and advertising use the same techniques of cynicism, irony, and absurdity in the interests of consumerism.

12. As discussed in chapter 2, the most common critical approaches to the grotesque are split into two camps. In the first, physical anomaly is seen as a metaphor for a chaotic world. The second mode, following Mikhail Bakhtin, takes up the figure of anomalous bodies for their transgressive potential. In concert with a poststructuralist bent toward heterogeneity and deconstruction, the carnivalesque is a liminal figure with the power to challenge conventional unities. I argue that both modes require an aestheticization of bodily difference in which the representation of abnormality produces only social or ontological critique. Physical and formal heterogeneity offers an avenue to describe a larger destabilization of trusted categories, but the street is one-way; there is no reciprocal attention to the subject position of disabled people.

In her essay "Dialogizing Postmodern Carnival," Catherine Nichols critiques the emphasis on liberation in Bakhtin-inspired criticism and wants to reassert an attention to the formation of grotesque figures. As she argues, the grotesque in Wallace's work is not a fleeting transgression of a more stable hegemony, but is the horrific *effect* of contemporary geopolitics. Excess and permeability in Wallace's world are not cause for celebration, but are the products of environmental "experialism" and pharmacological overdependence. While I agree with Nichols's revision, her work largely considers disabled characters a means to an end: Wallace's ecological critique. Like the more dominant modes of reading the grotesque, Nichols sees disabled characters as a sign of social and political excesses.

13. For more on these dynamics, see Shapiro.

14. For Siebers, realism is not an inherently exploitative genre, but offers the chance to effect change. In his essay "Disability in Theory," Siebers argues that the emphasis on discourse in contemporary theory empties out the corporeal experience of disability. He advocates a turn to the "real" and "realism," claiming that current attitudes about disability are so entrenched in expectations about the body that even radical changes in policy and attitudes will be inadequate to changing these expectations.

15. Kristeva 3.

16. In N. Katherine Hayles's essay "The Illusion of Autonomy and the Fact of Recursivity: Virtual Ecologies, Entertainment, and *Infinite Jest*," she argues that "another way to think about abjection is as an attempt to preserve the autonomy of the self in the face of an unavoidable confrontation with interconnection. Instead of acknowledging the coproduction that binds together the subject and the environment, the self clings to its precious autonomy and creates a liminal space in which the distinction between inside and outside, self and other, momentarily blurs" (684-685). These lines offer an interesting example of critical "interconnection" as our essays come together around the concept of abjection and then split along related, but distinct, threads of inquiry. Where Hayles critiques the illusion of autonomy by identifying recursivity as the shared heart of both virtual and natural environments, my argument against individualism and exploration of interdependence is animated by my homology of textual, physical, and social bodies.

17. In *Narrative Prosthesis*, David Mitchell and Sharon Snyder offer an extensive lineage of the use of disability as a tool in characterization.

Conclusion

1. At least two fascinating instances of political theater mark the passage of the ADA. Many scholars would argue that the spring 1990 ADAPT (American Disabled for Accessible Public Transit) protest, where wheelchair users left their chairs to crawl up the stairs of the Capitol building, left an indelible impression in the national imagination. More subtly, Ruth Colker argues that Ronald Reagan's "joke" regarding presidential candidate Michael Dukakis's record of psychiatric treatment—"Look, I'm not going to pick on an invalid"—pressed candidate and Vice President George H. W. Bush to publicly support early versions of the proposed legislation during the 1988 campaign. These examples demonstrate the ways in which public narratives structure legislative process.

2. In *States of Injury*, Wendy Brown discusses the ways in which legal redress aligns injury with identity. Brown describes two important effects of this turn to the law to address oppression. First, legal redress casts the law and the state as "neutral arbiters of injury rather than as themselves invested with the power to injure" (27). Second, in turning to the law for resolution, "political ground is ceded to moral and juridical ground . . . ; injury is thereby rendered intentional and individual [and] politics is reduced to punishment" (27-28). Legal redress, then, shrinks oppression from the sphere of complex political conditions to an isolatable case of injury and compensatory cure. For Tobin Siebers's critique of Brown and his contrasting model of identity politics as not merely a case of "wounded attachments" (Brown's term), but a coalition involved in political process, see *Disability Theory*, especially 95, 105, 193, 204.

3. In her 2003 book *Imagine Otherwise*, Kandice Chuh makes a similar point regarding the calcification of the rubric "Asian America," advocating a critical turn to the critique it inspires rather than hanging on to pan-ethnicity as an expression of subjectivity. She writes, "We can reinhabit and rearticulate difference not as the otherness constructed by certain practices of power . . . but instead as the basis for unification. . . . Thinking deconstructively, we can understand that identity is contingent upon difference, that difference precedes and constitutes identity" (247).

4. Mol's essay details the many ways in which variables are privileged or weeded out and how parameters are constructed. In another example of the influence of narrative

practice, medical practitioners and researchers commonly manage these complexities by recasting patients' stories into discrete, quantifiable numbers. The anxiety and
psychic costs of surgery and a hospital stay, for example, were measured in one clinical
evaluation by researchers who "subtracted 6 days from the life expectancy of someone
who undergoes an operation, because that is the number of days they spend in the
hospital" (Mol 235). The striking unevenness between the depth of this experience
and the shallowness of subtracting "6 days of life expectancy" may prompt a lament
over the inadequacies of the medical model to account for the complexities of life. Mol
argues, however, that conflicting impulses toward simplicity or heterogeneity should
not arrest our analysis of complexity; she invites, "It is an urgent task to find ways of
avoiding dreams of rationality and order, as well as equally pure dreams of holistic
sensitivity or true messy wildness" (248).

5. Foucault most famously inaugurated such objections with his claim, "Where
there is power, there is resistance, and yet, or rather consequently, this resistance is
never in a position of exteriority to power" (*History of Sexuality* 95). For an extended
discussion of the political implication of this idea, see Wendy Brown's *States of Injury*.

BIBLIOGRAPHY

Americans with Disabilities Act of 1990. Pub. L. 101–336. 26 July 1990. Stat. 104.327.

Adams, Rachel. *Sideshow U.S.A.* Chicago: University of Chicago Press, 2001.

Anderson, Benedict R. *Imagined Communities: Reflections on the Origin and Spread of Nationalism.* London: Verso, 1991.

Appadurai, Arjun. *Modernity at Large: Cultural Dimensions of Globalization.* Public Worlds. Minneapolis: University of Minnesota Press, 1996.

Arieli, Yehoshua. *Individualism and Nationalism in American Ideology.* Baltimore, MD: Penguin Books, 1966.

Armstrong, Tim. *Modernism, Technology and the Body.* Cambridge: Cambridge University Press, 1998.

Asals, Frederick. *Flannery O'Connor: The Imagination of Extremity.* Athens: University of Georgia Press, 1982.

Bakhtin, Mikhail. *Rabelais and His World.* Trans. Hélène Iswolsky. Bloomington: Indiana University Press, 1968.

Barabak, Mark Z. "The Democrats' 'Poster Boy.'" *Los Angeles Times Magazine,* 18 July 2004, 14.

Barnes, Elizabeth. *States of Sympathy: Seduction and Democracy in the American Novel.* New York: Columbia University Press, 1997.

Baynton, Douglas C. "Disability and the Justification of Inequality in American History." *The New Disability History: American Perspectives.* Ed. Paul K. Longmore and Lauri Umansky. New York: New York University Press, 2001. 33–57.

Beidler, Philip D. *American Literature and the Experience of the Vietnam War.* Athens: University of Georgia Press, 1982.

Beiner, Ronald. *Theorizing Citizenship.* SUNY Series in Political Theory. Albany: State University of New York Press, 1995.

Berlant, Lauren. *The Queen of America Goes to Washington City: Essays on Sex and Citizenship.* Durham, NC: Duke University Press, 1997.

Bertolini, Joseph C. *The Serpent within Politics: Literature and American Individualism.* Oxford: University Press of America, 1997.

Bérubé, Michael. "Citizenship and Disability." *Dissent* 50.2 (2003): 52–57.

Bibby, Michael. *Hearts and Minds: Bodies, Poetry, and Resistance in the Vietnam Era.* New Brunswick, NJ: Rutgers University Press, 1996.

Black, Shameem. "Fertile Cosmofeminism: Ruth L. Ozeki and Transnational Reproduction." *Meridians: Feminism, Race, Transnationalism* 5.1 (2004): 226–256.

Bonn, Maria S. "A Different World: The Vietnam Veteran Comes Home." *Fourteen Landing Zones: Approaches to Vietnam Literature.* Ed. Philip K. Jackson. Iowa City: University of Iowa Press, 1991. 1–14.

Boudreau, Kristin. *Sympathy in American Literature: American Sentiments from Jefferson to the Jameses.* Gainesville: University Press of Florida, 2002.

Brennan, Timothy. "The National Longing for Form." *Nation and Narration.* Ed. Homi K. Bhabha. London: Routledge, 1990. 44–70.

Brown, Bill. "Monstrosity." *The Material Unconscious: American Amusement, Stephen Crane, and the Economies of Play.* Cambridge, MA: Harvard University Press, 1996. 199–245.

———. *A Sense of Things: The Object Matter of American Literature.* Chicago: University of Chicago Press, 2003.

Brown, Gillian. *Domestic Individualism: Imagining Self in Nineteenth-Century America.* Berkeley: University of California Press, 1990.

Brown, Wendy. *States of Injury: Power and Freedom in Late Modernity.* Princeton, NJ: Princeton University Press, 1995.

———. "The Impossibility of Women's Studies." *Differences* 9.5 (1997): 79–101.

Burn, Stephen. *David Foster Wallace's "Infinite Jest": A Reader's Guide.* Continuum Contemporaries. New York: Continuum Books, 2003.

Butler, Judith. *Bodies That Matter: On the Discursive Limits of "Sex."* New York: Routledge, 1993.

Campbell, James. "Coming Home: Difference and Reconciliation in Narratives of Return to 'the World.'" *The United States and Viet Nam from War to Peace: Papers from an Interdisciplinary Conference on Reconciliation.* Ed. Robert M. Slabey. Jefferson, NC: MacFarland, 1996. 198–207.

Carlisle, Greg. *Elegant Complexity: A Study of David Foster Wallace's "Infinite Jest."* Universal City, CA: Sideshow Media Group, 2007.

Carr, Virginia Spencer. *The Lonely Hunter: A Biography of Carson McCullers.* New York: Carroll and Graff, 1975.

Caruso, Teresa. *"On the Subject of the Feminist Business": Re-reading Flannery O'Connor.* New York: Peter Lang, 2004.

Cassuto, Leonard. *The Inhuman Race: The Racial Grotesque in American Literature and Culture*. New York: Columbia University Press, 1997.

Chakrabarty, Dipesh. "Time of History and Times of Gods." *The Politics of Culture in the Shadow of Capital*. Ed. Lisa Lowe and David Lloyd. Durham, NC: Duke University Press, 1997. 35–60.

Charlton, James I. *Nothing about Us without Us: Disability Oppression and Empowerment*. Berkeley: University of California Press, 1998.

Chinn, Sarah E. *Technology and the Logic of American Racism: A Cultural History of the Body as Evidence*. Critical Research in Material Culture. London: Continuum, 2000.

Chiu, Monica. "Postnational Globalization and (En)Gendered Meat Production in Ruth L. Ozeki's *My Year of Meats*." *LIT* 12.1 (2001): 99–128.

Chuh, Kandice. *Imagine Otherwise: On Asian Americanist Critique*. Durham, NC: Duke University Press, 2003.

Clark, Beverly Lyon, and Melvin J. Friedman. *Critical Essays on Carson McCullers*. New York: G. K. Hall, 1996.

Cleland, Max. "Former Senator Max Cleland Introduces Senator John Kerry." 24 March 2005. http://www.pbs.org/newshour/vote2004/demconvention/speeches/cleland.html.

Colker, Ruth. *The Disability Pendulum: The First Decade of the Americans with Disabilities Act*. New York: New York University Press, 2005.

Corker, Mairian, and Tom Shakespeare, eds. *Disability/Postmodernity: Embodying Disability Theory*. London: Continuum, 2002.

Coulter, Ann. "Cleland Drops a Political Grenade." 2004. http://www.townhall.com/columnists/anncoulter/printac20040212.shtml.

Cox, James M. *Mark Twain: The Fate of Humor*. Princeton, NJ: Princeton University Press, 1966.

Crenshaw, Kimberle. "Demarginalizing the Intersection of Race and Sex: A Black Feminist Critique of Antidiscrimination Doctrine, Feminist Theory, and Antiracist Politics." *Feminism and Politics*. Ed. Anne Phillips. Oxford: Oxford University Press, 1998. 314–343.

Culler, Jonathan. "Anderson and the Novel." *Diacritics* 29.4 (1999): 20–39.

Davis, Lennard J. *Enforcing Normalcy: Disability, Deafness, and the Body*. London: Verso, 1995.

———. *Bending over Backwards: Disability, Dismodernism, and Other Difficult Positions*. New York: New York University Press, 2002.

Deutsch, Helen, and Felicity Nussbaum, eds. *"Defects": Engendering the Modern Body*. Corporealities. Ann Arbor: University of Michigan Press, 2000.

Di Renzo, Anthony. *American Gargoyles: Flannery O'Connor and the Medieval Grotesque*. Carbondale: Southern Illinois University Press, 1993.

Dimock, Wai-Chee. *Empire for Liberty: Melville and the Poetics of Individualism*. Princeton, NJ: Princeton University Press, 1989.

Douglas, Ann. *The Feminization of American Culture*. New York: Alfred A. Knopf, 1977.

Duden, Barbara. *The Woman beneath the Skin: A Doctor's Patients in Eighteenth-Century Germany*. Cambridge, MA: Harvard University Press, 1991.

Dunn, Katherine. *Geek Love*. New York: Vintage Books, 2002.

Ecker, Gisela. "Eating Identities—from Migration to Lifestyle: Mary Antin, Ntozake Shange, Ruth Ozeki." *Wandering Selves: Essays on Migration and Multiculturalism*. Ed. Michael Porsche and Christian Berkemeier. Essen, Germany: Blaue Eule, 2000. 171–183.

Edelman, Lee. *No Future: Queer Theory and the Death Drive*. Durham, NC: Duke University Press, 2004.

Ellis, Markman. *The Politics of Sensibility: Race, Gender, and Commerce in the Sentimental Novel*. Cambridge: Cambridge University Press, 1996.

Elshtain, Jean Bethke, ed. *Public Man, Private Woman: Women in Social and Political Thought*. Princeton, NJ: Princeton University Press, 1981.

Fiedler, Leslie. *Freaks: Myths and Images of the Secret Self*. New York: Simon and Schuster, 1978.

Figley, Charles R., and Seymour Leventman. *Strangers at Home: Vietnam Veterans since the War*. New York: Praeger, 1980.

Fine, Michelle, and Adrienne Asch. *Women with Disabilities: Essays in Psychology, Culture, and Politics*. Philadelphia: Temple University Press, 1988.

Foucault, Michel. *The Birth of the Clinic: An Archaeology of Medical Perception*. World of Man (London, England). New York: Pantheon Books, 1973.

———. *Discipline and Punish: The Birth of the Prison*. London: Allen Lane, 1977.

———. "Nietzsche, Genealogy, History." *Language, Counter-Memory, Practice: Selected Essays and Interviews by Michel Foucault*. Ed. Donald F. Bouchard. Ithaca, NY: Cornell University Press, 1977. 139–164.

———. *The History of Sexuality*. Vol. 1. New York: Vintage Books, 1990.

Foucault, Michel, et al. *Abnormal: Lectures at the Collège de France, 1974–1975*. New York: Picador, 2003.

Fracher, Jeffery, and Michael S. Kimmel. "Hard Issues and Soft Spots: Counseling Men about Sexuality." *Men's Lives*. Ed. Jeffery Fracher and Michael S. Kimmel. New York: Macmillan, 1989. 471–481.

Fraser, Nancy. "Rethinking the Public Sphere: A Contribution to the Critique of Actually Existing Democracy." *Social Text* 25/26 (1990): 56–80.

———. "Recognition or Redistribution? A Critical Reading of Iris Young's Justice and the Politics of Difference." *Journal of Political Philosophy* 3.2 (1995): 166–180.

Fredericks, Nancy. "Twain's Indelible Twins." *Nineteenth-Century Literature* 43.4 (1989): 484–499.

Freud, Sigmund. "The Uncanny." *The Standard Edition of the Complete Psychological Works of Sigmund Freud*. Ed. and trans. James Strachey. Vol. 17. London: Hogarth, 1953. 219–252.

Garland-Thomson, Rosemarie. *Freakery: Cultural Spectacles of the Extraordinary Body*. New York: New York University Press, 1996.

———. *Extraordinary Bodies: Figuring Physical Disability in American Culture and Literature*. New York: Columbia University Press, 1997.

———. "Feminist Disability Studies: A Review Essay." *Signs* 30.2 (2005): 1557–1587.

———. *Staring: How We Look*. New York: Oxford University Press, 2009.

Gentry, Marshall Bruce. *Flannery O'Connor's Religion of the Grotesque*. Jackson: University Press of Mississippi, 1986.

———. "The Eye vs. the Body: Individual and Communal Grotesquerie in *Wise Blood*." *The Critical Response to Flannery O'Connor*. Ed. Douglas Robillard. Westport, CT: Praeger, 2004. 223–228.

Gibson, James William. *The Perfect War: Technowar in Vietnam*. Boston: Atlantic Monthly Press, 1986.

Gillman, Susan. *Dark Twins: Imposture and Identity in Mark Twain's America*. Chicago: University of Chicago Press, 1989.

Gillman, Susan, and Forrest G. Robinson. *Mark Twain's "Pudd'nhead Wilson": Race, Conflict, and Culture*. Durham, NC: Duke University Press, 1990.

Gilmore, Michael T. *Surface and Depth: The Quest for Legibility in American Culture*. Oxford: Oxford University Press, 2003.

Gleeson-White, Sarah. *Strange Bodies: Gender and Identity in the Novels of Carson McCullers*. Tuscaloosa: University of Alabama Press, 2003.

Goffman, Erving. *Stigma: Notes on the Management of Spoiled Identity*. New York: Simon and Schuster, 1986.

———. *The Presentation of Self in Everyday Life*. Anchor Books. New York: Doubleday, 1990.

Greiff, Louis K. "In the Name of the Brother: Larry Heinemann's *Paco's Story* and Male America." *Critique: Studies in Contemporary Fiction* 41.4 (2000): 381–389.

Grosz, Elizabeth. *Volatile Bodies: Toward a Corporeal Feminism*. Bloomington: Indiana University Press, 1994.

———. "Intolerable Ambiguity: Freaks as/at the Limit." *Freakery: Cultural Spectacles of the Extraordinary Body*. Ed. Rosemarie Garland-Thomson. New York: New York University Press, 1996. 55–66.

Gunsteren, Herman R. van. *A Theory of Citizenship: Organizing Plurality in Contemporary Democracies*. Boulder, CO: Westview Press, 1998.

Gysin, Fritz. *The Grotesque in American Negro Fiction: Jean Toomer, Richard Wright, and Ralph Ellison*. Cooper Monographs on English and American Language and Literature. Bern, Switzerland: Francke, 1975.

Haar, Maria. *The Phenomenon of the Grotesque in Modern Southern Fiction: Some Aspects of Its Form and Function*. Stockholm, Sweden: Universitetet i Umeå/Almqvist & Wiksell International, 1983.

Halberstam, Judith. *Skin Shows: Gothic Horror and the Technology of Monsters*. Durham, NC: Duke University Press, 1995.

Haraway, Donna Jeanne. "A Cyborg Manifesto: Science, Technology, and Socialist-Feminism in the Late Twentieth Century." *Simians, Cyborgs, and Women: The Reinvention of Nature.* New York: Routledge, 1991.

Hardin, Michael. "Fundamentally Freaky: Collapsing the Freak/Norm Binary in *Geek Love.*" *Critique* 45.4 (2004): 337–346.

Harpham, Geoffrey Galt. *On the Grotesque: Strategies of Contradiction in Art and Literature.* Princeton, NJ: Princeton University Press, 1982.

Hayles, N. Katherine. "Postmodern Parataxis: Embodied Texts, Weightless Information." *American Literary History* 2.3 (1990): 394–421.

———. "The Illusion of Autonomy and the Fact of Recursivity: Virtual Ecologies, Entertainment and *Infinite Jest.*" *New Literary History* 30.3 (1999): 675–697.

———. *How We Became Posthuman: Virtual Bodies in Cybernetics, Literature, and Informatics.* Chicago: University of Chicago Press, 1999.

Hays, Peter L. *The Limping Hero: Grotesques in Literature.* New York: New York University Press, 1971.

Heinemann, Larry. *Paco's Story.* New York: Farrar Straus Giroux, 1986.

———. "Foreword: A Word to the Reader." *Paco's Story.* New York: Penguin Books, 1987. ix–x.

Heller, Thomas C., Morton Sosna, and David E. Wellbery. *Reconstructing Individualism: Autonomy, Individuality, and the Self in Western Thought.* Stanford, CA: Stanford University Press, 1986.

Hellmann, John. *American Myth and the Legacy of Vietnam.* New York: Columbia University Press, 1986.

Henderson, Carol E., and Hazel Arnett Ervin. "The 'Walking Wounded': Rethinking Black Women's Identity in Ann Petry's *The Street.*" *The Critical Response to Ann Petry.* Ed. Hazel Arnett Ervin. Critical Responses in Arts and Letters. Westport, CT: Praeger, 2005. 264–278.

Herndl, Diane Price. *Invalid Women: Figuring Feminine Illness in American Fiction and Culture, 1840–1940.* Chapel Hill: University of North Carolina Press, 1993.

Herr, Michael. *Dispatches.* New York: Vintage International, 1991.

Hicks, Heather. "'This Strange Communion': Surveillance and Spectatorship in Ann Petry's *The Street.*" *African American Review* 37.1 (2003): 21–37.

Hillyer, Barbara. *Feminism and Disability.* Norman: University of Okalahoma Press, 1993.

Hoover, Herbert. *American Individualism.* Garden City, NY: Doubleday, Page & Company, 1922.

Horne, A. D., ed. *The Wounded Generation: America after Vietnam.* Englewood Cliffs, NJ: Prentice-Hall, 1981.

Huet, Marie Hélène. *Monstrous Imagination.* Cambridge, MA: Harvard University Press, 1993.

Jeffords, Susan. *The Remasculinization of America: Gender and the Vietnam War.* Bloomington: Indiana University Press, 1989.

———. "Tattoos, Scars, Diaries, and Writing Masculinity." *The Vietnam War and American Culture*. Ed. John Carlos Rowe and Rick Berg. New York: Columbia University Press, 1991. 208–225.

Jehlen, Myra. *American Incarnation: The Individual, the Nation, and the Continent*. Cambridge, MA: Harvard University Press, 1986.

———. "The Ties That Bind: Race and Sex in *Pudd'nhead Wilson*." *Mark Twain's "Pudd'nhead Wilson": Race, Conflict, and Culture*. Ed. Susan Gillman and Forrest G. Robinson. Durham, NC: Duke University Press, 1990. 105–120.

Joseph, May. *Nomadic Identities*. Minneapolis: University of Minnesota Press, 1999.

Kakutani, Michiko. "Novelists and Vietnam: The War Goes On." *New York Times*, 15 April 1984, sec 7.1.

Kantorowicz, Ernst Hartwig. *The King's Two Bodies: A Study in Mediaeval Political Theology*. Princeton, NJ: Princeton University Press, 1957.

Kaplan, Amy. "'Left Alone with America': The Absence of Empire in the Study of American Culture." *Cultures of United States Imperialism*. Ed. Amy Kaplan and Donald Pease. Durham, NC: Duke University Press, 1993. 3–21.

Kayser, Wolfgang Johannes. *The Grotesque in Art and Literature*. New York: Columbia University Press, 1981.

Kennelly, Laura B. "Exhortation in *Wise Blood*: Rhetorical Theory as an Approach to Flannery O'Connor." *Flannery O'Connor: New Perspectives*. Ed. Sura P. Rath and Mary Neff Shaw. Athens: University of Georgia Press, 1996. 152–168.

Kenschaft, Lori J. "Homoerotics and Human Connections: Reading Carson McCullers 'As a Lesbian.'" *Critical Essays on Carson McCullers*. Ed. Beverly Lyon Clark and Melvin J. Friedman. New York: G. K. Hall, 1996. 221–233.

Klages, Mary. *Woeful Afflictions: Disability and Sentimentality in Victorian America*. Philadelphia: University of Pennsylvania Press, 1999.

Kovic, Ron. *Born on the Fourth of July*. New York: McGraw-Hill, 1976.

Kristeva, Julia. *Powers of Horror: An Essay on Abjection*. New York: Columbia University Press, 1982.

Kunz, Don. "Oliver Stone's Film Adaptation of *Born on the Fourth of July*: Redefining Masculine Heroism." *War, Literature, and the Arts* 2.2 (1990): 1–25.

Law, John, and Annemarie Mol. *Complexities: Social Studies of Knowledge Practices*. Science and Cultural Theory. Durham, NC: Duke University Press, 2002.

Lawson, Jacqueline E. "'She's a Pretty Woman . . . for a Gook': The Misogyny of the Vietnam War." *Fourteen Landing Zones: Approaches to Vietnam Literature*. Ed. Philip K. Jackson. Iowa City: University of Iowa Press, 1991. 15–37.

LeClair, Tom. "The Prodigious Fiction of Richard Powers, William Vollmann, and David Foster Wallace." *Critique* 38.1 (1996): 12–37.

Lee, Rachel. "Notes from the (Non)Field: Teaching and Theorizing Women of Color." *Meridians: Feminism, Race, Transnationalism* 1.1 (2000): 85–109.

Linton, Simi. *Claiming Disability: Knowledge and Identity.* New York: New York University Press, 1998.

Lipset, Seymour Martin, and Leo Lowenthal. *Culture and Social Character: The Work of David Riesman Reviewed.* New York: Free Press of Glencoe, 1961.

Longmore, Paul K. "Conspicuous Contribution and American Cultural Dilemmas: Telethon Rituals of Cleansing and Renewal." *The Body and Physical Difference: Discourses of Disability.* Ed. David T. Mitchell and Sharon L. Snyder. Ann Arbor: University of Michigan Press, 1997. 134–158.

Lott, Eirc. *Love and Theft: Blackface Minstrelsy and the American Working Class.* New York: Oxford University Press, 1993.

Macpherson, C. B. *The Political Theory of Possessive Individualism: Hobbes to Locke.* Oxford: Oxford University Press, 1983.

Marcus, George E. "'What Did He Reckon Would Become of the Other Half If He Killed His Half?': Doubled, Divided, and Crossed Selves in *Pudd'nhead Wilson*; or, Mark Twain as Cultural Critic in His Times and Ours." *Mark Twain's "Pudd'nhead Wilson": Race, Conflict, Culture.* Ed. Susan Gillman and Forrest G. Robinson. Durham, NC: Duke University Press, 1990. 190–210.

Marshall, Thomas Humphrey. *Citizenship and Social Class and Other Essays.* Cambridge: Cambridge University Press, 1950.

Martin, Emily. "Body Narratives, Body Boundaries." *Cultural Studies.* Ed. Cary Nelson, Lawrence Grossberg, and Paula A. Treichler. New York: Routledge, 1992. 409–419.

———. *Flexible Bodies: Tracking Immunity in American Culture from the Days of Polio to the Age of AIDS.* Boston: Beacon Press, 1994.

Matson, John, and E. Berger Sidney. "The Text That Wrote Itself: Identifying the Automated Subject in *Pudd'nhead Wilson* and *Those Extraordinary Twins*." *"Pudd'nhead Wilson" and "Those Extraordinary Twins."* 2nd ed. Norton Critical Edition. New York: W. W. Norton, 2005. 347–369.

McBride, Kecia Driver. "Fear, Consumption, and Desire: Naturalism and Ann Petry's *The Street*." *Twisted from the Ordinary: Essays on American Literary Naturalism.* Ed. Mary E. Papke. Knoxville: University of Tennessee Press, 2003. 304–322.

McClure, Kirstie M. "On the Subject of Rights: Pluralism, Plurality, and Political Identity." *Dimensions of Radical Democracy: Pluralism, Citizenship, Community.* Ed. Chantal Mouffe. London: Verso, 1992.

McCullers, Carson. *The Heart Is a Lonely Hunter.* New York: Modern Library, 1993.

———. *Illumination and Night Glare: The Unfinished Autobiography of Carson McCullers.* Ed. C. L. Barney Dews. Wisconsin Studies in Autobiography. Madison: University of Wisconsin Press, 1999.

McElroy, Bernard. *Fiction of the Modern Grotesque.* Basingstoke, UK: Macmillan, 1989.

McInerney, Peter. "'Straight' and 'Secret' History in Vietnam War Literature." *Contemporary Literature* 22.2 (1981): 187–204.

McRuer, Robert. *Crip Theory: Cultural Signs of Queerness and Disability*. Cultural Front. New York: New York University Press, 2006.

McWilliams, Wilson Carey. *"Pudd'nhead Wilson* on Democratic Governance." *Mark Twain's "Pudd'nhead Wilson": Race, Conflict, and Culture*. Ed. Susan Gillman and Forrest G. Robinson. Durham, NC: Duke University Press, 1990. 177–189.

Meindl, Dieter. *American Fiction and the Metaphysics of the Grotesque*. Columbia: University of Missouri Press, 1996.

Melling, Philip H. *Vietnam in American Literature*. Boston: Twayne, 1990.

Meyer, John W. "Myths of Socialization and of Personality." *Reconstructing Individualism: Autonomy, Individuality, and the Self in Western Thought*. Ed. Thomas C. Heller, Morton Sosna, and David E. Wellbery. Stanford, CA: Stanford University Press, 1986. 208–221.

Michaels, Walter Benn. *Our America: Nativism, Moderism, and Pluralism*. Durham, NC: Duke University Press, 1995.

Miller, Perry. *Errand into the Wilderness*. Cambridge, MA: Harvard University Press, 1956.

Mills, Alice. *Seriously Weird Papers on the Grotesque*. Studies on Themes and Motifs in Literature. New York: Peter Lang, 1999.

Mitchell, David T., and Sharon L. Snyder. *Narrative Prosthesis: Disability and the Dependencies of Discourse*. Ann Arbor: University of Michigan Press, 2000.

Mol, Annemarie. "Cutting Surgeons, Walking Patients: Some Complexities Involved in Comparing." *Complexities: Social Studies of Knowledge Practices*. Ed. John Law and Annemarie Mol. Durham, NC: Duke University Press, 2002. 218–253.

Morris, Gregory L. "Telling War Stories: Larry Heinemann's *Paco's Story* and the Serio-Comic Tradition." *Critique: Studies in Contemporary Fiction* 36.1 (1994): 58–68.

Mouffe, Chantal. *Dimensions of Radical Democracy: Pluralism, Citizenship, Community*. London, New York: Verso, 1992.

Muller, Gilbert H. *Nightmares and Visions: Flannery O'Connor and the Catholic Grotesque*. Athens: University of Georgia Press, 1972.

Muñoz, José Esteban. *Disidentifications: Queers of Color and the Performance of Politics*. Cultural Studies of the Americas. Minneapolis: University of Minnesota Press, 1999.

Nancy, Jean-Luc. "Corpus." *Thinking Bodies*. Ed. Juliet Flower MacCannell and Laura Zakarin. Stanford, CA: Stanford University Press, 1994. 17–31.

Neilson, Jim. *Warring Fictions: Cultural Politics and the Vietnam War Narrative*. Jackson: University Press of Mississippi, 1998.

Newman, John, with Ann Hilfinger. *Vietnam War Literature: An Annotated*

Bibliography of Imaginative Works about Americans Fighting in Vietnam.
Metuchen, NJ: Scarecrow Press, 1988.

Nichols, Catherine. "Dialogizing Postmodern Carnival: David Foster Wallace's *Infinite Jest.*" *Studies in Contemporary Fiction* 43 (Fall 2001): 3–16.

Nguyen, Viet Thanh. *Race and Resistance: Literature and Politics in Asian America.* Oxford: Oxford University Press, 2002.

Norden, Martin F. "Portrait of a Disabled Veteran: Alex Cutter in Cutter's Way." *From Hanoi to Hollywood: The Vietnam War in American Film.* Ed. Linda Dittmar and Gene Michaud. New Brunswick, NJ: Rutgers University Press, 1990. 217–225.

O'Connor, Flannery. *Three by Flannery O'Connor: "Wise Blood"/"The Violent Bear It Away"/ "Everything That Rises Must Converge."* Signet Classic. New York: New America Library, 1983.

———. *Mystery and Manners: Occasional Prose.* Ed. Sally and Robert Fitzgerald. New York: Farrar, Strauss & Giroux, 1969.

O'Connor, William Van. *The Grotesque: An American Genre and Other Essays.* Crosscurrents/Modern Critiques. Carbondale: Southern Illinois University Press, 1962.

Ong, Aihwa. *Flexible Citizenship: The Cultural Logics of Transnationality.* Durham, NC: Duke University Press, 1999.

Ortiz, Ricardo L. "Sexuality Degree Zero: Pleasure and Power in the Novels of John Rechy, Arturo Islas, and Michael Nava." *Journal of Homosexuality* 26.2–3 (1993): 111.

Ozeki, Ruth L. *My Year of Meats.* New York: Penguin Books, 1999.

Parker, Hershel. "Jack-Leg Author, Unreadable Text, and Sense-Making Critics." *Flawed Texts and Verbal Icons: Literary Authority in American Fiction.* Evanston, IL: Northwestern University Press, 1984. 115–145.

Pernick, Martin S. "Defining the Defective: Eugenics, Aesthetics, and Mass Culture in Early-Twentieth-Century America." *The Body and Physical Difference: Discourses of Disability.* Ed. David T. Mitchell and Sharon L. Snyder. Ann Arbor: University of Michigan Press, 1997. 89–110.

Petchesky, Rosalind Pollack. "The Body as Property: A Feminist Revision." *Conceiving the New World Order: The Global Politics of Reproduction.* Ed. Faye D. Ginsburg and Rayna Rapp. Berkeley: University of California Press, 1995. 387–406.

Petry, Ann Lane. *The Street.* Virago Modern Classics. London: Virago, 1986.

Phelan, Peggy. *Unmarked: The Politics of Performance.* London: Routledge, 1993.

Punday, Daniel. "Narrative Performance in the Contemporary Monster Story." *Modern Language Review* 97.4 (2002): 803–820.

Ramlow, Todd R. "Bad Boys: Abstractions of Difference and the Politics of Youth 'Deviance.'" *GLQ: A Journal of Lesbian and Gay Studies* 9.1–2 (2003): 107–132.

Rath, Sue P., and Mary Neff Shaw. *Flannery O'Connor: New Perspectives.* Athens: University of Georgia Press, 1996.

Reesman, Jeanne Campbell. "Women, Language, and the Grotesque in Flannery O'Connor and Eudora Welty." *Flannery O'Connor: New Perspectives.* Ed. Sura P. Rath and Mary Neff Shaw. Athens: University of Georgia Press, 1996. 38–56.

Riesman, David. *The Lonely Crowd: A Study of the Changing American Character.* New Haven, CT: Yale University Press, 1961.

Rignalda, Don. *Fighting and Writing the Vietnam War.* Jackson: University Press of Mississippi, 1994.

Roach, Joseph R. *Cities of the Dead: Circum-Atlantic Performance.* Social Foundations of Aesthetic Forms. New York: Columbia University Press, 1996.

Robertson, Alton Kim. *The Grotesque Interface: Deformity, Debasement, Dissolution.* Frankfurt am Main, Madrid: Iberoamericana/Vervuert, 1996.

Robillard, Douglas. *The Critical Response to Flannery O'Connor.* Critical Responses in Arts and Letters. Westport, CT: Praeger, 2004.

Robinson, Forrest G. "The Sense of Disorder in *Pudd'nhead Wilson.*" *Mark Twain's "Pudd'nhead Wilson": Race, Conflict, and Culture.* Ed. Susan Gillman and Forrest G. Robinson. Durham, NC: Duke University Press, 1990. 22–45.

Rogin, Michael Paul. *"Ronald Reagan," the Movie: And Other Episodes in Political Demonology.* Berkeley: University of California Press, 1987.

———. "Francis Galton and Mark Twain: The Natal Autograph in *Pudd'nhead Wilson.*" *Mark Twain's "Pudd'nhead Wilson": Race, Conflict, and Culture.* Ed. Susan Gillman and Forrest G. Robinson. Durham, NC: Duke University Press, 1990. 73–85.

Rowe, John Carlos. "Fatal Speculations: Murder, Money, and Manners in *Pudd'nhead Wilson.*" *Mark Twain's "Pudd'nhead Wilson": Race, Conflict, and Culture.* Ed. Susan Gillman and Forrest G. Robinson. Durham, NC: Duke University Press, 1990. 137–154.

Rowe, John Carlos, and Rick Berg. *The Vietnam War and American Culture.* New York: Columbia University Press, 1991.

Rubin, Louis D., Jr. "Carson McCullers: The Aesthetic of Pain." *Critical Essays on Carson McCullers.* Ed. Clark Beverly Lyon and Melvin J. Friedman. New York: G. K. Hall, 1996. 111–123.

Russo, Mary J. "Female Grotesques: Carnival and Theory." *Feminist Studies, Critical Studies.* Ed. Teresa De Lauretis. Bloomington: Indiana University Press, 1986. 213–229.

———. *The Female Grotesque: Risk, Excess, and Modernity.* New York: Routledge, 1995.

Saldívar, José David. *Border Matters: Remapping American Cultural Studies.* Berkeley: University of California Press, 1997.

Samuels, Ellen. "Critical Divides: Judith Butler's Body Theory and the Question of Disability." *NWSA Journal* 14.3 (2002): 58–76.

———. "My Body, My Closet: Invisible Disability and the Limits of Coming-out Discourse." *GLQ: A Journal of Gay and Lesbian Studies* 9.1–2 (2003): 233–255.

Samuels, Shirley. "The Identity of Slavery." *The Culture of Sentiment: Race, Gender, and Sentimentality in Nineteenth-Century America*. Ed. Shirley Samuels. New York: Oxford University Press, 1992. 157–171.

Sánchez-Eppler, Karen. "Bodily Bonds: The Intersecting Rhetorics of Feminism and Abolition." *The Culture of Sentiment: Race, Gender, and Sentimentality in Nineteenth-Century America*. Ed. Shirley Samuels. New York: Oxford University Press, 1992. 92–114.

Sandoval, Chela. "US Third-World Feminism: The Theory and Method of Oppositional Consciousness in the Postmodern World." *Feminist Postcolonial Theory: A Reader*. Ed. Reina Lewis and Sara Mills. Edinburgh: Edinburgh University Press, 2003. 75–99.

Scarry, Elaine. *The Body in Pain: The Making and Unmaking of the World*. New York: Oxford University Press, 1985.

Schweik, Susan. *Ugly Laws: Disability in Public*. History of Disability. New York: New York University Press, 2009.

Scott, Grant F. "*Paco's Story* and the Ethics of Violence." *Critique: Studies in Contemporary Fiction* 36.1 (1994): 69–81.

Searle, William J. "Walking Wounded: Vietnam War Novels of Return." *Search and Clear: Critical Responses to Selected Literature and Films of the Vietnam War*. Ed. William J. Searle. Bowling Green, OH: Bowling Green State University Popular Press, 1988. 147–159.

Sedgwick, Eve. "Queer and Now." *Tendencies*. Durham, NC: Duke University Press, 1993. 1–20.

Seltzer, Mark. *Bodies and Machines*. New York: Routledge, 1992.

Shapiro, Joseph P. *No Pity: Disabled People Forging a New Civil Rights Movement*. New York: Times Books, 1994.

Shildrick, Margrit. *Embodying the Monster: Encounters with the Vulnerable Self*. London: SAGE, 2002.

Shor, Fran. "Transcending the Myths of Patriotic Militarized Masculinity: Armoring, Wounding, and Transfiguration in Ron Kovic's *Born on the Fourth of July*." *Journal of Men's Studies* 8.3 (2000): 375–385.

Showalter, Elaine. *The New Feminist Criticism: Essays on Women, Literature and Theory*. New York: Pantheon Books, 1985.

Siebers, Tobin. "My Withered Limb." *Points of Contact: Disability, Art, and Culture*. Ed. Susan Crutchfield and Marcy Epstein. Ann Arbor: University of Michigan Press, 2000. 21–30.

———. "Disability in Theory: From Social Constructionism to the New Realism of the Body." *American Literary History* 13.4 (2001): 737–754.

———. *Disability Theory*. Corporealities: Discourses of Disability. Ann Arbor: University of Michigan Press, 2008.

Silverman, Kaja. *Male Subjectivity at the Margins*. New York: Routledge, 1992.

Smetak, Jacqueline R. "The Antiwar Activist in Vietnam War Fiction." *Fourteen Landing Zones: Approaches to Vietnam War Literature*. Ed. Philip K. Jackson. Iowa City: University of Iowa Press, 1991. 141–165.

Smith, Adam. *The Theory of Moral Sentiments*. Ed. D. D. Raphael and A. L. Macfie. Oxford: Clarendon Press, 1976.

Snyder, Sharon L., Brenda Jo Brueggemann, and Rosemarie Garland-Thomson. *Disability Studies: Enabling the Humanities*. New York: Modern Language Association of America, 2002.

Sobchack, Vivian. "Beating the Meat/Surviving the Text, or How to Get Out of This Century Alive." *Cyberspace/Cyberbodies/Cyberpunk: Cultures of Technological Embodiment*. Ed. Mike Featherstone and Roger Burrows. London: Sage Publications, 1995. 205–215.

———. *Carnal Thoughts: Embodiment and Moving Image Culture*. Berkeley: University of California Press, 2004.

Sontag, Susan. *Illness as Metaphor*. New York: Farrar, Strauss & Giroux, 1978.

Spivak, Gayatri Chakravorty. "Response to Jean-Luc Nancy." *Thinking Bodies*. Ed. Juliet Flower MacCannell and Laura Zakarin. Stanford, CA: Stanford University Press, 1994. 32–51.

———. "A Feminist Reading: McCullers's *Heart Is a Lonely Hunter*." *Critical Essays on Carson McCullers*. Ed. Beverly Lyon Clark and Melvin J. Friedman. New York: G. K. Hall, 1996. 129–142.

Stallybrass, Peter, and Allon White. *The Politics and Poetics of Transgression*. Ithaca, NY: Cornell University Press, 1986.

Stern, Julia A. *The Plight of Feeling: Sympathy and Dissent in the Early American Novel*. Chicago: University of Chicago Press, 1997.

Stewart, Susan. *On Longing: Narratives of the Miniature, the Gigantic, the Souvenir, the Collection*. Durham, NC: Duke University Press, 1993.

Sundquist, Eric J. "Mark Twain and Homer Plessy." *To Wake the Nations: Race in the Making of American Literature*. Cambridge, MA: Belknap Press, 1993. 225–270.

Switzer, Jacqueline Vaughn. *Disabled Rights: American Disability Policy and the Fight for Equality*. Washington, DC: Georgetown University Press, 2003.

Tal, Kali. "Speaking the Language of Pain: Vietnam War Literature in the Context of a Literature of Trauma." *Fourteen Landing Zones: Approaches to Vietnam Literature*. Ed. Philip K. Jackson. Iowa City: University of Iowa Press, 1991. 217–250.

———. *Worlds of Hurt: Reading the Literatures of Trauma*. Cambridge: Cambridge University Press, 1996.

Thomson, Philip J. *The Grotesque*. Critical Idiom. London: Methuen, 1972.

Tichi, Cecelia. *Embodiment of a Nation: Human Form in American Places*. Cambridge, MA: Harvard University Press, 2001.

Tocqueville, Alexis de. *Democracy in America*. Ed. Harvey Claflin Mansfield and Delba Winthrop. Chicago: University of Chicago Press, 2000.

Tompkins, Jane. *Sensational Designs: The Cultural Work of American Fiction, 1790–1860.* New York: Oxford University Press, 1985.

Tremain, Shelley. "On the Subject of Impairment." *Disability/Postmodernity: Embodying Disability Theory.* Ed. Mairian Corker and Tom Shakespeare. London: Continuum, 2002. 32–47.

Twain, Mark. *Roughing It. The Complete Works of Mark Twain.* American Artists Edition. Vol. 6. New York: Harper, 1913.

———. "The Siamese Twins." *The Writings of Mark Twain: Sketches Old and New.* Ed. Paine Albert Bigelow. New York: Harper & Brothers, 1917. 248–253.

———. *Innocents Abroad; or, The New Pilgrims' Progress.* New York: Heritage Press, 1962.

———. *"Pudd'nhead Wilson" and "Those Extraordinary Twins."* 2nd ed. Norton Critical Edition. New York: W. W. Norton, 2005.

Wald, Priscilla. *Constituting Americans: Cultural Anxiety and Narrative Form.* New Americanists. Durham, NC: Duke University Press, 1995.

———. "Minefields and Meeting Grounds: Transnational Analyses and American Studies." *American Literary History* 10.1 (1998): 199–218.

Walker, Alice. "Beyond the Peacock: The Reconstruction of Flannery O'Connor." *In Search of Our Mother's Gardens.* San Francisco: Harcourt Brace Jovanovich, 1984. 42–59.

Wallace, David Foster. *Infinite Jest: A Novel.* Boston: Little, Brown, 1996.

———. "E Unibus Pluram: Television and U.S. Fiction." *A Supposedly Fun Thing I'll Never Do Again.* New York: Little, Brown, 1997. 21–82.

Warner, Michael. *Publics and Counterpublics.* New York: Zone Books, 2002.

Warren, Victoria. "American Tall Tale/Tail: Katherine Dunn's *Geek Love* and the Paradox of American Individualism." *Critique* 45.4 (2004): 323–336.

Weese, Katherine. "Normalizing Freakery: Katherine Dunn's *Geek Love* and the Female Grotesque." *Critique* 41.4 (2000): 349–364.

Wendell, Susan. *The Rejected Body: Feminist Philosophical Reflections on Disability.* New York: Routledge, 1996.

Westling, Louise Hutchings. *Sacred Groves and Ravaged Gardens: The Fiction of Eudora Welty, Carson McCullers, and Flannery O'Connor.* Athens: University of Georgia Press, 1985.

Wiegman, Robin. *American Anatomies: Theorizing Race and Gender.* Durham, NC: Duke University Press, 1995.

Wills, David. *Prosthesis.* Stanford, CA: Stanford University Press, 1995.

Wise, Gene. "'Paradigm Dramas' in American Studies: A Cultural and Institutional History of the Movement." *American Quarterly* 31.3 (1979): 293–337.

Wright, Richard. "Inner Landscape." *New Republic* 103 (1940): 195.

Wu, Cynthia. "The Siamese Twins in Late-Nineteenth-Century Narratives of Conflict and Resolution." *American Literature* 80.1 (2008): 29–55.

Yaeger, Patricia. "Flannery O'Connor and the Aesthetics of Torture." *Flannery*

O'Connor: New Perspectives. Ed. Sue P. Rath and Mary Neff Shaw. Athens: University of Georgia Press, 1996. 183–206.

Yarborough, Richard, and Hazel Arnett Ervin. "The Quest for the American Dream in Three Afro-American Novels: *If He Hollers Let Him Go, The Street,* and *Invisible Man.*" *The Critical Response to Ann Petry.* Ed. Hazel Arnett Ervin. Critical Responses in Arts and Letters. Westport, CT: Praeger, 2005. 53–67.

Young, Iris Marion. "Polity and Group Difference: A Critique of the Ideal of Universal Citizenship." *Ethics* 99.2 (1989): 250–274.

Žižek, Slavoj. *The Sublime Object of Ideology.* London: Verso, 1989.

INDEX

Gallaudet University, 99
Galton, Francis, 175, 210n13
Garland-Thomson, Rosemarie: on
cultural expectations, 50; on disability
and race, gender, and class, 10,
11–12; on Emerson and self-reliance,
5; *Extraordinary Bodies*, 5, 10, 18,
30–31, 50, 179, 211n22; on freak shows,
211n22; on liberal individualism and
disability, 30–31; on normate body,
14, 175; on sentimental fiction, 18,
210n10; *Staring*, 48; on tension between
uniqueness and uniformity, 179; on
visual encounters, 48, 101
Gates, Henry Louis, Jr., 13
Geek Love (Dunn), 159–169; ambiguity in,
168; Americana in, 136, 137–139, 219n4;
Arturism, 133, 165–168; Browning's
Freaks compared with, 159, 167;
carnival circuit in, 137–139; cast of
characters, 136; central conceit of, 134;
conceives America through logic of
embodiment, 133, 169; on conception,
160, 164–165; as critique of dominant
norms through disability, 19–20, 135–
136; on disability, 160–161, 166–167;
episodic structure of, 133; essentialism
of, 164–166; on freakish body as gift,
135; on freaks as born not made, 133–
134; on heterogeneity within difference,
166; hierarchy of disability in, 166; as
hybrid of fantasy and realism, 142;
language and social apprehension of
difference in, 17; masculine authority
in, 161–162; "Mutant Mystery" exhibit,
162–163; nature-nurture tension in,
163; reproduction in, 134, 135, 160–169;
siblings in, 133; on social and economic
value as related, 161; two temporal
registers of, 164; in works of disability
studies, 18
gender: deviation from norms, 150;
disability compared with, 11–12,
41; spectacle as gendered, 92–93;
transgressive identities, 221n12;
triumph of traditional roles in *The
Heart Is a Lonely Hunter*, 94–95. *See
also* women
Gender Trouble (Butler), 15
Gentry, Marshall Bruce, 216n15

Gibson, James, 98, 99, 102, 110–111, 129,
216n1
Gillman, Susan, 57
Gleeson-White, Sarah, 95, 216n18
Grosz, Elizabeth, 11, 208n6
grotesque, the: Bakhtinian, 60, 68, 92;
body, 60–61, 68, 71, 76–84, 95–96, 117,
215n12; as boundary transgressing, 78,
92–93; central categories of, 61, 79–80;
as comment on its context, 215n10;
critical approaches to, 60, 223n12;
definitions of, 60; in fiction, 59–60, 64;
as gendered, 92–93; in *Infinite Jest*, 191;
literary, 17, 19, 28, 62, 68, 95–96, 215n12;
materiality of, 60, 61, 62; as metaphor,
7; modernity, 80–84; realism, 68–76, 79,
84; in representation of disability, 60–61,
212n1; simultaneity of, 72; and Southern
literature, 213n5, 214n6; tension between
symbolic and real in, 62–63
Grotesque in Art and Literature, The
(Kayser), 215n11
Gulf War (1991), 129, 139, 140

"Hands" (Anderson), 81
Hardin, Michael, 221n16, 221n17
Harkin, Tom, 200
Harpham, Geoffrey, 60
Harwood, Richard, 130
Hayles, N. Katherine, 167, 224n16
Heart Is a Lonely Hunter, The (McCullers),
59–96; affinity for freaks in, 59, 61,
71; blood in, 70; central problems in,
81–82; characters with disabilities
in, 214n7; on disability and social
connection, 74–76, 80, 88; five central
characters, 61, 74; grotesque bodies as
relics in, 76–77; on grotesque body as
effect of modern world, 80–82, 83; on
language as unreliable, 67–68; pain as
antidote for modern alienation in, 69–
70, 80; physical difference represents
alienating modern state in, 19, 62, 96;
preoccupation with the crowd, 84, 85,
87–88; reception and marketing of,
84–85; threatening female body in,
93–95; vision in, 65
heimlich, 56, 211n25
Heinemann, Larry. See *Paco's Story*
(Heinemann)
Helms, Jesse, 2

About the Author

Emily Russell is an assistant professor of American literature at Rollins College in Winter Park, Florida. Her research interests include twentieth- and twenty-first-century fiction, the multiethnic novel, and theories of embodiment.